C-165   CAREER EXAMINATION SERIES

This is your
PASSBOOK for...

Correction Captain

Test Preparation Study Guide
Questions & Answers

COPYRIGHT NOTICE

This book is SOLELY intended for, is sold ONLY to, and its use is RESTRICTED to individual, bona fide applicants or candidates who qualify by virtue of having seriously filed applications for appropriate license, certificate, professional and/or promotional advancement, higher school matriculation, scholarship, or other legitimate requirements of education and/or governmental authorities.

This book is NOT intended for use, class instruction, tutoring, training, duplication, copying, reprinting, excerption, or adaptation, etc., by:

1) Other publishers
2) Proprietors and/or Instructors of "Coaching" and/or Preparatory Courses
3) Personnel and/or Training Divisions of commercial, industrial, and governmental organizations
4) Schools, colleges, or universities and/or their departments and staffs, including teachers and other personnel
5) Testing Agencies or Bureaus
6) Study groups which seek by the purchase of a single volume to copy and/or duplicate and/or adapt this material for use by the group as a whole without having purchased individual volumes for each of the members of the group
7) Et al.

Such persons would be in violation of appropriate Federal and State statutes.

PROVISION OF LICENSING AGREEMENTS – Recognized educational, commercial, industrial, and governmental institutions and organizations, and others legitimately engaged in educational pursuits, including training, testing, and measurement activities, may address request for a licensing agreement to the copyright owners, who will determine whether, and under what conditions, including fees and charges, the materials in this book may be used them. In other words, a licensing facility exists for the legitimate use of the material in this book on other than an individual basis. However, it is asseverated and affirmed here that the material in this book CANNOT be used without the receipt of the express permission of such a licensing agreement from the Publishers. Inquiries re licensing should be addressed to the company, attention rights and permissions department.

All rights reserved, including the right of reproduction in whole or in part, in any form or by any means, electronic or mechanical, including photocopying, recording, or by any information storage and retrieval system, without permission in writing from the Publisher.

Copyright © 2024 by
National Learning Corporation

212 Michael Drive, Syosset, NY 11791
(516) 921-8888 • www.passbooks.com
E-mail: info@passbooks.com

PASSBOOK® SERIES

THE *PASSBOOK® SERIES* has been created to prepare applicants and candidates for the ultimate academic battlefield – the examination room.

At some time in our lives, each and every one of us may be required to take an examination – for validation, matriculation, admission, qualification, registration, certification, or licensure.

Based on the assumption that every applicant or candidate has met the basic formal educational standards, has taken the required number of courses, and read the necessary texts, the *PASSBOOK® SERIES* furnishes the one special preparation which may assure passing with confidence, instead of failing with insecurity. Examination questions – together with answers – are furnished as the basic vehicle for study so that the mysteries of the examination and its compounding difficulties may be eliminated or diminished by a sure method.

This book is meant to help you pass your examination provided that you qualify and are serious in your objective.

The entire field is reviewed through the huge store of content information which is succinctly presented through a provocative and challenging approach – the question-and-answer method.

A climate of success is established by furnishing the correct answers at the end of each test.

You soon learn to recognize types of questions, forms of questions, and patterns of questioning. You may even begin to anticipate expected outcomes.

You perceive that many questions are repeated or adapted so that you can gain acute insights, which may enable you to score many sure points.

You learn how to confront new questions, or types of questions, and to attack them confidently and work out the correct answers.

You note objectives and emphases, and recognize pitfalls and dangers, so that you may make positive educational adjustments.

Moreover, you are kept fully informed in relation to new concepts, methods, practices, and directions in the field.

You discover that you are actually taking the examination all the time: you are preparing for the examination by "taking" an examination, not by reading extraneous and/or supererogatory textbooks.

In short, this PASSBOOK®, used directedly, should be an important factor in helping you to pass your test.

CORRECTION CAPTAIN

DUTIES:
Under general supervision, Captains (Correction) are in charge of Correction Officers assigned to the care and custody of prison inmates. They monitor the supervision of inmates; supervise and evaluate work performance of subordinates; oversee inmate movement; authorize and direct search activities; respond to reports of emergences; confer with staff of all ranks to give and/or receive instructions and to make and/or receive reports; perform related work.

EXAMPLES OF TYPICAL TASKS
Monitors supervision of inmates; supervises and evaluates work performance of subordinates; supervises inmate movement; authorizes and directs search activities; responds to reports of emergencies; conducts investigation of unusual incidents; confers with staff of all ranks to give and/or receive instructions and to make and/or receive reports; conducts roll call; inspects officers, posts and assigned work area; enforces and carries out the Department rules, regulations, policies and procedures; supervises inmate feeding; ensures that programs and services are made available to inmates as mandated; receives and classifies new admissions in accordance with department guidelines; ensures inmates are discharged in accordance with department guidelines; prepares, completes and/or reviews records, logs and reports.

TESTS
The written test will be of the multiple-choice type and may include questions on supervision and development of staff; including aspects of communication and public relations; institution operations, including, but not limited to, custody and security, and riot control, classification, and searching; rules and regulations of the Department; principles and practices in the fields of criminology and penology; and comprehension of written material, interpretation of tables, charts, and graphs; and related areas.

The written test may also test for the following abilities; ability to apply technical knowledge in job-related situations; ability to understand and apply written material and communications; ability to plan, prioritize, coordinate and delegate work; ability to gather information, identify problems, analyze details and make appropriate judgments in determining the best feasible solutions; ability to prepare, complete and/or review records, logs and reports; ability to appraise a situation or work product to determine to what extent criteria have been met; ability to identify hidden contraband; ability to accurately perform numerical operations; ability to recognize and consider the feelings, needs and points of view of others when taking actions that affect them.

The written test may include material that correction captains must deal with in the performance of their duties in such areas as coordinating shift transition at the beginning and end of shifts; searches; inspections, emergency responses; admission and discharge of inmates; supervision of uniformed staff, civilians and inmates; and other related areas.

TASKS/AREAS TO BE TESTED ARE AS FOLLOWS:
- Conducts Inspections, Searches and Tours: These tasks involve the monitoring and supervision of inspections of Correction Officers, searches of inmates and tours of a Department of Correction facility.
- Responds to Conflicts, Emergencies and Other Unusual Situations: These tasks involve the direction and supervision of staff in conflicts and other emergencies and follow-up procedures.

HOW TO TAKE A TEST

I. YOU MUST PASS AN EXAMINATION

A. *WHAT EVERY CANDIDATE SHOULD KNOW*

Examination applicants often ask us for help in preparing for the written test. What can I study in advance? What kinds of questions will be asked? How will the test be given? How will the papers be graded?

As an applicant for a civil service examination, you may be wondering about some of these things. Our purpose here is to suggest effective methods of advance study and to describe civil service examinations.

Your chances for success on this examination can be increased if you know how to prepare. Those "pre-examination jitters" can be reduced if you know what to expect. You can even experience an adventure in good citizenship if you know why civil service exams are given.

B. *WHY ARE CIVIL SERVICE EXAMINATIONS GIVEN?*

Civil service examinations are important to you in two ways. As a citizen, you want public jobs filled by employees who know how to do their work. As a job seeker, you want a fair chance to compete for that job on an equal footing with other candidates. The best-known means of accomplishing this two-fold goal is the competitive examination.

Exams are widely publicized throughout the nation. They may be administered for jobs in federal, state, city, municipal, town or village governments or agencies.

Any citizen may apply, with some limitations, such as the age or residence of applicants. Your experience and education may be reviewed to see whether you meet the requirements for the particular examination. When these requirements exist, they are reasonable and applied consistently to all applicants. Thus, a competitive examination may cause you some uneasiness now, but it is your privilege and safeguard.

C. *HOW ARE CIVIL SERVICE EXAMS DEVELOPED?*

Examinations are carefully written by trained technicians who are specialists in the field known as "psychological measurement," in consultation with recognized authorities in the field of work that the test will cover. These experts recommend the subject matter areas or skills to be tested; only those knowledges or skills important to your success on the job are included. The most reliable books and source materials available are used as references. Together, the experts and technicians judge the difficulty level of the questions.

Test technicians know how to phrase questions so that the problem is clearly stated. Their ethics do not permit "trick" or "catch" questions. Questions may have been tried out on sample groups, or subjected to statistical analysis, to determine their usefulness.

Written tests are often used in combination with performance tests, ratings of training and experience, and oral interviews. All of these measures combine to form the best-known means of finding the right person for the right job.

II. HOW TO PASS THE WRITTEN TEST

A. NATURE OF THE EXAMINATION

To prepare intelligently for civil service examinations, you should know how they differ from school examinations you have taken. In school you were assigned certain definite pages to read or subjects to cover. The examination questions were quite detailed and usually emphasized memory. Civil service exams, on the other hand, try to discover your present ability to perform the duties of a position, plus your potentiality to learn these duties. In other words, a civil service exam attempts to predict how successful you will be. Questions cover such a broad area that they cannot be as minute and detailed as school exam questions.

In the public service similar kinds of work, or positions, are grouped together in one "class." This process is known as *position-classification*. All the positions in a class are paid according to the salary range for that class. One class title covers all of these positions, and they are all tested by the same examination.

B. FOUR BASIC STEPS

1) Study the announcement

How, then, can you know what subjects to study? Our best answer is: "Learn as much as possible about the class of positions for which you've applied." The exam will test the knowledge, skills and abilities needed to do the work.

Your most valuable source of information about the position you want is the official exam announcement. This announcement lists the training and experience qualifications. Check these standards and apply only if you come reasonably close to meeting them.

The brief description of the position in the examination announcement offers some clues to the subjects which will be tested. Think about the job itself. Review the duties in your mind. Can you perform them, or are there some in which you are rusty? Fill in the blank spots in your preparation.

Many jurisdictions preview the written test in the exam announcement by including a section called "Knowledge and Abilities Required," "Scope of the Examination," or some similar heading. Here you will find out specifically what fields will be tested.

2) Review your own background

Once you learn in general what the position is all about, and what you need to know to do the work, ask yourself which subjects you already know fairly well and which need improvement. You may wonder whether to concentrate on improving your strong areas or on building some background in your fields of weakness. When the announcement has specified "some knowledge" or "considerable knowledge," or has used adjectives like "beginning principles of…" or "advanced … methods," you can get a clue as to the number and difficulty of questions to be asked in any given field. More questions, and hence broader coverage, would be included for those subjects which are more important in the work. Now weigh your strengths and weaknesses against the job requirements and prepare accordingly.

3) Determine the level of the position

Another way to tell how intensively you should prepare is to understand the level of the job for which you are applying. Is it the entering level? In other words, is this the position in which beginners in a field of work are hired? Or is it an intermediate or advanced level? Sometimes this is indicated by such words as "Junior" or "Senior" in the class title. Other jurisdictions use Roman numerals to designate the level – Clerk I, Clerk II, for example. The word "Supervisor" sometimes appears in the title. If the level is not indicated by the title, check the description of duties. Will you be working under very close supervision, or will you have responsibility for independent decisions in this work?

4) Choose appropriate study materials

Now that you know the subjects to be examined and the relative amount of each subject to be covered, you can choose suitable study materials. For beginning level jobs, or even advanced ones, if you have a pronounced weakness in some aspect of your training, read a modern, standard textbook in that field. Be sure it is up to date and has general coverage. Such books are normally available at your library, and the librarian will be glad to help you locate one. For entry-level positions, questions of appropriate difficulty are chosen – neither highly advanced questions, nor those too simple. Such questions require careful thought but not advanced training.

If the position for which you are applying is technical or advanced, you will read more advanced, specialized material. If you are already familiar with the basic principles of your field, elementary textbooks would waste your time. Concentrate on advanced textbooks and technical periodicals. Think through the concepts and review difficult problems in your field.

These are all general sources. You can get more ideas on your own initiative, following these leads. For example, training manuals and publications of the government agency which employs workers in your field can be useful, particularly for technical and professional positions. A letter or visit to the government department involved may result in more specific study suggestions, and certainly will provide you with a more definite idea of the exact nature of the position you are seeking.

III. KINDS OF TESTS

Tests are used for purposes other than measuring knowledge and ability to perform specified duties. For some positions, it is equally important to test ability to make adjustments to new situations or to profit from training. In others, basic mental abilities not dependent on information are essential. Questions which test these things may not appear as pertinent to the duties of the position as those which test for knowledge and information. Yet they are often highly important parts of a fair examination. For very general questions, it is almost impossible to help you direct your study efforts. What we can do is to point out some of the more common of these general abilities needed in public service positions and describe some typical questions.

1) General information

Broad, general information has been found useful for predicting job success in some kinds of work. This is tested in a variety of ways, from vocabulary lists to questions about current events. Basic background in some field of work, such as sociology or economics, may be sampled in a group of questions. Often these are principles which have become familiar to most persons through exposure rather than through formal training. It is difficult to advise you how to study for these questions; being alert to the world around you is our best suggestion.

2) Verbal ability

An example of an ability needed in many positions is verbal or language ability. Verbal ability is, in brief, the ability to use and understand words. Vocabulary and grammar tests are typical measures of this ability. Reading comprehension or paragraph interpretation questions are common in many kinds of civil service tests. You are given a paragraph of written material and asked to find its central meaning.

3) Numerical ability

Number skills can be tested by the familiar arithmetic problem, by checking paired lists of numbers to see which are alike and which are different, or by interpreting charts and graphs. In the latter test, a graph may be printed in the test booklet which you are asked to use as the basis for answering questions.

4) Observation

A popular test for law-enforcement positions is the observation test. A picture is shown to you for several minutes, then taken away. Questions about the picture test your ability to observe both details and larger elements.

5) Following directions

In many positions in the public service, the employee must be able to carry out written instructions dependably and accurately. You may be given a chart with several columns, each column listing a variety of information. The questions require you to carry out directions involving the information given in the chart.

6) Skills and aptitudes

Performance tests effectively measure some manual skills and aptitudes. When the skill is one in which you are trained, such as typing or shorthand, you can practice. These tests are often very much like those given in business school or high school courses. For many of the other skills and aptitudes, however, no short-time preparation can be made. Skills and abilities natural to you or that you have developed throughout your lifetime are being tested.

Many of the general questions just described provide all the data needed to answer the questions and ask you to use your reasoning ability to find the answers. Your best preparation for these tests, as well as for tests of facts and ideas, is to be at your physical and mental best. You, no doubt, have your own methods of getting into an exam-taking mood and keeping "in shape." The next section lists some ideas on this subject.

IV. KINDS OF QUESTIONS

Only rarely is the "essay" question, which you answer in narrative form, used in civil service tests. Civil service tests are usually of the short-answer type. Full instructions for answering these questions will be given to you at the examination. But in case this is your first experience with short-answer questions and separate answer sheets, here is what you need to know:

1) Multiple-choice Questions

Most popular of the short-answer questions is the "multiple choice" or "best answer" question. It can be used, for example, to test for factual knowledge, ability to solve problems or judgment in meeting situations found at work.

A multiple-choice question is normally one of three types—
- It can begin with an incomplete statement followed by several possible endings. You are to find the one ending which *best* completes the statement, although some of the others may not be entirely wrong.
- It can also be a complete statement in the form of a question which is answered by choosing one of the statements listed.

- It can be in the form of a problem – again you select the best answer.

Here is an example of a multiple-choice question with a discussion which should give you some clues as to the method for choosing the right answer:

When an employee has a complaint about his assignment, the action which will *best* help him overcome his difficulty is to
- A. discuss his difficulty with his coworkers
- B. take the problem to the head of the organization
- C. take the problem to the person who gave him the assignment
- D. say nothing to anyone about his complaint

In answering this question, you should study each of the choices to find which is best. Consider choice "A" – Certainly an employee may discuss his complaint with fellow employees, but no change or improvement can result, and the complaint remains unresolved. Choice "B" is a poor choice since the head of the organization probably does not know what assignment you have been given, and taking your problem to him is known as "going over the head" of the supervisor. The supervisor, or person who made the assignment, is the person who can clarify it or correct any injustice. Choice "C" is, therefore, correct. To say nothing, as in choice "D," is unwise. Supervisors have and interest in knowing the problems employees are facing, and the employee is seeking a solution to his problem.

2) True/False Questions

The "true/false" or "right/wrong" form of question is sometimes used. Here a complete statement is given. Your job is to decide whether the statement is right or wrong.

SAMPLE: A roaming cell-phone call to a nearby city costs less than a non-roaming call to a distant city.

This statement is wrong, or false, since roaming calls are more expensive.

This is not a complete list of all possible question forms, although most of the others are variations of these common types. You will always get complete directions for answering questions. Be sure you understand *how* to mark your answers – ask questions until you do.

V. RECORDING YOUR ANSWERS

Computer terminals are used more and more today for many different kinds of exams.

For an examination with very few applicants, you may be told to record your answers in the test booklet itself. Separate answer sheets are much more common. If this separate answer sheet is to be scored by machine – and this is often the case – it is highly important that you mark your answers correctly in order to get credit.

An electronic scoring machine is often used in civil service offices because of the speed with which papers can be scored. Machine-scored answer sheets must be marked with a pencil, which will be given to you. This pencil has a high graphite content which responds to the electronic scoring machine. As a matter of fact, stray dots may register as answers, so do not let your pencil rest on the answer sheet while you are pondering the correct answer. Also, if your pencil lead breaks or is otherwise defective, ask for another.

Since the answer sheet will be dropped in a slot in the scoring machine, be careful not to bend the corners or get the paper crumpled.

The answer sheet normally has five vertical columns of numbers, with 30 numbers to a column. These numbers correspond to the question numbers in your test booklet. After each number, going across the page are four or five pairs of dotted lines. These short dotted lines have small letters or numbers above them. The first two pairs may also have a "T" or "F" above the letters. This indicates that the first two pairs only are to be used if the questions are of the true-false type. If the questions are multiple choice, disregard the "T" and "F" and pay attention only to the small letters or numbers.

Answer your questions in the manner of the sample that follows:

32. The largest city in the United States is
 A. Washington, D.C.
 B. New York City
 C. Chicago
 D. Detroit
 E. San Francisco

1) Choose the answer you think is best. (New York City is the largest, so "B" is correct.)
2) Find the row of dotted lines numbered the same as the question you are answering. (Find row number 32)
3) Find the pair of dotted lines corresponding to the answer. (Find the pair of lines under the mark "B.")
4) Make a solid black mark between the dotted lines.

VI. BEFORE THE TEST

Common sense will help you find procedures to follow to get ready for an examination. Too many of us, however, overlook these sensible measures. Indeed, nervousness and fatigue have been found to be the most serious reasons why applicants fail to do their best on civil service tests. Here is a list of reminders:

- Begin your preparation early – Don't wait until the last minute to go scurrying around for books and materials or to find out what the position is all about.
- Prepare continuously – An hour a night for a week is better than an all-night cram session. This has been definitely established. What is more, a night a week for a month will return better dividends than crowding your study into a shorter period of time.
- Locate the place of the exam – You have been sent a notice telling you when and where to report for the examination. If the location is in a different town or otherwise unfamiliar to you, it would be well to inquire the best route and learn something about the building.
- Relax the night before the test – Allow your mind to rest. Do not study at all that night. Plan some mild recreation or diversion; then go to bed early and get a good night's sleep.
- Get up early enough to make a leisurely trip to the place for the test – This way unforeseen events, traffic snarls, unfamiliar buildings, etc. will not upset you.
- Dress comfortably – A written test is not a fashion show. You will be known by number and not by name, so wear something comfortable.

- Leave excess paraphernalia at home – Shopping bags and odd bundles will get in your way. You need bring only the items mentioned in the official notice you received; usually everything you need is provided. Do not bring reference books to the exam. They will only confuse those last minutes and be taken away from you when in the test room.
- Arrive somewhat ahead of time – If because of transportation schedules you must get there very early, bring a newspaper or magazine to take your mind off yourself while waiting.
- Locate the examination room – When you have found the proper room, you will be directed to the seat or part of the room where you will sit. Sometimes you are given a sheet of instructions to read while you are waiting. Do not fill out any forms until you are told to do so; just read them and be prepared.
- Relax and prepare to listen to the instructions
- If you have any physical problem that may keep you from doing your best, be sure to tell the test administrator. If you are sick or in poor health, you really cannot do your best on the exam. You can come back and take the test some other time.

VII. AT THE TEST

The day of the test is here and you have the test booklet in your hand. The temptation to get going is very strong. Caution! There is more to success than knowing the right answers. You must know how to identify your papers and understand variations in the type of short-answer question used in this particular examination. Follow these suggestions for maximum results from your efforts:

1) Cooperate with the monitor

The test administrator has a duty to create a situation in which you can be as much at ease as possible. He will give instructions, tell you when to begin, check to see that you are marking your answer sheet correctly, and so on. He is not there to guard you, although he will see that your competitors do not take unfair advantage. He wants to help you do your best.

2) Listen to all instructions

Don't jump the gun! Wait until you understand all directions. In most civil service tests you get more time than you need to answer the questions. So don't be in a hurry. Read each word of instructions until you clearly understand the meaning. Study the examples, listen to all announcements and follow directions. Ask questions if you do not understand what to do.

3) Identify your papers

Civil service exams are usually identified by number only. You will be assigned a number; you must not put your name on your test papers. Be sure to copy your number correctly. Since more than one exam may be given, copy your exact examination title.

4) Plan your time

Unless you are told that a test is a "speed" or "rate of work" test, speed itself is usually not important. Time enough to answer all the questions will be provided, but this does not mean that you have all day. An overall time limit has been set. Divide the total time (in minutes) by the number of questions to determine the approximate time you have for each question.

5) Do not linger over difficult questions

If you come across a difficult question, mark it with a paper clip (useful to have along) and come back to it when you have been through the booklet. One caution if you do this – be sure to skip a number on your answer sheet as well. Check often to be sure that you have not lost your place and that you are marking in the row numbered the same as the question you are answering.

6) Read the questions

Be sure you know what the question asks! Many capable people are unsuccessful because they failed to *read* the questions correctly.

7) Answer all questions

Unless you have been instructed that a penalty will be deducted for incorrect answers, it is better to guess than to omit a question.

8) Speed tests

It is often better NOT to guess on speed tests. It has been found that on timed tests people are tempted to spend the last few seconds before time is called in marking answers at random – without even reading them – in the hope of picking up a few extra points. To discourage this practice, the instructions may warn you that your score will be "corrected" for guessing. That is, a penalty will be applied. The incorrect answers will be deducted from the correct ones, or some other penalty formula will be used.

9) Review your answers

If you finish before time is called, go back to the questions you guessed or omitted to give them further thought. Review other answers if you have time.

10) Return your test materials

If you are ready to leave before others have finished or time is called, take ALL your materials to the monitor and leave quietly. Never take any test material with you. The monitor can discover whose papers are not complete, and taking a test booklet may be grounds for disqualification.

VIII. EXAMINATION TECHNIQUES

1) Read the general instructions carefully. These are usually printed on the first page of the exam booklet. As a rule, these instructions refer to the timing of the examination; the fact that you should not start work until the signal and must stop work at a signal, etc. If there are any *special* instructions, such as a choice of questions to be answered, make sure that you note this instruction carefully.

2) When you are ready to start work on the examination, that is as soon as the signal has been given, read the instructions to each question booklet, underline any key words or phrases, such as *least, best, outline, describe* and the like. In this way you will tend to answer as requested rather than discover on reviewing your paper that you *listed without describing*, that you selected the *worst* choice rather than the *best* choice, etc.

3) If the examination is of the objective or multiple-choice type – that is, each question will also give a series of possible answers: A, B, C or D, and you are called upon to select the best answer and write the letter next to that answer on your answer paper – it is advisable to start answering each question in turn. There may be anywhere from 50 to 100 such questions in the three or four hours allotted and you can see how much time would be taken if you read through all the questions before beginning to answer any. Furthermore, if you come across a question or group of questions which you know would be difficult to answer, it would undoubtedly affect your handling of all the other questions.

4) If the examination is of the essay type and contains but a few questions, it is a moot point as to whether you should read all the questions before starting to answer any one. Of course, if you are given a choice – say five out of seven and the like – then it is essential to read all the questions so you can eliminate the two that are most difficult. If, however, you are asked to answer all the questions, there may be danger in trying to answer the easiest one first because you may find that you will spend too much time on it. The best technique is to answer the first question, then proceed to the second, etc.

5) Time your answers. Before the exam begins, write down the time it started, then add the time allowed for the examination and write down the time it must be completed, then divide the time available somewhat as follows:
    - If 3-1/2 hours are allowed, that would be 210 minutes. If you have 80 objective-type questions, that would be an average of 2-1/2 minutes per question. Allow yourself no more than 2 minutes per question, or a total of 160 minutes, which will permit about 50 minutes to review.
    - If for the time allotment of 210 minutes there are 7 essay questions to answer, that would average about 30 minutes a question. Give yourself only 25 minutes per question so that you have about 35 minutes to review.

6) The most important instruction is to *read each question* and make sure you know what is wanted. The second most important instruction is to *time yourself properly* so that you answer every question. The third most important instruction is to *answer every question*. Guess if you have to but include something for each question. Remember that you will receive no credit for a blank and will probably receive some credit if you write something in answer to an essay question. If you guess a letter – say "B" for a multiple-choice question – you may have guessed right. If you leave a blank as an answer to a multiple-choice question, the examiners may respect your feelings but it will not add a point to your score. Some exams may penalize you for wrong answers, so in such cases *only*, you may not want to guess unless you have some basis for your answer.

7) Suggestions
    a. Objective-type questions
        1. Examine the question booklet for proper sequence of pages and questions
        2. Read all instructions carefully
        3. Skip any question which seems too difficult; return to it after all other questions have been answered
        4. Apportion your time properly; do not spend too much time on any single question or group of questions

5. Note and underline key words – *all, most, fewest, least, best, worst, same, opposite,* etc.
6. Pay particular attention to negatives
7. Note unusual option, e.g., unduly long, short, complex, different or similar in content to the body of the question
8. Observe the use of "hedging" words – *probably, may, most likely,* etc.
9. Make sure that your answer is put next to the same number as the question
10. Do not second-guess unless you have good reason to believe the second answer is definitely more correct
11. Cross out original answer if you decide another answer is more accurate; do not erase until you are ready to hand your paper in
12. Answer all questions; guess unless instructed otherwise
13. Leave time for review

b. Essay questions
1. Read each question carefully
2. Determine exactly what is wanted. Underline key words or phrases.
3. Decide on outline or paragraph answer
4. Include many different points and elements unless asked to develop any one or two points or elements
5. Show impartiality by giving pros and cons unless directed to select one side only
6. Make and write down any assumptions you find necessary to answer the questions
7. Watch your English, grammar, punctuation and choice of words
8. Time your answers; don't crowd material

8) Answering the essay question

Most essay questions can be answered by framing the specific response around several key words or ideas. Here are a few such key words or ideas:

M's: manpower, materials, methods, money, management
P's: purpose, program, policy, plan, procedure, practice, problems, pitfalls, personnel, public relations

  a. Six basic steps in handling problems:
    1. Preliminary plan and background development
    2. Collect information, data and facts
    3. Analyze and interpret information, data and facts
    4. Analyze and develop solutions as well as make recommendations
    5. Prepare report and sell recommendations
    6. Install recommendations and follow up effectiveness

  b. Pitfalls to avoid
    1. *Taking things for granted* – A statement of the situation does not necessarily imply that each of the elements is necessarily true; for example, a complaint may be invalid and biased so that all that can be taken for granted is that a complaint has been registered

2. *Considering only one side of a situation* – Wherever possible, indicate several alternatives and then point out the reasons you selected the best one
3. *Failing to indicate follow up* – Whenever your answer indicates action on your part, make certain that you will take proper follow-up action to see how successful your recommendations, procedures or actions turn out to be
4. *Taking too long in answering any single question* – Remember to time your answers properly

IX. AFTER THE TEST

Scoring procedures differ in detail among civil service jurisdictions although the general principles are the same. Whether the papers are hand-scored or graded by machine we have described, they are nearly always graded by number. That is, the person who marks the paper knows only the number – never the name – of the applicant. Not until all the papers have been graded will they be matched with names. If other tests, such as training and experience or oral interview ratings have been given, scores will be combined. Different parts of the examination usually have different weights. For example, the written test might count 60 percent of the final grade, and a rating of training and experience 40 percent. In many jurisdictions, veterans will have a certain number of points added to their grades.

After the final grade has been determined, the names are placed in grade order and an eligible list is established. There are various methods for resolving ties between those who get the same final grade – probably the most common is to place first the name of the person whose application was received first. Job offers are made from the eligible list in the order the names appear on it. You will be notified of your grade and your rank as soon as all these computations have been made. This will be done as rapidly as possible.

People who are found to meet the requirements in the announcement are called "eligibles." Their names are put on a list of eligible candidates. An eligible's chances of getting a job depend on how high he stands on this list and how fast agencies are filling jobs from the list.

When a job is to be filled from a list of eligibles, the agency asks for the names of people on the list of eligibles for that job. When the civil service commission receives this request, it sends to the agency the names of the three people highest on this list. Or, if the job to be filled has specialized requirements, the office sends the agency the names of the top three persons who meet these requirements from the general list.

The appointing officer makes a choice from among the three people whose names were sent to him. If the selected person accepts the appointment, the names of the others are put back on the list to be considered for future openings.

That is the rule in hiring from all kinds of eligible lists, whether they are for typist, carpenter, chemist, or something else. For every vacancy, the appointing officer has his choice of any one of the top three eligibles on the list. This explains why the person whose name is on top of the list sometimes does not get an appointment when some of the persons lower on the list do. If the appointing officer chooses the second or third eligible, the No. 1 eligible does not get a job at once, but stays on the list until he is appointed or the list is terminated.

X. HOW TO PASS THE INTERVIEW TEST

The examination for which you applied requires an oral interview test. You have already taken the written test and you are now being called for the interview test – the final part of the formal examination.

You may think that it is not possible to prepare for an interview test and that there are no procedures to follow during an interview. Our purpose is to point out some things you can do in advance that will help you and some good rules to follow and pitfalls to avoid while you are being interviewed.

What is an interview supposed to test?

The written examination is designed to test the technical knowledge and competence of the candidate; the oral is designed to evaluate intangible qualities, not readily measured otherwise, and to establish a list showing the relative fitness of each candidate – as measured against his competitors – for the position sought. Scoring is not on the basis of "right" and "wrong," but on a sliding scale of values ranging from "not passable" to "outstanding." As a matter of fact, it is possible to achieve a relatively low score without a single "incorrect" answer because of evident weakness in the qualities being measured.

Occasionally, an examination may consist entirely of an oral test – either an individual or a group oral. In such cases, information is sought concerning the technical knowledges and abilities of the candidate, since there has been no written examination for this purpose. More commonly, however, an oral test is used to supplement a written examination.

Who conducts interviews?

The composition of oral boards varies among different jurisdictions. In nearly all, a representative of the personnel department serves as chairman. One of the members of the board may be a representative of the department in which the candidate would work. In some cases, "outside experts" are used, and, frequently, a businessman or some other representative of the general public is asked to serve. Labor and management or other special groups may be represented. The aim is to secure the services of experts in the appropriate field.

However the board is composed, it is a good idea (and not at all improper or unethical) to ascertain in advance of the interview who the members are and what groups they represent. When you are introduced to them, you will have some idea of their backgrounds and interests, and at least you will not stutter and stammer over their names.

What should be done before the interview?

While knowledge about the board members is useful and takes some of the surprise element out of the interview, there is other preparation which is more substantive. It *is* possible to prepare for an oral interview – in several ways:

1) Keep a copy of your application and review it carefully before the interview

This may be the only document before the oral board, and the starting point of the interview. Know what education and experience you have listed there, and the sequence and dates of all of it. Sometimes the board will ask you to review the highlights of your experience for them; you should not have to hem and haw doing it.

2) Study the class specification and the examination announcement

Usually, the oral board has one or both of these to guide them. The qualities, characteristics or knowledges required by the position sought are stated in these documents. They offer valuable clues as to the nature of the oral interview. For example, if the job involves supervisory responsibilities, the announcement will usually indicate that knowledge of modern supervisory methods and the qualifications of the candidate as a supervisor will be tested. If so, you can expect such questions, frequently in the form of a hypothetical situation which you are expected to solve. NEVER go into an oral without knowledge of the duties and responsibilities of the job you seek.

3) Think through each qualification required

Try to visualize the kind of questions you would ask if you were a board member. How well could you answer them? Try especially to appraise your own knowledge and background in each area, *measured against the job sought*, and identify any areas in which you are weak. Be critical and realistic – do not flatter yourself.

4) Do some general reading in areas in which you feel you may be weak

For example, if the job involves supervision and your past experience has NOT, some general reading in supervisory methods and practices, particularly in the field of human relations, might be useful. Do NOT study agency procedures or detailed manuals. The oral board will be testing your understanding and capacity, not your memory.

5) Get a good night's sleep and watch your general health and mental attitude

You will want a clear head at the interview. Take care of a cold or any other minor ailment, and of course, no hangovers.

What should be done on the day of the interview?

Now comes the day of the interview itself. Give yourself plenty of time to get there. Plan to arrive somewhat ahead of the scheduled time, particularly if your appointment is in the fore part of the day. If a previous candidate fails to appear, the board might be ready for you a bit early. By early afternoon an oral board is almost invariably behind schedule if there are many candidates, and you may have to wait. Take along a book or magazine to read, or your application to review, but leave any extraneous material in the waiting room when you go in for your interview. In any event, relax and compose yourself.

The matter of dress is important. The board is forming impressions about you – from your experience, your manners, your attitude, and your appearance. Give your personal appearance careful attention. Dress your best, but not your flashiest. Choose conservative, appropriate clothing, and be sure it is immaculate. This is a business interview, and your appearance should indicate that you regard it as such. Besides, being well groomed and properly dressed will help boost your confidence.

Sooner or later, someone will call your name and escort you into the interview room. *This is it.* From here on you are on your own. It is too late for any more preparation. But remember, you asked for this opportunity to prove your fitness, and you are here because your request was granted.

What happens when you go in?

The usual sequence of events will be as follows: The clerk (who is often the board stenographer) will introduce you to the chairman of the oral board, who will introduce you to the other members of the board. Acknowledge the introductions before you sit down. Do not be surprised if you find a microphone facing you or a stenotypist sitting by. Oral interviews are usually recorded in the event of an appeal or other review.

Usually the chairman of the board will open the interview by reviewing the highlights of your education and work experience from your application – primarily for the benefit of the other members of the board, as well as to get the material into the record. Do not interrupt or comment unless there is an error or significant misinterpretation; if that is the case, do not hesitate. But do not quibble about insignificant matters. Also, he will usually ask you some question about your education, experience or your present job – partly to get you to start talking and to establish the interviewing "rapport." He may start the actual questioning, or turn it over to one of the other members. Frequently, each member undertakes the questioning on a particular area, one in which he is perhaps most competent, so you can expect each member to participate in the examination. Because time is limited, you may also expect some rather abrupt switches in the direction the questioning takes, so do not be upset by it. Normally, a board member will not pursue a single line of questioning unless he discovers a particular strength or weakness.

After each member has participated, the chairman will usually ask whether any member has any further questions, then will ask you if you have anything you wish to add. Unless you are expecting this question, it may floor you. Worse, it may start you off on an extended, extemporaneous speech. The board is not usually seeking more information. The question is principally to offer you a last opportunity to present further qualifications or to indicate that you have nothing to add. So, if you feel that a significant qualification or characteristic has been overlooked, it is proper to point it out in a sentence or so. Do not compliment the board on the thoroughness of their examination – they have been sketchy, and you know it. If you wish, merely say, "No thank you, I have nothing further to add." This is a point where you can "talk yourself out" of a good impression or fail to present an important bit of information. Remember, *you close the interview yourself*.

The chairman will then say, "That is all, Mr. _____, thank you." Do not be startled; the interview is over, and quicker than you think. Thank him, gather your belongings and take your leave. Save your sigh of relief for the other side of the door.

How to put your best foot forward

Throughout this entire process, you may feel that the board individually and collectively is trying to pierce your defenses, seek out your hidden weaknesses and embarrass and confuse you. Actually, this is not true. They are obliged to make an appraisal of your qualifications for the job you are seeking, and they want to see you in your best light. Remember, they must interview all candidates and a non-cooperative candidate may become a failure in spite of their best efforts to bring out his qualifications. Here are 15 suggestions that will help you:

1) Be natural – Keep your attitude confident, not cocky

If you are not confident that you can do the job, do not expect the board to be. Do not apologize for your weaknesses, try to bring out your strong points. The board is interested in a positive, not negative, presentation. Cockiness will antagonize any board member and make him wonder if you are covering up a weakness by a false show of strength.

2) Get comfortable, but don't lounge or sprawl

Sit erectly but not stiffly. A careless posture may lead the board to conclude that you are careless in other things, or at least that you are not impressed by the importance of the occasion. Either conclusion is natural, even if incorrect. Do not fuss with your clothing, a pencil or an ashtray. Your hands may occasionally be useful to emphasize a point; do not let them become a point of distraction.

3) Do not wisecrack or make small talk

This is a serious situation, and your attitude should show that you consider it as such. Further, the time of the board is limited – they do not want to waste it, and neither should you.

4) Do not exaggerate your experience or abilities

In the first place, from information in the application or other interviews and sources, the board may know more about you than you think. Secondly, you probably will not get away with it. An experienced board is rather adept at spotting such a situation, so do not take the chance.

5) If you know a board member, do not make a point of it, yet do not hide it

Certainly you are not fooling him, and probably not the other members of the board. Do not try to take advantage of your acquaintanceship – it will probably do you little good.

6) Do not dominate the interview

Let the board do that. They will give you the clues – do not assume that you have to do all the talking. Realize that the board has a number of questions to ask you, and do not try to take up all the interview time by showing off your extensive knowledge of the answer to the first one.

7) Be attentive

You only have 20 minutes or so, and you should keep your attention at its sharpest throughout. When a member is addressing a problem or question to you, give him your undivided attention. Address your reply principally to him, but do not exclude the other board members.

8) Do not interrupt

A board member may be stating a problem for you to analyze. He will ask you a question when the time comes. Let him state the problem, and wait for the question.

9) Make sure you understand the question

Do not try to answer until you are sure what the question is. If it is not clear, restate it in your own words or ask the board member to clarify it for you. However, do not haggle about minor elements.

10) Reply promptly but not hastily

A common entry on oral board rating sheets is "candidate responded readily," or "candidate hesitated in replies." Respond as promptly and quickly as you can, but do not jump to a hasty, ill-considered answer.

11) Do not be peremptory in your answers

A brief answer is proper – but do not fire your answer back. That is a losing game from your point of view. The board member can probably ask questions much faster than you can answer them.

12) Do not try to create the answer you think the board member wants

He is interested in what kind of mind you have and how it works – not in playing games. Furthermore, he can usually spot this practice and will actually grade you down on it.

13) Do not switch sides in your reply merely to agree with a board member

Frequently, a member will take a contrary position merely to draw you out and to see if you are willing and able to defend your point of view. Do not start a debate, yet do not surrender a good position. If a position is worth taking, it is worth defending.

14) Do not be afraid to admit an error in judgment if you are shown to be wrong

The board knows that you are forced to reply without any opportunity for careful consideration. Your answer may be demonstrably wrong. If so, admit it and get on with the interview.

15) Do not dwell at length on your present job

The opening question may relate to your present assignment. Answer the question but do not go into an extended discussion. You are being examined for a *new* job, not your present one. As a matter of fact, try to phrase ALL your answers in terms of the job for which you are being examined.

Basis of Rating

Probably you will forget most of these "do's" and "don'ts" when you walk into the oral interview room. Even remembering them all will not ensure you a passing grade. Perhaps you did not have the qualifications in the first place. But remembering them will help you to put your best foot forward, without treading on the toes of the board members.

Rumor and popular opinion to the contrary notwithstanding, an oral board wants you to make the best appearance possible. They know you are under pressure – but they also want to see how you respond to it as a guide to what your reaction would be under the pressures of the job you seek. They will be influenced by the degree of poise you display, the personal traits you show and the manner in which you respond.

ABOUT THIS BOOK

This book contains tests divided into Examination Sections. Go through each test, answering every question in the margin. We have also attached a sample answer sheet at the back of the book that can be removed and used. At the end of each test look at the answer key and check your answers. On the ones you got wrong, look at the right answer choice and learn. Do not fill in the answers first. Do not memorize the questions and answers, but understand the answer and principles involved. On your test, the questions will likely be different from the samples. Questions are changed and new ones added. If you understand these past questions you should have success with any changes that arise. Tests may consist of several types of questions. We have additional books on each subject should more study be advisable or necessary for you. Finally, the more you study, the better prepared you will be. This book is intended to be the last thing you study before you walk into the examination room. Prior study of relevant texts is also recommended. NLC publishes some of these in our Fundamental Series. Knowledge and good sense are important factors in passing your exam. Good luck also helps. So now study this Passbook, absorb the material contained within and take that knowledge into the examination. Then do your best to pass that exam.

EXAMINATION SECTION

EXAMINATION SECTION
TEST 1

DIRECTIONS: Each question or incomplete statement is followed by several suggested answers or completions. Select the one that BEST answers the question or completes the statement. *PRINT THE LETTER OF THE CORRECT ANSWER IN THE SPACE AT THE RIGHT.*

1. In a uniformed correction force, the limits of authority and responsibility of each position should be clearly defined. Of the following, the MAIN reason for this is to

    A. avoid overlapping authority and possible conflicts
    B. facilitate an exchange of viewpoints at parallel levels of authority
    C. improve the training and therefore the competence of personnel
    D. provide well-defined promotional levels for personnel

    1._____

2. When some correction officers complained about a new Department order, a captain remarked, *I agree with you but you can't fight Central Office.* Such a remark is unwise chiefly because

    A. correction officers may assume that the captain will back them when they do not enforce the order
    B. correction officers will be motivated to have doubts about all other orders
    C. the captain cannot know all the reasons for the promulgation of the order
    D. the captain is undermining discipline by his criticism of Department policies

    2._____

3. Correction Officer A is asked a question by Correction Officer B concerning a matter which is primarily B's responsibility. Although Correction Officer A is not sure of the correct answer, he gives one to the best of his knowledge, not giving any indication of his uncertainty. A's action in this instance was

    A. *acceptable;* B has the basic responsibility in this matter and is most likely seeking only A's informal opinion
    B. *not acceptable;* A should not have answered B's question since the matter is B's responsibility
    C. *acceptable;* the search for absolute certainty prior to making a decision leads to undesirable delay
    D. *not acceptable;* B may act on the basis of the uncertain answer given by A

    3._____

4. Since a correction captain expects subordinates to carry out commands to the letter, it is most important for the captain to

    A. check on the execution of all commands immediately
    B. issue commands clearly and make sure they are understood
    C. issue only commands that seem obviously reasonable to anyone
    D. make only one officer responsible for the execution of any command

    4._____

5. A new correction officer under your supervision lacks confidence in her/his ability to perform the duties of the position. Of the following, it would be BEST for you as captain to

    5._____

A. assign simple and routine tasks to this officer for a few months
B. recommend that the officer be dropped at the end of probation if no improvement is shown
C. assign this officer to work along with and under the guidance of an experienced officer for a while
D. recommend to your superior that this officer be returned to the academy for extended and intensive classroom training

6. In evaluating the capability of a correction officer to use independent judgment, the one of the following to which the captain should usually give GREATEST consideration is the

   A. ability of the officer to establish good relationships with people
   B. number of times the officer speaks to the captain
   C. officer's record of emotional stability
   D. decisions made by the officer in previous work situations

7. If a captain is to be an effective leader of the correction officers he/she commands, the captain must

   A. assign to each officer an equal amount of responsibility and authority
   B. develop the individual capabilities of each officer and motivate them all to work for the good of the institution as a whole
   C. give them close and strict supervision at all times
   D. permit them to follow their own initiative whenever they strongly disagree with established procedures

8. A captain notices that one correction officer does not get along too well with the other officers. Of the following, the BEST thing for the captain to do in such a situation is to

   A. make an effort to learn the reasons for the difficulty in an effort to resolve the problem
   B. overlook the matter since the work will probably be unaffected
   C. prepare a report of the situation to a superior officer and be guided by the latter's decision
   D. tell all the officers they must work together harmoniously or risk disciplinary action

9. You observe that a correction officer under your command is not carrying out a specific assignment in accordance with the instructions you gave. Of the following, the MOST important reason why you should have this officer repeat the instructions you gave is that

   A. instructions can be misunderstood even by excellent correction officers
   B. it will indicate that incorrect instructions were given
   C. inefficiency usually has serious consequences
   D. oral instructions should be repeated when issued as a safeguard that they are understood

10. It is generally considered that the use of a police training program for the purpose of training correction personnel would be undesirable mainly because

A. those attracted to correctional work would for the most part not be interested in police work
B. the two uniformed forces should be kept distinct, the one from the other
C. emphasis in police work is on the apprehension of law violators
D. correction training facilities do not measure up to those available to police forces

11. When correction officers ask a certain captain's advice about handling specific work problems, the captain now and then responds to the request by first asking the correction officer what the latter thinks should be done. This practice by the captain is generally   11.____

    A. *bad,* since subordinates will not ask questions in the future
    B. *good,* since it motivates subordinates to think about possible solutions
    C. *bad,* since correction officers will question the motives of the captain
    D. *good,* since poorly thought out action can lead to undesirable results

12. If a correction officer comes to a captain with a minor grievance that seems of great importance to the officer, it would be BEST for the captain to   12.____

    A. explain that supervisory personnel should not be involved in petty grievances
    B. explain why the grievance is of no importance
    C. listen attentively and give the grievance serious consideration
    D. redirect the officer's attention to a major department problem

13. When delivering a training talk to new correction officers, a captain who uses technical terms which may not be familiar to the *rookies* acts correctly provided that he/she   13.____

    A. explains such terms as soon as he/she uses them
    B. invites the *rookies* to ask questions about anything they do not understand
    C. questions the *rookies* at the end of the lecture to evaluate their grasp of the material
    D. tells the *rookies* the names of standard correctional works in which they are to look up the terms

14. The captain whose subordinates never have any complaints about anything should probably reappraise his role as a supervisor. Upon such a reappraisal, the captain is *most likely* to discover that   14.____

    A. supervision is too strict
    B. the officers are afraid
    C. the officers are well satisfied with everything
    D. communication is poor

15. It is generally bad for subordinate employees to become aware of pending or contemplated changes in policy via the *grapevine* mainly because   15.____

    A. subordinates may feel that the administration thinks the staff cannot be trusted with the information
    B. subordinates may feel that the administration lacks the courage to make an unpopular announcement
    C. information circulated by this method is seldom completely accurate and often spreads needless apprehension among the staff
    D. evidence that a responsible official has proven to be secretive will undermine confidence

16. The one of the following training methods likely to be MOST effective in developing in correction officers a specific skill, such as taking inmate counts, is

    A. meticulously planned lectures
    B. repeated and supervised practice
    C. selected and comprehensive readings
    D. well-designed demonstrations using visual aids

17. For a captain to give equally close supervision to all correction officers would be

    A. *desirable;* all correction officers can benefit from the captain's guidance
    B. *undesirable;* the degree of supervision needed varies with the capabilities of each officer
    C. *desirable;* all subordinates would be assured of fair and equal treatment
    D. *undesirable;* the demands on the captain's time would be too great

18. Of the following, the BEST technique for a captain to use in training correction officers is to

    A. encourage them to ask questions at all times
    B. change their assignments frequently
    C. teach them how to analyze important facts in order to make their own decisions
    D. teach them how to evaluate inmate morals

19. A captain should not permit correction officers who have just been appointed to learn institutional procedures entirely on the basis of their own experience mainly because they

    A. learn more quickly under correct guidance
    B. learn quickest when left to their own resources
    C. remember best what they learn first
    D. will lose too much time worrying about whether they are learning the proper things in the proper manner

20. Captains may find that some correction officers who have been on the job a long time require more supervision than correction officers with less experience. Of the following, the CHIEF implication of this statement for the captain as a supervisor is that

    A. correction officers with years of experience generally break more minor regulations than do the newer correction officers
    B. the ability of correction officers does not increase with years of experience
    C. the newer correction officers are usually better acquainted with the detailed rules and regulations of the Department
    D. the number of years of experience a correction officer has may not be a reliable index of the amount of supervision needed

21. When instructing correction officers under his/her supervision, a captain should realize that

    A. after the age of 20, a person's ability to learn decreases progressively at a slow rate
    B. learning should be uniform if instruction is uniform
    C. learning should be uniform if there is active participation by each learner
    D. persons of the same age differ in the amount they can learn in a given time

22. A captain must be strict in enforcing discipline, but at the same time should also show sympathy and understanding toward subordinates. The captain who BEST illustrates this is the one who

   A. gives orders that are precise and unambiguous
   B. overlooks minor infractions
   C. seeks to discover the reasons behind an officer's misconduct
   D. shows no favoritism toward anyone

23. Which one of the following is the LEAST desirable supervisory practice for a captain to follow?

   A. Discuss with correction officers theoretical situations which they may conceivably encounter in their work and their possible solutions
   B. Observe for a few days the mistakes a correction officer makes and then discuss these mistakes with the officer
   C. Praise a correction officer for good work in the presence of other correction officers
   D. Question correction officers from time to time on provisions of the rules and regulations relating to their work

24. When a captain must often take disciplinary action against subordinates, the captain should realize that

   A. this is normal practice if officers are to be well disciplined
   B. he/she was probably assigned to this troublesome group because he/she had the ability to handle it
   C. it would be best to ask for a new assignment for the good of the Department
   D. his/her methods of supervision need self-review to determine whether they are faulty

25. Captain A, just before instructing a correction officer in the correct method of searching a cell for contraband, explained to the officer why it was important to follow the correct procedure. The captain's action was

   A. *good;* a procedure is less likely to be forgotten if its purpose is understood
   B. *poor;* since the importance of searching for contraband is obvious, the explanation is a waste of time
   C. *good;* repetition is an effective aid in learning an operation
   D. *poor;* such an explanation will distract the correction officer from the main points in the instruction

26. The use of positive discipline by a captain will enhance the morale of the institution. Of the following, the BEST example of positive discipline is

   A. assigning unpleasant duties purely as an educational device
   B. reprimanding in private and very soon after the negligent act
   C. suggesting methods of work improvement when reviewing work that is poorly done
   D. adjusting the severity of the punishment to the severity of the offense

27. If a correction officer wants to talk to the captain about a personal problem, the captain should

   A. be willing to discuss the matter with the officer
   B. refer the officer to the Assistant Deputy so as to keep the captain-correction officer relationship impersonal
   C. tell the officer to discuss the matter with another correction officer with whom he/she is friendly
   D. tell the officer that personal problems should not be discussed on the job

28. Assume you are a correction captain. Another captain has been newly assigned to your institution. For you to tell this new captain the strengths and weaknesses of some of the individual correction officers he/she will supervise would be

   A. *bad;* bias will be introduced unknowingly into the work situation
   B. *good;* the new captain will be able to make various assignments of officers more intelligently
   C. *bad;* it will delay the new captain's adjustment to new responsibilities
   D. *good;* the abilities of a correction officer change from day to day due to various factors

29. Of the following, the BEST way of helping to assure that procedures on a particular post will be carried out uniformly is to

   A. assign officers of approximately the same ability to this post
   B. assign the same officers to this post as much as possible
   C. have the same captain instruct any personnel assigned to this post for the first time
   D. require that every officer assigned to the post read and know the procedural orders and job analysis of the post

30. A captain on patrol of a cell block at night sees an inmate writhing on the floor in apparent pain. In this situation, the captain should

   A. bear in mind that the inmate may be feigning and take necessary precautions
   B. enter the cell immediately to get the inmate back on the bed and give first aid
   C. notify the officer in command of the tour right away
   D. summon a doctor immediately and wait for him to arrive

31. Of the following, the BEST method of counting inmates in an open area is to have

   A. the most capable officer make two successive counts
   B. two officers make the count simultaneously
   C. one officer make the count with a second officer watching for any movement of inmates
   D. one officer make one count and then immediately after have another officer make an independent count

32. Strict limitation and control of telephone calls by inmates of a correctional institution is

   A. *desirable;* it is a necessary security precaution
   B. *undesirable;* it causes a loss of incentive for good behavior
   C. *desirable;* the number of available telephone instruments is limited
   D. *undesirable;* it is destructive of morale

33. Of the following prisoners, which one is LEAST likely to attempt to escape? One   33._____

    A. about to complete his sentence
    B. afraid of being assaulted by other prisoners
    C. just denied parole
    D. with no family ties

34. Of the following, the main purpose of the tool shadow board is to   34._____

    A. enable employees to locate needed tools quickly
    B. indicate when a tool is missing
    C. provide a central place for the storage of tools
    D. reduce accidents by storing tools in a safe place

35. Which one of the following is a problem of LEAST immediate concern at the time of admission of a new inmate to a correctional institution?   35._____

    A. Exclusion of contraband
    B. Safeguarding the inmate's money and valuables
    C. Proper work assignment
    D. Safeguarding the institution from vermin and disease

36. Assume a riot of prison inmates is in progress. Of the following, it would be LEAST desirable for the prison authorities to   36._____

    A. separate the apparent ringleaders from the rest of the inmates as soon as practicable
    B. keep a reserve group of officers away from the riot area until the situation has been assessed
    C. follow a pre-established emergency plan for riots
    D. bargain with the rioting inmates if their complaints seem legitimate

37. A correction officer in a court pen searches police cases delivered to the pen for temporary detention before he/she assumes custody of these prisoners. The prisoners are later taken before the judge. For the correction officer to search the prisoners again when they are returned to the pen is   37._____

    A. *foolish* because the prisoners have not been out of the building and have been under surveillance at all times
    B. *sensible* because the prisoners may have acquired contraband when they were out of the pen
    C. *foolish* because the prisoners were searched very thoroughly the first time
    D. *sensible* because prisoners in court pens should be searched several times each day

38. Which one of the following statements about firearms is the MOST accurate?   38._____

    A. A correction officer's personal safety can be absolutely guaranteed only when he carries a gun.
    B. An armory tower is usually a very poor place for storing firearms.
    C. A supply of firearms coming into an institution should be clearly labeled.
    D. The best place for storing firearms is right next to the inmate housing area, for easy accessibility when needed.

39. The practice of receiving a new prisoner and admitting him to the institution without a complete strip shakedown is

    A. *desirable* only if the officer delivering the prisoner gives written assurance that the prisoner has been frisked and is free of contraband
    B. *not desirable* under any circumstances
    C. *desirable* only if the prisoner has been brought directly from another jail
    D. *not desirable* except with material witnesses

40. *A captain should patrol at irregular and unexpected times throughout his tour.* This method of patrol is preferable to regular patrols at scheduled times mainly because

    A. the captain has greater flexibility in scheduling the day's activities
    B. patrols will not be forgotten or reduced if they become habitual
    C. officers on post know that the captain will be around to inspect their work
    D. it gives a truer picture of actual conditions on the different posts

41. A well-trained correction officer, if he/she is alert, will know at all times how many prisoners he/she has and where they are. Of the following, the CHIEF implication of this statement for the captain as a supervisor is that the

    A. responsibility for the proper custody, security, and control of inmates is primarily that of the line officer
    B. captain, as well as the officer, should know at all times how many prisoners each officer has in his/her charge and where each is assigned
    C. captain should repeatedly test the alertness of subordinates by questioning them as to the number and the whereabouts of the prisoners under their supervision
    D. most thorough grounding of officers in proper methods of custody and security will be nullified if they are not also imbued with an understanding of the importance of being always attentive to duty

42. Of the following, the LEAST desirable procedure to follow in the control of contraband is to search

    A. cells at regular intervals in accordance with a fixed schedule
    B. both incoming and outgoing vehicles
    C. *trusties* often
    D. the visitor when an inmate is authorized to have an open type visit

43. In a well-run correctional institution, it should not be too difficult for an inmate to bring to the attention of the administration a matter that he considers important.
    However, a danger that must be guarded against in keeping communication between inmates and staff open is that

    A. inmates may gradually assume some staff functions
    B. introvert inmates may not utilize the established channels of communication
    C. there may be an accompanying weakening of inmate discipline
    D. certain classes of inmates may consume administrators' time needlessly

44. Extra security precautions are generally advisable in the supervision of prisoners at mess. This is so mainly because

A. different classes of inmates mingle together freely at mess
B. large numbers of prisoners are concentrated together in one place
C. prisoners are usually dissatisfied with institution food
D. prison riots may begin anywhere

45. In a certain correctional institution, a captain discharging an inmate asked the latter some personal questions such as, *Where do your parents live?*, *What is your mother's name?*, etc. The purpose of asking these questions was probably to

    A. check the accuracy of the information on the discharge papers
    B. motivate the inmate to renew his family ties
    C. prevent a substitution of inmates
    D. show an interest in the inmate's welfare

46. Which one of the following is NOT a recommended procedure when searching a large group of inmates, such as a work detail?

    A. After search of inmates is completed, officer searches area where they were standing.
    B. Each inmate in turn approaches officer for search, arms outstretched, back to officer.
    C. First inmate searched starts a new line at a distance from those not yet searched.
    D. Inmates in a circle, far apart from each other, the officer in the center where he/she can see all the inmates.

47. For a correction officer to keep a type of cover over the prison keys that he/she carries is a

    A. *good* idea; it will prevent the inmates from studying the shapes of the keys
    B. *poor* idea; the inmates are likely to resent such extraordinary precautionary measures
    C. *good* idea; it will prevent loss of keys
    D. *poor* idea; it will cause a correction officer undue delay in reaching for a key in an emergency

48. As a general rule, delay by uniformed personnel in considering inmate complaints is

    A. *desirable;* it will discourage complaints
    B. *undesirable;* it may create inmate unrest
    C. *desirable;* most inmate complaints are not justified
    D. *undesirable;* the cause of the complaint may disappear if action is delayed

49. *In every prison population there are a few inmates, probably not over 5 percent of the total, who are constantly attempting to agitate trouble for the administration. These individuals are frequently model prisoners on the surface.* Of the following, the MOST practical way to prevent these habitual agitators from causing any great amount of harm is to

    A. keep them under constant observation
    B. keep the rest of the inmates satisfied by providing good prison conditions
    C. let these troublesome inmates know that the administration knows who they are and that any attempt to start trouble will be dealt with swiftly
    D. segregate them

50. Of the following, the best justification for NOT keeping large amounts of gas munitions on hand at an institution is that

    A. a large supply creates a security problem
    B. additional supplies can be obtained quickly if trouble is suspected
    C. gas shouldn't be used in large quantities
    D. the effectiveness of gas munitions depreciates quickly

---

KEY (CORRECT ANSWERS)

1. A	11. B	21. D	31. C	41. D
2. D	12. C	22. C	32. A	42. A
3. D	13. A	23. B	33. A	43. D
4. B	14. D	24. D	34. B	44. B
5. C	15. C	25. A	35. C	45. C
6. D	16. B	26. B	36. D	46. D
7. B	17. B	27. A	37. B	47. A
8. A	18. C	28. B	38. C	48. B
9. A	19. A	29. D	39. B	49. B
10. C	20. D	30. A	40. D	50. D

TEST 2

DIRECTIONS: Each question or incomplete statement is followed by several suggested answers or completions. Select the one that BEST answers the question or completes the statement. *PRINT THE LETTER OF THE CORRECT ANSWER IN THE SPACE AT THE RIGHT.*

1. Which one of the following principles is it LEAST desirable to follow in a good system of key control?　　1.____

    A. A listing of all keys should be maintained which should include the trade name of the lock.
    B. Keys should not be issued from several locations of an institution.
    C. No duplicate keys should be kept at the institution.
    D. The location of each lock for which there is a key should be recorded.

2. Of the following, the BEST way for a captain to avoid unintentional infractions of the institution's rules by inmates is to　　2.____

    A. enforce the rules uniformly and impartially
    B. make sure the officers know the rules, so they can enforce them
    C. post the rules conspicuously where they will always command the attention of inmates
    D. see that inmates are instructed thoroughly in these rules

3. For a captain to occasionally research a correction officer's detail of inmates after the latter has completed his/her search is a　　3.____

    A. *desirable* practice because it discourages a lackadaisical attitude in the searching of inmates
    B. *undesirable* practice because it impairs the officer's confidence
    C. *desirable* practice because even the officer who consistently employs the most thoroughgoing methods of searching should be checked regularly
    D. *undesirable* practice because it weakens the officer's control of the inmates

4. Suppose that a study of prison inmates shows that the rate of recidivism increases as the number of the offense increases. For example, 10% of first offenders become second offenders, 30% of second offenders become third offenders, 70% of third offenders become fourth offenders, etc. If the findings of this study are valid, then it is MOST reasonable to assume that　　4.____

    A. environment plays a minor role in the predisposition towards criminal behavior
    B. exposure to prison life inevitably leads to the commission of further crimes
    C. first offenders represent the most fruitful field for intensive rehabilitative efforts
    D. it would be desirable in an institution to house together offenders who have committed the same number of offenses

5. Which one of the following statements about the psychopathic or sociopathic personality is TRUE?　　5.____

    A. All criminals are sociopathic in varying degree.
    B. The sociopath has frequent guilt feelings about his non-conformist behavior.
    C. The sociopath seldom has guilt feelings about his non-conformist behavior.
    D. The sociopath responds well to psychotherapy or mental treatment.

11

6. A captain instructed subordinates NEVER, under any circumstances, to use force against an inmate. The captain's instructions were

   A. *foolish;* the use of force against an inmate is justified in certain situations
   B. *sensible;* the use of force may accidentally cause the death of an inmate
   C. *foolish;* each correction officer should use common sense in each situation
   D. *sensible;* unless force is absolutely prohibited, some officers are bound to use it to excess

7. Which one of the following is LEAST characteristic of an inmate who has a paranoid personality?
   He

   A. forgets an imagined offense quickly
   B. thinks other people are hostile to him
   C. thinks other people are jealous of him
   D. tries to prove the institution is not well run

8. Model behavior in prison is not always a good guide to the inmate's success on parole because

   A. adjustment to the complexities of civilian life is as difficult as adjustment to prison life
   B. experience has shown that parolees very often violate the terms of their parole
   C. inmates are individuals and generalized conclusions cannot be drawn regarding their behavior
   D. prison-wise inmates will often behave well in prison merely to hasten the date of release

9. The practice of using inmate *trusties* to perform responsible tasks in a correctional institution is generally considered by progressive prison administrators to be

   A. desirable only with inmates nearing the end of their sentence
   B. of doubtful value
   C. of value if used with discretion
   D. unacceptable

10. The one of the following that is a characteristic of the schizoid type of personality encountered in correctional work is

    A. an exaggerated degree of socialization with other inmates
    B. assertiveness
    C. a tendency to become emotionally involved with certain inmates
    D. a tendency to excessive daydreaming

11. It is generally considered undesirable, as a disciplinary practice, to restrict an inmate's letter writing privilege UNLESS the

    A. inmate is not unduly harmed by this restriction
    B. offense being punished is in violation of the regulations relating to this privilege
    C. restriction is for a short time
    D. restriction is used in conjunction with other forms of punishment

12. Of the following, one of the MAIN theories underlying use of the indeterminate sentence is that the

    A. punishment should be adjusted to the severity of the offense
    B. rate of improvement should be a factor in determining the length of imprisonment
    C. sentencing of offenders should be left entirely to the discretion of the courts
    D. variation in sentences for the same offense is destructive of inmate morale

13. Since inmate programs of work, recreation, vocational training, etc. have not been effective in reducing crime or the rate of recidivism, they should be abandoned.
    A basic weakness of this criticism is that it fails to take into account that these programs

    A. are also needed to keep inmates occupied
    B. are not intended to achieve the purposes stated
    C. can not influence the majority of criminals, since they are not apprehended
    D. have been tried for only a very short time

14. Contrasting the responsibility of prison management for rehabilitating inmates with its responsibility for secure custody and control of inmates, which one of the following statements is MOST accurate?

    A. Both responsibilities have equal priority.
    B. Good control can be consistently realized without rehabilitative treatment.
    C. Methods for effective rehabilitative treatment can operate only in an atmosphere where control is maintained.
    D. The more fundamental responsibility is the rehabilitation of inmates.

15. In a correctional institution, it is usually desirable to vest responsibility for the general enforcement of discipline and the administration of punishment in a single disciplinary officer, who is usually the head of the institution or one of her/his deputies. This system for the enforcement of discipline is desirable mainly because

    A. discipline, if inflexible, will do more harm than good
    B. greater uniformity in the enforcement of discipline and the application of punishments will result
    C. the list of infractions and punishments should be well publicized
    D. the officer responsible for the enforcement of discipline should not be too far removed from the offender

16. In all probability, the behavior of a recalcitrant inmate serving an indefinite sentence would be MOST influenced by a threatened

    A. isolation and restricted diet
    B. loss of family visits
    C. loss of good time
    D. suspension of privileges

17. Is it desirable for indeterminate sentence prisoners to be familiar with the general procedures of the parole board?

    A. *No;* it would lead to attempts by inmates to interfere with the parole board.
    B. *Yes;* it will lead to greater public acceptance of parole boards.
    C. *No;* parole board procedures and practices change from time to time.
    D. *Yes;* it would lessen prisoner resentment caused by ignorance against actions of the parole board.

18. While we cannot tell to what extent individuals are predisposed toward crime at birth, there is no doubt that some are so formed that in an unfavorable environment they are more apt to be lead into crime than others.
    This statement suggests *most nearly* that

    A. all individuals have some pre-disposition toward crime from birth but most are able to overcome this
    B. if exposure to unfavorable environment were eliminated, crime would be eliminated
    C. it is possible to foretell criminal behavior
    D. under the same circumstances, some persons will react criminally because of hereditary factors, while others will not

19. Of the following, the PRINCIPAL reason for controlling the amount of money an inmate may spend weekly for commissary items is generally to

    A. check gambling and attempts at bribery
    B. control smuggling of contraband
    C. keep the commissary staff at a moderate size
    D. make it easier to operate the commissary

20. In prostitution cases, the courts have little choice but to decide whether the offense actually occurred as charged, rather than the more desirable alternative of determining whether the particular offender is a social misfit in need of rehabilitation. This statement implies *most directly* that

    A. a very large proportion of women who are social misfits resort to prostitution
    B. the determination of whether a prostitution offender is a social misfit is up to the courts
    C. there is the wrong legal emphasis in prostitution cases
    D. with an effort at rehabilitation prostitution would be eliminated

21. Special privileges which are not open to all the inmates of a correctional institution must not be permitted to particular individuals. This statement means to imply that

    A. some classes of inmates should not be permitted special privileges
    B. any inmate should be able, by good conduct and proper attitude, to earn any privilege which another inmate enjoys
    C. no inmate should enjoy a privilege which all the other inmates do not also enjoy at the same time
    D. there should not be any special privileges for inmates to enjoy

22. Of the following, the MAIN drawback of placing chief or sole emphasis in a prison recreation program on active games and sports is that it

    A. deprives those not physically fit of the opportunity to participate
    B. fosters an unhealthy competitive spirit
    C. requires money for equipment
    D. requires the inmate to expend too much physical energy

23. The experience of several leading cottage type correctional institutions for women with inmate *student government* programs has shown them to be

    A. *desirable;* they develop a sense of group responsibility in the inmate
    B. *undesirable;* they tend to become a type of kangaroo court
    C. *desirable;* they have effectively fixed responsibility for the maintenance of discipline in each cottage on the cottage committee
    D. *undesirable;* they must be directed by staff, and inmates lose interest

24. Institutions for women have made notable contributions to correctional progress because public opinion has not stood in the way of experimentation with new methods and techniques by women superintendents. Of the following, the CHIEF reason for this attitude on the part of the public is probably that

    A. a more chivalrous attitude toward women is a cultural phenomenon of our society that has carried over into the public's attitude toward the heads of women's institutions
    B. the number of women offenders is smaller than the number of men offenders
    C. the public is not as well-informed about women's institutions
    D. women offenders do not generally commit acts of violence or present a threat to the public in the same way as male offenders

25. Which one of the following statements about the homosexual inmate is LEAST accurate?

    A. Individuals who habitually engage in such conduct are quite easy to identify.
    B. Some, but not all such inmates, have certain distinctive mannerisms.
    C. Some inmates who engage in homosexual practices in prison are sexually normal outside of prison.
    D. When housed in dormitories with normal inmates, they will be deterred from engaging in homosexual practices with such inmates.

26. According to the Rules and Regulations of the Department of Correction, a captain is NOT required to

    A. be responsible for handling records, fines, bails, and entries in the register of prisoners when in charge of a tour
    B. be responsible for the identification and discharge of prisoners when in charge of a tour
    C. immediately send home a correction officer under her/his command who reports to work intoxicated
    D. report in writing all latenesses of correction officers under her/his command

27. A member of the immediate family of an inmate who is confined in a Department of Correction institution may visit the inmate provided said family member is not less than _____ years old.

    A. 16   B. 17   C. 18   D. 19

28. Assume that in a sampling of inmates, three-fifths are found to be over 30 years old. One-third of the remainder are under 20 years of age. Then, of all the inmates in this sampling, the number between the ages of 20 and 30 inclusive is *most nearly* _____ of the total.

    A. 1/15   B. 4/15   C. 3/16   D. 2/7

29. Suppose your institution's census decreased 15% from 2000 to 2002, increased 10% from 2002 to 2004, and increased 5% from 2004 to 2006. The number of inmates in 2006 is most nearly what percent of the number of inmates in 2006?

    A. 98% B. 99% C. 99.5% D. 100%

30. According to the Rules and Regulations of the Department of Correction, prisoners sentenced in night court to one day are to be discharged

    A. on the day and hour specified by the judge
    B. after the court has adjourned
    C. at 9:00 A.M. the next morning
    D. at 4:00 P.M. the next afternoon

31. When an officer finds narcotics in the possession of an unauthorized person at a Department of Correction institution, the officer is required to take possession of the narcotics, place them in a sealed envelope or package, and make certain notations on the outside of such envelope or package. Such notations do NOT include the

    A. name of witnesses
    B. status of the person on whom the narcotics was found
    C. time the incident occurred
    D. type of narcotics that was found

32. A criminal court procedure designed to speed up justice and to provide relief for a universally denounced process is:

    A. More extensive use of probation with certain classes of minor offenders
    B. Release on their own recognizance of certain offenders who cannot furnish bail
    C. Setting up of a 24-hour arraignment part of Criminal Court in each county
    D. Speeding up court calendars by assignment of rotating panels of judges

33. A captain has been notified by a correction officer under his supervision that an inmate has committed an infraction of discipline important enough to necessitate action. The FIRST thing that the captain should do is to

    A. inform the disciplinary officer or board of the institution so that a hearing can be held quickly
    B. investigate the complaint to see if the facts warrant disciplinary action
    C. notify the inmate that he is in a punishment status pending a hearing
    D. place the inmate in segregation pending investigation

34. If a member of a work gang in a Department of Correction institution escapes, the officer in charge of the gang should FIRST

    A. inform his superior officer of the name and number of the escapee
    B. inform the Police Department of the escape
    C. line up all the remaining members of the work gang
    D. question the other inmates of the gang to find out who saw the inmate last, when, and where

35. Assume you are preparing a summary of all the inmates serving definite sentence in your institution, grouped according to length of sentence. You have the following totals: the number of inmates serving a definite sentence of more than 6 months; the number of inmates serving a definite sentence of more than 3 months; and the number of inmates serving a definite sentence of 3 months or less. To find what fraction the inmates serving more than 6 months constitute of all the inmates serving a definite sentence, you should

    A. divide the number of inmates serving more than 6 months by the number serving 3 months or less, then by the number serving more than 3 months, and add the two
    B. divide the number of inmates serving more than 6 months by the sum of the inmates serving 3 months or less and the inmates serving more than 3 months
    C. divide twice the number of inmates serving more than 6 months by the total of all the inmates serving definite sentences
    D. subtract the number of inmates serving more than 6 months from the total of all the inmates serving definite sentences and then divide by the total number of inmates serving definite sentence

36. According to the Rules and Regulations of the Department of Correction, the officer on duty is NOT required to inspect an inmate placed in isolation or solitary confinement more often than

    A. once a day
    B. once every hour
    C. twice a day
    D. twice every hour

37. A captain is instructing a correction officer assigned to a court pen in the proper procedure for the receipt of new or direct admissions from the police. The captain need NOT instruct the correction officer to

    A. ask the patrolman to sign his name and write his precinct or command in the proper section on the back of the commitment
    B. require the prisoner to sign his name on the commitment while the patrolman is there
    C. take a print of the prisoner's left index finger on the commitment
    D. tell the patrolman the reason for the procedures the correction officer must follow before assuming custody of the prisoner

38. Unless otherwise stated on the commitment papers, an inmate in a Department of Correction institution on 2 separate commitments must serve the sentences consecutively if the sentences are

    A. being served in default of payment of respective fines
    B. for the same offense
    C. from the same court
    D. from the same court and the court did not indicate the order in which they are to be served

39. When contraband is found on a prisoner who is received from the police at a court detention pen, the correction officer should

   A. deliver the contraband to the property clerk of the court
   B. notify the person designated by the prisoner to pick it up
   C. take charge of it pending disposition of the case
   D. have the police officer take it from the prisoner

40. The Department of Correction will conduct a lineup for the purpose of identification of an inmate at the written request of the Police Department or Office of the District Attorney. Which one of the following is NOT a part of the lineup procedure as conducted by the Department of Correction?

   A. A record is kept of the names of all inmates presented at the lineup.
   B. The suspected inmate must be advised of the reason he is being called.
   C. The names of any police officers present during the lineup must be recorded.
   D. Each individual lineup is made up of nine inmates, including the person suspected.

41. The one of the following which BEST exemplifies *negative motivation* is:

   A. A feeling on the part of the officer that the work is significant
   B. Monetary rewards offered the officer for high levels of output
   C. Reducing or withholding the officer's incentive rewards when performance is mediocre
   D. Non-monetary rewards given the officer such as publicizing a good suggestion

42. Which one of the following measures to deal with addicts may be deemed MOST coercive?

   A. Compulsory commitment of addicts to correctional institutions upon application to the court by a member of the addict's family
   B. Dispensing of limited amounts of drugs to addicts by doctors
   C. Involuntary commitment of addicts to hospitals for treatment
   D. Stiffer prison sentences for narcotics users

43. Which one of the following is part of the standard operating procedure whenever a payment for a fine is made at an institution of the Department?

   A. A certified or teller's check will be accepted in payment.
   B. The duplicate copy of the receipt is given to the person paying the fine.
   C. The payment will be accepted even if other detainers exist in the case.
   D. The serial numbers of all bills received in payment must be entered on the receipt form.

44. A captain is explaining security precautions to an officer who is to escort an inmate to a public clinic for required treatment. The captain should instruct the officer to

   A. call him/her for permission to remove the inmate's handcuffs if there is an emergency and the inmate's life is in danger
   B. keep the inmate handcuffed at all times and under no circumstances remove the handcuffs
   C. remove the inmate's handcuffs while the inmate is being treated by the physician
   D. telephone him/her for security instructions to be taken if the doctor asks that the handcuffs be removed

45. When a prisoner is to be discharged from a court detention pen, the name of the prisoner and the statement of charge on the order of discharge must be compared with this information on the commitment. However, if the prisoner was transferred to the court pen from an institution of the Department, this comparison is also to be made with the information on the _____ card.

   A. accompanying
   B. inmate detention record
   C. inmate identification
   D. records and statistics

46. A captain who is asked for information about the Department by a visiting member of the public should

   A. advise the individual that information about the Department is restricted
   B. give the individual the information requested unless it is restricted
   C. refer the individual to the office of the Commissioner
   D. refer the individual to the office of the Director of Operations

47. Suppose that an inmate's date of release falls on Independence Day, Monday, July 4. The inmate should be discharged

   A. the day before
   B. two days before
   C. three days before
   D. the day after

48. Which one of the following statements about the *Manhattan Bail Project* is NOT true?

   A. Its work has been taken over by the Office of Probation.
   B. It was a project launched by the Vera Foundation.
   C. Of the cases released on recognizance and later convicted, the majority received suspended sentences.
   D. Only 25% of defendants released on recognizance failed to return to court when required.

49. While the available data reveal that the typical offender in the institutions of the Department of Correction has a background of family failure, the rehabilitative efforts of the Department must nevertheless be directed toward the offender as an individual, rather than toward the family. This is so mainly because

   A. family patterns cannot be influenced
   B. it has not been proven that there is any direct relationship between environment and criminal behavior
   C. the Department of Correction does not have the capability to reach out and change the family background
   D. the typical offender does not have any firm family ties

50. *Jottings on Jails and Jailers* is

   A. a feature of the American Journal of Correction
   B. a publication of the California Department of Correction
   C. the title of a magazine on correction
   D. the title of a recent book by a well-known retired warden

KEY (CORRECT ANSWERS)

1. C	11. B	21. B	31. D	41. C
2. D	12. B	22. A	32. C	42. C
3. A	13. A	23. A	33. B	43. C
4. C	14. C	24. D	34. C	44. D
5. B	15. B	25. A	35. B	45. A
6. A	16. C	26. C	36. D	46. B
7. A	17. D	27. C	37. D	47. C
8. D	18. D	28. B	38. A	48. D
9. C	19. A	29. A	39. D	49. C
10. D	20. C	30. B	40. B	50. A

EXAMINATION SECTION
TEST 1

DIRECTIONS: Each question or incomplete statement is followed by several suggested answers or completions. Select the one that BEST answers the question or completes the statement. *PRINT THE LETTER OF THE CORRECT ANSWER IN THE SPACE AT THE RIGHT.*

1. When a correction officer who has been efficient and conscientious suddenly becomes less attentive to duty and makes numerous mistakes, the cause of such a change

    A. is usually that the officer is responding to a subtle change or modification in the job situation
    B. is usually apparent to a discerning supervisor and to observant fellow correction officers
    C. may be readily discovered by a close study of reports and personnel records
    D. may have no direct relationship to the job or to the supervisory situation

    1.____

2. In spite of a fairly common feeling among the staff of an institution that many procedures are superfluous and are just *red tape,* the BEST justification for such procedures and so-called *red tape* is that

    A. certain standard procedures are needed to help achieve the overall objectives of an institution
    B. standard procedures insure accuracy although slowing down the pace of work
    C. standard procedures usually result in the creation of important and necessary records
    D. uniform procedures have the definite merit of eliminating opportunities for favoritism and special privilege

    2.____

3. Forms for reporting work, which in the past were often criticized as just some more paperwork, are considered by progressive management today as a(n)

    A. effective system for informing higher management echelons of goals at which to aim
    B. effective way to record and to control work and assignments
    C. way of taking the monotony factor out of report keeping
    D. method of arriving at a fairly precise measure of an employee's morale

    3.____

4. The principal purpose of a formal employee grievance procedure should be to

    A. demonstrate that top management is interested in staff morale
    B. prevent employee grievances from building up to a point where they may receive undesirable publicity in the public press
    C. provide a safety valve for employees who might otherwise resort to quite serious misconduct
    D. reveal the existence of inequitable situations and afford an opportunity for their correction

    4.____

5. One of the most important relationships involving employees in an organization is called the employee *grapevine*. A characteristic of this employee *grapevine* is that it, generally,

   A. is informally organized and operates vertically rather than horizontally
   B. has a well-defined structure and is an indication of a breakdown in communications
   C. is quite informally organized and thrives on information not openly available to the entire group
   D. has a well-defined structure and may or may not serve the proper ends of an organization

6. The MOST accurate of the following statements about employee supervision is that the

   A. abler the employee, the more likely the employee will benefit from intelligent supervision
   B. less exacting the supervisor, the better the quality but not the quantity of work performed by employees
   C. more dedicated the employee, the less the employee can accept supervision
   D. more incapable the employee, the more likely the employee will benefit from intelligent supervision

7. If one of your officers disagrees with your evaluation of his (her) work, the BEST way to handle such a problem is for you to

   A. avoid discussing your actual evaluation but indicate the employee's specific strengths as well as the weaknesses
   B. explain the basis of your evaluation and discuss it with the officer
   C. indicate that in any person-to-person evaluation some individuals must necessarily receive less than a perfect rating
   D. point out that by virtue of your supervisory role you are in a better position to appraise an employee's work

8. In the forced distribution method of rating job performance, all the employees are considered in relation to each other and each is usually placed into one of three groups which represent levels of performance, such as the top 25%, middle 50%, and bottom 25%. The one of the following which is TRUE about such a rating system is that

   A. it is useful for large employee groups
   B. personal strengths and weaknesses of employees are meticulously indicated
   C. raters make very precise distinctions between all employees
   D. all raters use the same standards

9. If a correction officer attempts to conceal from the captain the fact that the officer has made an error, the MOST important assumption the captain should make in such a situation is that the

   A. officer-captain relationship needs study and improvement
   B. error was not serious since otherwise it would have been revealed in the regular course of institutional operations
   C. officer is willing to take a chance that the error will not be discovered until later
   D. officer may be shielding someone else who was also responsible

10. As a captain, you have received from the head of the institution an order with which you disagree, concerning a new method to be used in institutional operations. You discuss the matter with the head of the institution, who declines to change the order, giving reasons therefor. Later you issue this order to your staff, and the correction officers find objections similar to yours. One of the officers asks to discuss the order with you. You should

    A. admit your agreement with this officer's views but state that the head of the institution wishes it done this way
    B. discuss the matter with the officer indicating why the head of the institution feels the new method is superior
    C. in company with, and reinforced by, the correction officer repeat your original objections to the head of the institution
    D. tactfully refrain from discussing the matter at all, out of loyalty to the head of the institution and in deference to the command structure

11. A group of correction officers strongly opposed a proposed change in procedure designed to reorganize the work of the institution. After a review of such protests, it was decided to institute the change on a trial basis with permanent adoption of the change if later indicated after such trial. Such a tactic is

    A. *good;* it is an indication that the administration is willing to surrender some of its authority in order to secure staff harmony
    B. *bad;* it is an indication that the administration is unwisely yielding to group pressure
    C. *good;* it is an indication that the realities of the situation are being considered by those in authority
    D. *bad;* it is an indication that employee organizations had not been consulted prior to announcing the proposed change

12. A correction officer has been complaining bitterly to fellow officers that another correction officer has received a desirable assignment by reason of influence. Via the grapevine, the captain learns of this allegation, but knows that it is untrue. In this situation, the captain should

    A. inform the complaining officer privately of the truth regarding the assignment
    B. confront the complaining officer in the presence of others and demand absolute proof of the charge immediately
    C. ignore the matter since it is not the captain's job to interfere in disagreements between officers
    D. tell the complaining officer to apply for a desirable assignment also

13. Your superior assigns you a new and difficult task which you honestly believe you will be unable to complete in the time set. The best procedure in such a situation would be to

    A. inform your superior at the outset that the job cannot be done in the time limit
    B. work as quickly as possible and periodically inform your superior of the progress of the job
    C. work as quickly as possible and when the deadline arrives remind your superior that the time allowance was insufficient
    D. work as quickly as possible, taking whatever shortcuts are possible, but finish the job in the time allotted even though it may be unacceptable

14. The one of the following which is generally regarded as a weakness of the lecture as a method of training is that it

    A. does not allow for the teaching of material in logical sequence
    B. is suitable mainly for teaching small groups
    C. is difficult to hold the interest of a group
    D. requires the use of many visual aid techniques

15. If a captain has a feeling that a certain correction officer is hostile to him, the captain should

    A. sound out some other correction officers as to whether this is really the case
    B. try to discover the basis for this attitude
    C. overlook the matter since first impressions are often valueless
    D. point out then and there his displeasure with the correction officer's attitude

16. Assume that there are certain duties that are not liked by correction officers. Because the work has to be done, the captain should, as much as practicable,

    A. assign these duties to the best natured officers
    B. assign these duties to the junior officers
    C. rotate these duties among subordinates
    D. assign these duties as punishment details

17. A special responsible job needs to be done in your area. The officer you should assign is the one who

    A. acts as captain in your absence
    B. has had the least opportunity for special assignments
    C. is the senior officer in your command
    D. through past performance seems best suited to do the job

18. The captain's chief function in regard to departmental policies is to

    A. determine when they should be applied
    B. interpret and transmit them to subordinates
    C. make decisions about conflicts in policy
    D. review them to see if they are workable

19. To serve as an effective deterrent to future rule infractions by inmates, punishment for infractions is most effective when its application is

    A. certain but delayed   B. certain and physical
    C. certain and prompt   D. prompt but moderate

20. Reprimanding an officer for inefficiency in the presence of fellow officers usually is apt to

    A. arouse the officer's resentment
    B. cause the officer to resign
    C. improve the performance of the crew
    D. stimulate the officer to improve

21. Organized rebellion by inmate leaders, except under very rare conditions, is not favored by the other inmates chiefly because

    A. it introduces an element of disagreement between the leaders and the followers
    B. it usually leads to greater restriction of privileges for most of the inmates
    C. the leaders are in the minority and therefore can not represent the wishes of the majority
    D. the leaders, due to their distorted thinking, and their need to make an impression, fail to take into account the realities of the situation

22. The Federal Bureau of Prisons, in its Correspondence Course for Jailers, states that, when an emergency alarm is sounded, be certain that all available officers do not rush to the scene. The principal reason given for this is that

    A. all officers will not have the opportunity nor the time to draw weapons from the armory
    B. a rear guard or reserve force should remain away from the scene of possible trouble
    C. it prevents uncontrollable panic from developing throughout the entire institution
    D. the alarm may later turn out to have been false or unnecessary

23. Select the one of the following statements which is most correct as a statement of fact. A trial inmate _____ refuse to appear in a *line-up* _____ refuse a request for an interview by a city police officer.

    A. cannot; but may
    B. can; but cannot
    C. can; and may
    D. cannot; and cannot

24. It must be borne in mind that a fire allowed to get out of control endangers the lives of all occupants who are locked in cells. The principal cause of deaths in such a situation is usually

    A. actual contact with flames
    B. panic
    C. shock
    D. suffocation

25. An attempt to encourage participation by inmates in the educational program of a correctional institution would be most effective if institution officials

    A. emphasized that an inmate is less likely to get into trouble in the institution by such participation
    B. indicated that such programs are in accord with the most progressive theories of penology
    C. tried to equate the amount of instruction with the length of sentence to be served by an individual inmate
    D. tried to show inmates the benefits to them individually of taking part in such a program

26. If a rule is unpopular with the inmates, the captain should

    A. appeal to all inmates to obey the rule in question thereby preparing the way for its possible repeal
    B. apply it especially against inmates who are disliked by the other inmates
    C. consistently enforce the rule regardless of its unpopularity
    D. continuously emphasize to all inmates the penalty for violating the rule

27. According to the manual of correctional standards, counts in dormitory or open-type units should always be made by more than one officer. The chief reason for this is that

    A. it assigns clear responsibility for a very important task to two men rather than to a single individual
    B. it is a desirable show of strength which impresses all concerned
    C. it minimizes the chance that inmates may move around undetected and thus cause an incorrect count
    D. the two officers can each make independent counts and thus check each other

28. According to authorities in prison administration, a pre-arranged plan for dealing with escapes should provide that officers on assigned posts may be moved only

    A. by the person in charge of the search operation
    B. by the senior officer present at the assigned post
    C. when such officers are positive such a move is desirable
    D. when such officers are relieved by any superior officer

29. The one of the following religions which has recently acquired a considerable number of converts among the inmates of prisons in this country is

    A. Buddhism   B. Islam
    C. Mormonism   D. Pantheism

30. *Velcro* is a trademark that refers to a type of

    A. clothing fastener
    B. identifying wristband
    C. intercommunication system
    D. tamperproof plumbing fixture

31. The library catalog in a correctional institution, to be worthwhile, must answer three questions. The one of the following questions it is NOT important for the catalog to answer is:

    A. Does the library contain a book with a certain title?
    B. How often is a certain book taken out by the readers?
    C. What books are there in the library on certain subjects?
    D. What books does the library contain by a certain author?

32. A good correctional program should be carried on in such a way that problem cases are revealed long before they reach a critical state. A correction officer could help most in carrying out such a program by

    A. consulting with superiors as to the type of disciplinary action to be taken with problem cases
    B. learning to recognize the signs of trouble and how to deal with them
    C. preparing a good case against the inmate in the event a disciplinary hearing is held
    D. getting the help of other correction officers in dealing with critical situations

33. Visual inspection of cell bars should be supplemented by tapping the bars with a leather hammer to detect the sound of a partially sawed bar. This sound can most accurately be characterized as a _____ sound.

    A. bell   B. clanging   C. dull   D. grating

34. In making a search of a cell, the officer should apply pressure against the shatterproof immovable glass fronting the compartment which houses the concealed cell light. If the glass yields to pressure, it is most probable that

    A. an attempt was made to remove the glass so it could be used as a weapon
    B. it is an unsuccessful attempt at vandalism
    C. the wiring in the lamp housing has been tampered with in order to cause a *short* and thereby create a disturbance
    D. an inmate may have tried to gain access to the light compartment as a possible hiding place for contraband

35. After the officer starts the movement of the cell doors where such doors are opened and closed by a mechanical arrangement detached from the cells proper, he should stop such motion for a fraction of a second in order to

    A. additionally test the proper mechanical operation of the doors
    B. be alert for any last minute instructions from superiors relative to opening or closing the doors
    C. clear the slide of debris
    D. give unmistakable warning to the occupants of the cells about the opening or the closing of the doors

36. The desire for special clothing in a correctional institution usually is concerned with

    A. shoes   B. sox   C. trousers   D. underwear

37. Several women's institutions have tried out student government programs in the form of cottage committees or of inmate councils representing the entire institution. About these programs, it is most correct to state that they

    A. can be of value both to the institution and to the inmates
    B. have no positive value for either the institution or the inmate
    C. may benefit some inmates but they are generally harmful to orderly administration
    D. may contribute to orderly administration but are harmful to inmates

38. All the processes in a correctional institution for women should lead toward educating the woman inmate for

    A. earning a living in a socially acceptable type of work
    B. marriage and motherhood
    C. successful community living
    D. making the best use of leisure time after release

39. A study entitled, *A preliminary evaluation of the relationship between group psychotherapy and the adjustment of adolescent inmates (16-21 years) in a short-term penal institution* was conducted by the Diagnostic Staff at Rikers Island. A conclusion which was drawn as a result of the study was that

    A. a repetition of the study was necessary with smaller therapy and non-therapy groups
    B. group psychotherapy subjects displayed a better institutional adjustment than those not receiving group therapy

C. no follow-up study was necessary because of the negative results from the original study
D. a smaller proportion of experimental group subjects improved after receiving group psychotherapy when compared to those who did not receive group therapy

40. The one of the following statements which is most accurate concerning group psychotherapy is that group psychotherapy

A. is in a way an outgrowth of the concept of inmate self-government
B. is of little value with deviant personality types
C. should make the group members resent help from their fellow inmates
D. reflects a punitive rather than a rehabilitative aim

41. In group counseling and psychotherapy, it is usually true that persons are more defensive and argumentative than in individualized counseling and therapy sessions. The reason for this tendency is that

A. individuals in a group setting feel it more necessary to protect their personality
B. people in group settings are motivated by the characteristically free atmosphere
C. people would rather argue in a group setting than in an individualized setting
D. the group session is more poorly organized and therefore uncontrolled

42. Research studies have revealed almost nothing, in an exact sense, of the possible effectiveness of any given approach to the problem of rehabilitation mainly because

A. of the lack of motivation of and failure to cooperate by inmates involved in such studies
B. proper control (non-treated) groups have rarely been included in any such studies of the problem
C. of the relatively brief period during which any such rehabilitative programs have been in effect
D. such studies cannot probe unduly into an inmate's post-release activities, as must be done if they are to be valid

43. It has been suggested that the Court of Appeals in the state be permitted to establish an Institute of Sentencing similar to the one set up by Federal law. The primary function of such an Institute would be to

A. render assistance to judges in achieving more uniformity of sentencing in accordance with recognized criteria
B. to curtail the sentencing freedom of the judiciary which has resulted in inequitable sentencing practices
C. shift the sentencing from the judiciary to the Institute
D. hear appeals from inequitable sentencing

44. Creative or guided restitution refers to a rehabilitation technique in which an offender, under appropriate supervision, is helped to

A. adjust to a normal social life after release from confinement
B. become familiar with agencies whose programs include aid for the released inmate
C. find a way to make amends to those he has hurt by his misconduct
D. rid himself of anti-social drives, desires, and associates

45. The success of a public relations program in a correctional agency can best be measured by the

   A. amount of favorable publicity acquired by the agency over a given time period through the medium of the public relations program
   B. creation of a satisfactory image of the correction officer as a custodial officer
   C. rate and extent of improvement in the correction employee's job
   D. degree to which the public relations program assists the correctional agency in accomplishing its general aims

46. Concerning tear gas and its use, it would be most correct to state that

   A. the only type of tear gas dispenser is the tear gas projection gun
   B. tear gas munitions deteriorate rapidly
   C. the pscyhological effect of using tear gas is negligible
   D. the use of tear gas in quelling prison disturbances is usually considered inhumane

47. The correction officer can contribute to the inmate's rehabilitation by helping him see for himself patterns of behavior which do not and will not bring satisfaction. This approach, to be most effective, is best used

   A. at critical moments of stress in institutional life
   B. when the inmate first shows signs of a satisfactory adjustment to institutional life
   C. when the officer-inmate relationship is strong and the inmate is himself discussing his problems
   D. when the officer-inmate relationship is strong, and the inmate is receptive to suggestion due to fatigue or depression

48. Of the following, the most important reason why psychiatric social workers find it difficult to achieve success in their work in prisons is that

   A. psychiatry and social work are not exact sciences
   B. neither inmates nor correctional officers are in sympathy with their work
   C. no precise goals have been established to guide them in their work
   D. they must deal with cases with which other treatment services have previously failed

49. The *Differential Association* theory of Sutherland holds that

   A. fundamentally, criminals are led into crime by socio-economic forces
   B. criminals learn criminal behavior in much the same way as they learn non-criminal behavior
   C. shrewder criminals induce individuals with low I.Q.'s to commit crime
   D. status in a crime-oriented group is achieved by the successful commission of dramatic criminal acts

50. A survey made in a large male correctional institution disclosed that 10% of the inmates had *nomadic tendencies*. Nomadic tendencies means MOST NEARLY _____ tendencies.

   A. assaultive   B. sadistic
   C. narcotic   D. wandering

KEY (CORRECT ANSWERS)

1. D	11. C	21. B	31. B	41. A
2. A	12. A	22. B	32. B	42. B
3. B	13. B	23. C	33. C	43. A
4. D	14. C	24. D	34. D	44. C
5. C	15. B	25. D	35. D	45. D
6. A	16. C	26. C	36. A	46. B
7. B	17. D	27. C	37. A	47. C
8. A	18. B	28. A	38. C	48. D
9. A	19. C	29. B	39. B	49. B
10. B	20. A	30. A	40. A	50. D

TEST 2

DIRECTIONS: Each question or incomplete statement is followed by several suggested answers or completions. Select the one that BEST answers the question or completes the statement. *PRINT THE LETTER OF THE CORRECT ANSWER IN THE SPACE AT THE RIGHT.*

1. There is a group of mentally ill inmates who have a *functional psychosis*. The word *functional* in this case indicates that

   A. it is an organic psychosis
   B. the psychosis is caused by alcoholism or drug addiction
   C. there are no demonstrable changes in the brain
   D. there are clinical findings of senile arteriosclerosis

   1.____

2. The term *sociopaths* describes

   A. confirmed narcotics addicts
   B. latent male homosexuals
   C. neurotic adolescents
   D. psychopathic personalities

   2.____

3. The incarceration of the geriatric presents many problems in correctional administration. The word *geriatric* means MOST NEARLY

   A. dipsomaniac (alcoholic)
   B. moronic (mentally deficient)
   C. pertaining to split personality types
   D. pertaining to individuals of advanced years

   3.____

4. Those sections of a city where unfortunates congregate is usually called Skid Row. It would be most accurate to state that on a typical Skid Row

   A. a high percentage of the men there are non-white
   B. the men prefer organized group recreation rather than being alone
   C. most of the men are over 40 years of age
   D. there is a higher proportion of married men than is found in the general population

   4.____

5. The lowest parole violation rate is generally shown by parolees who have been sentenced for homicide and

   A. burglary
   B. forgery
   C. robbery
   D. sex offenses

   5.____

6. Jobs for ex-inmates can most often be found in

   A. big corporations
   B. domestic service
   C. government agencies
   D. small private enterprises

   6.____

7. The one of the following which probably could make a contribution in the correctional field that would be most productive of long range desirable results is the _____ sciences.

   A. behavioral
   B. medical
   C. physical
   D. statistical

   7.____

31

8. The one of the following statements about basket making as a prison handicraft which is most accurate is that

   A. it cannot be used for occupational therapy
   B. the work involved is too simple and cannot hold inmate interest
   C. tools are not usually needed in basket making
   D. the end-products of basket making do not find widespread use

9. The one of the following which would be considered a leading question in interrogating an inmate is:

   A. How old was your wife when you married her?
   B. Tell me something about your wife.
   C. Do you want your wife to visit you?
   D. You don't seem to like your wife, do you?

10. There are 21 Borstal institutions in England. These Borstal institutions are designed to take

    A. only female inmates
    B. only the most hardened offenders
    C. the criminally insane
    D. offenders over 16 and under 21

11. Highfields is an institution in New Jersey that is mainly concerned with

    A. adult narcotics addicts
    B. adult recidivists
    C. juvenile delinquents
    D. juvenile narcotics addicts

12. A characteristic of the teaching machine used in the Department of Correction is that it

    A. is extremely costly to buy and to operate
    B. has a built-in reward factor to stimulate use and study
    C. is apt to be too inflexible and to permit no changeover to different subjects
    D. requires close supervision while the student is operating it

13. The state Department of Correction has established conservation work camps and several of these are now operating. The one of the following statements about these camps which is TRUE is that

    A. offenders assigned to them are a mixture of wayward youths and older felons
    B. the parole violation rate of inmates paroled from the camps has been disappointingly high
    C. there is a definite age limit set for inmates assigned to them
    D. transfers to these camps from other institutions are made on a non-voluntary basis

14. A treatment program for alcoholics in correctional institutions is usually handicapped by the fact that

    A. alcoholics are extremely resistive to any kind of treatment
    B. alcoholics feel superior to the institutional environment and will not cooperate

C. other inmates resent any special attention given to alcoholics
D. the sentence of most alcoholics is too short to permit effective treatment

15. A psychoanalyst prominent in forensic (legal) psychiatry has written that a criminal act is the sum of a person's criminalistic tendencies plus his total situation, divided by the amount of his resistance; or, expressed symbolically, $C = \frac{T+S}{R}$. According to this statement, if a given individual's R is great, then it is most probable that

    A. it will exactly cancel out the T (criminalistic tendencies) and no criminal act will occur
    B. it will increase just enough to annul the potentiality for crime implicit in S (total situation)
    C. the criminal offense, if and when committed, will be great
    D. the criminal offense is less likely to be committed

16. In the history of American penology, there is a period roughly from 1870 to 1900, characterized as the *reformatory system,* which began with the building of the Elmira, New York, Reformatory. The one of the following which was a characteristic of this *reformatory system* was that it

    A. had no provision for institutional industries
    B. introduced the indeterminate sentence
    C. made no provision for parole
    D. was used chiefly for recidivists

17. The one of the following statements about the Board of Correction which is TRUE is that

    A. it consists of nine members
    B. the members receive a salary for their services
    C. the stated term of office is five years
    D. it is an all-male body

18. The one of the following which is normally the responsibility of the First Deputy Commissioner of Correction is the

    A. examination and approval of an extraordinary request from a lawyer for an interview or visit with an inmate
    B. conduct of an investigation and evaluation of an unusual occurrence or complaint from the inmate population
    C. issuance of information concerning correctional activities through press releases
    D. participation in the weekly conference of the city parole commission

19. Of the following vocational training courses suitable for a women's institution, the one which has special value, more so than the others, because of its effect on institutional morale, is a course in

    A. beauty culture   B. homemaking
    C. practical nursing   D. child care

20. A recent amendment to the state law relating to credit for time served prior to conviction and sentencing gives credit for such time to

    A. city workhouse, reformatory, or penitentiary inmates under definite sentence
    B. city workhouse, reformatory, or penitentiary inmates under an indeterminate sentence
    C. inmates of state penal institutions serving definite sentence
    D. inmates of state penal institutions serving indeterminate sentence

21. The Department of Correction is the only municipal correctional agency in the state that houses sentenced inmates on indefinite sentences up to three years. This is due to the fact that the

    A. city has created a city parole commission
    B. city is the only city in the state of the first class, i.e., having more than a million population
    C. *home rule* feature of the State Constitution requires it
    D. State Parole Commission mandates this practice

22. It has not been possible to include all employed inmates under the Pilot Inmate Wage Incentive Plan of the Department of Correction. However, the one of the following groups which is included is the _____ work force.

    A. housekeeping   B. kitchen
    C. laundry   D. maintenance

23. Promotion and the raising of pay levels in the Pilot Inmate Wage Incentive Plan is accomplished by

    A. a type of collective bargaining, with the inmates and institutional staff as the two parties
    B. recommendation of the individual shop supervisors to the Warden
    C. reference to the general wage rates prevailing in private industry
    D. a work performance merit measurement of the individual inmate

24. The term *state use,* in the correctional field, means that

    A. goods manufactured by inmate labor are for use by state departments and other political subdivisions
    B. inmate labor must be paid
    C. the state, by virtue of its sovereignty, has the right to make use of prison labor within limits as it sees fit
    D. the state has a prior claim on inmate labor before cities and counties

25. With respect to sentenced inmates in institutions of the Department of Correction, the one of the following statements that is INCORRECT is that the

    A. greatest percentage had only a common school education
    B. majority fall into the 21 to 30 year age group
    C. majority are native born
    D. majority are unmarried

26. Of the following, the MOST appropriate use of staff conferences is to enable the supervisor to 26._____

    A. inform staff of the latest administrative policies
    B. give dissatisfied employees a chance to voice their grievances
    C. let staff know that he is aware of violations of personnel policies
    D. obtain the benefits of collective thinking about a problem

27. State legislation effective for two decades has made it possible for the city to appoint *public defenders*. Such public defenders would 27._____

    A. assist the District Attorney to prosecute crimes of extreme violence
    B. concentrate on crimes of subversion and espionage
    C. encourage citizens to press charges against individuals suspected of having committed certain sex crimes
    D. represent indigent (poor) defendants charged with a felony

28. A recent survey made by the City Parole Commission revealed that the average amount of pre-sentence city jail time spent by inmates is about _____ days for adults and about _____ days for adolescents. 28._____

    A. 30; 30   B. 90; 30   C. 90; 90   D. 30; 90

29. With respect to the Cottage Plan Separation Unit of the Department of Correction, it would be most accurate to state that 29._____

    A. admissions to the Cottage Unit are scheduled so that there is a complete inmate population turnover every four weeks
    B. a psychiatric social worker is available for service, but a psychiatrist is not
    C. the Cottage Supervisor, who is the administrator of the Unit, is a member of the custodial staff
    D. the correction officers assigned thereto function in a house-father relationship

30. In most states in the United States, the test of insanity is whether or not the defendant knew right from wrong at the time of the crime and whether or not the defendant 30._____

    A. is declared by qualified experts to be sane or insane
    B. at the time of the crime gave sufficient evidence to support a finding of sanity or insanity
    C. appreciated the nature and consequences of his act
    D. by his actions at the time of the crime met the test of rationality

31. The use of an *information* in the prosecution of a misdemeanor does NOT 31._____

    A. serve as the basis for the warrant arresting the accused
    B. serve as a ground for holding the accused in custody until trial
    C. protect the accused from the jeopardy of a further trial for the same crime
    D. prohibit the granting of bail to the accused

32. The section of the Criminal Procedure Law entitled *Preparation for Trial* states that, *After his plea, the defendant is entitled to at least two days to prepare for his trial* 32._____

    A. if he requires it
    B. if the court so directs
    C. if he is not represented by counsel
    D. with the consent of the district attorney

33. The Criminal Procedure Law, concerning the right of a defendant, upon arrest, contains a provision which states that the defendant must, in all cases, be taken before the judge

    A. with all deliberate speed
    B. as soon as practicable
    C. without unnecessary delay
    D. forthwith

34. Writs of *coram nobis*, a type of writ of error, sometimes operate to free prisoners from incarceration. Such a writ usually refers to an error or errors committed by the

    A. court where judgment was rendered
    B. District Attorney who had refused to permit bail for a bailable offense or crime
    C. law enforcement officers who made the original arrest
    D. prison authorities where the inmate is incarcerated

35. The principal disadvantage of using a punch clock system in connection with regular tours of inspection in a correctional institution, similar to that used by night watchmen in factories or in warehouses, is that

    A. it is subject to excessive tampering and vandalism
    B. it is too costly unless it is a part of the original electro-mechanical control system
    C. it tends to emphasize clock punching to the detriment of actual inspections
    D. *ringing in* can be faked by untrustworthy personnel

36. Correction officers derive their peace officer status from the Correction Law and the

    A. Administrative Code
    B. Criminal Procedure Law
    C. City Charter
    D. Penal Law

37. A commitment which sets aside another commitment is called a(n) _____ commitment.

    A. direct
    B. indirect
    C. interdepartmental
    D. superseding

38. The Grand Jury may decide that a crime has been committed but the evidence does not indicate a crime of felony grade. In this event, the Grand Jury usually

    A. directs the appropriate court to issue a court summons
    B. has no further duty in the matter
    C. will request the Police Department or a court officer to make an arrest
    D. will instruct the district attorney to file an information

39. Assume that you are asked to study and report on employee turnover in several agency units which vary widely as to total number of employees and the number of employees involved in turnover. In order to present an accurate picture of turnover, your report should show, with regard to persons leaving, both actual numbers and

    A. central tendencies
    B. raw data
    C. percentages
    D. rounded totals

40. When *shaking down* an inmate, the officer should 40.____

   A. always have the inmate strip
   B. be casual in order to put the inmate off guard
   C. order the inmate to face forward if there is a suspicion that the inmate may have a weapon
   D. when bending over, hold his head to the side of the inmate for protection

41. Of the following, a term used to describe how a supervisor may determine whether he is communicating effectively with his staff is called 41.____

   A. backlash   B. delegation
   C. implementation   D. feedback

42. False rumors about unpleasant possibilities such as employee cutbacks can do serious damage to morale. Most rumors of this kind in large organizations and public agencies are caused by 42.____

   A. over-permissiveness and general laxity of supervision
   B. employees who distort the facts for their own purposes
   C. a breakdown in communication between management and employees
   D. newspaper articles planted by special interest groups

43. A method attempted to overcome the lack of nursing personnel in the Department of Correction was the development of a training program for inmate nurses' aides. This program failed mainly because of the 43.____

   A. inability to obtain qualified teachers of nursing
   B. opposition of the medical profession
   C. requirements of the state law regarding licensing of nurses
   D. security and contraband risks involved

44. In the House of Detention for Women, all women charged with prostitution undergo an examination to determine evidences of venereal disease. This examination takes place 44.____

   A. after arraignment, and treatment is begun if indicated
   B. after arraignment, but treatment is deferred until sentence
   C. before arraignment, and treatment is begun if indicated
   D. before arraignment, but treatment is deferred until sentence

45. Of the following, staff meetings are LEAST likely to be productive when 45.____

   A. only four or five people are present
   B. the chairman conducts the meeting in a formal manner
   C. private discussions are not allowed
   D. discussion is kept to a minimum

KEY (CORRECT ANSWERS)

1. C	11. C	21. A	31. D	41. D
2. D	12. B	22. C	32. A	42. C
3. D	13. C	23. D	33. C	43. A
4. C	14. D	24. A	34. A	44. C
5. D	15. D	25. B	35. C	45. D
6. D	16. B	26. D	36. B	
7. A	17. A	27. D	37. D	
8. C	18. B	28. B	38. D	
9. D	19. A	29. D	39. C	
10. D	20. B	30. C	40. D	

EXAMINATION SECTION
TEST 1

DIRECTIONS: Each question or incomplete statement is followed by several suggested answers or completions. Select the one that BEST answers the question or completes the statement. *PRINT THE LETTER OF THE CORRECT ANSWER IN THE SPACE AT THE RIGHT.*

1. The MOST accurate statement concerning inmate living quarters is:
The
   A. open dormitory encourages harmonious group relations and is ordinarily the best approach
   B. open dormitory is usually preferred by inmates who find difficulty in establishing social relationships since it gives them a wider area from which to form close friendships
   C. private room with no window but with a barred cell door facing a corridor is the best approach since the existence of a window fosters unconscious suicidal tendencies
   D. private room with outside window establishes *individuality and territory* and is considered the best approach

1.____

2. If a group of rioting inmates demands that they negotiate directly with the Governor of the state, the request should PROBABLY be
   A. *denied;* leading political figures can always be depended upon to make false or unworkable promises in order to get credit for ending the riot
   B. *denied;* the granting of such a request lends encouragement to other inmates of other institutions to repeat the same show on another stage
   C. *granted;* inmates who do not receive satisfaction will torture hostages and destroy property
   D. *granted;* the public regrettably has a greater confidence in the ability of a governor to handle a riot than in the abilities of correction officials

2.____

3. Assume that you are a superior. An inmate comes to you with a request arising out of a grievance he has which he believes to be legitimate. You can see that the inmate is making a request which is important to him. You consider the inmate's request carefully and decide that you cannot grant the inmate's request.
It would be BEST for you to
   A. give the inmate a firm *no* answer and your reason for doing so
   B. grant the inmate's request because of its importance but point out to him that there were very good reasons for not granting the request
   C. tell the inmate that his request is an important one and you will let him know in the not too distant future whether his request can be granted
   D. tell the inmate that there are two sides to his request and that you will ask the Deputy Warden to frame a written response to the inmate

3.____

4. Assume that you are a superior and that the early warning signs of an inmate disturbance are present in your institution. One of the officers you supervise behaves in a very nervous, insecure way in the presence of inmates. You try to encourage the officer to behave in a confident manner but the officer is unable to do so.
In the circumstances, it would probably be BEST to

4.____

39

A. hold a brief meeting with the other line officers who comprise your staff and ask for suggestions on dealing with the officer
B. order the officer to straighten up or face disciplinary charges
C. recommend that the officer be temporarily assigned to a less sensitive area
D. shock the officer into proper behavior by asking him if he intends to turn *yellow* should trouble break out

5. There is a strong disagreement among correctional administrators concerning the use of inmate councils.
   The MOST feasible approach concerning the use of inmate councils is generally the

   A. elimination of inmate advisory groups, since membership in such a group gives the inmate member an opportunity to exploit other inmate members
   B. formation of inmate advisory groups to deal with particular problems, with such groups dissolving as soon as the problem is resolved
   C. popular election by inmates of an inmate advisory group to meet at frequent periodic intervals
   D. taking of formal surveys by supervisory correction personnel to determine inmate attitudes

5.___

6. Which of the following may spark a prison riot or major prison disturbance?

   A. Absence of clearly defined and easily understood rules and regulations
   B. Indecisive actions on legitimate inmate grievances
   C. Poor communications
   D. All of the above

6.___

7. Which of the following is NOT true?

   A. A disproportionate share of individuals who are prone to violent behavior are to be found in correctional institutions.
   B. Inmates have high self-esteem and are fully committed to the major goal of making large sums of money.
   C. Inmates are more apt to be mentally deficient than persons who are not in correctional institutions.
   D. Inmates are frequently the product of broken homes, are unskilled, and have unstable work records.

7.___

8. Of the following, the MOST correct statement is:
   Riots

   A. are caused by a conscious desire to bring about revolutionary improvements in the American social system and to put an end to the devaluation of certain elements of the population by those who are in positions of power
   B. come about because institutional life is monotonous and because inmates feel a sense of being hopelessly oppressed and stripped of all human dignity
   C. are complex phenomena for which simple explanations do not in reality exist
   D. are violent acts contrary to law and are proof positive of the moral deterioration of middle-class America

8.___

9. Assume that you have made an informal count of a small inmate work crew assigned to a small area on a site that has never known an escape. There is doubt in your mind as to the correctness of your count.
   Your BEST reaction is that

   A. there is no cause for immediate alarm, since only formal crew counts are recorded
   B. you should first count the crew again
   C. you should waste no time in reporting an inmate missing and then, after the report is made, count the crew again
   D. you should ask the crew whether one of the inmates is missing

10. The BASIC function of a correctional institution is

    A. to operate at maximum efficiency
    B. to make certain that every department understands that teamwork is vital and that all departments are important
    C. the protection of society and the rehabilitation of the inmates
    D. the recognition that correctional institutions face a more difficult problem than at any time in the history of our country

11. It is sometimes necessary for a correction officer to order an inmate to do something the officer knows the inmate will not like to do.
    In these circumstances, the following is the recommended BEST procedure:

    A. Convince the inmate of the merit of your order before the inmate carries it out
    B. Do not insist upon immediate compliance with the order but give the inmate time to come to the realization that it is best to comply with an officer's order
    C. If faced with total refusal, restructure the order and emphasize a different aspect of the original order
    D. Make sure that the order is carried out completely

12. The use of food for payment of work or for special privileges has no justification and such practice should never be permitted and will very likely get completely out of control and develop a usage of large amounts of luxury goods.
    Which one of the following would be an EXCEPTION to the preceding passage?

    A. The giving of large portions of meat to those who are given arduous work assignments
    B. An officer who gives extra portions of food to those inmates who have been helpful to the officer during the day
    C. The giving of an extra large piece of pastry by a kitchen helper to an officer while on duty in the dining hall
    D. An officer who allows the kitchen help to keep leftovers which are storable

13. The MAJOR purpose of a perimeter search is to

    A. assure that all cell blocks are secure
    B. discover whether any tools have been taken from the work area
    C. keep illegal items from being passed among the inmates while in open courtyards
    D. make sure contraband doesn't enter from the outside

4 (#1)

14. A major point of emphasis in the instruction of a correction officer concerns security and the causes of breach of security.
Experience has shown that MOST escapes are traceable directly to

    A. relatives who smuggle escape instruments to inmates
    B. officers who smuggle contraband to inmates
    C. the haphazard handling of keys and tools
    D. the lack of knowledge among inmates as to the possible consequences of escape

15. Reception centers have been established in several of the larger states.
The BASIC idea behind the reception centers is that

    A. before an offender has been found guilty in court, a sound orientation program should be instituted designed to facilitate good adjustment to healthy social life
    B. before an offender has been found guilty in court, the decision as to the value of lenient treatment should be decided by specialists in the correctional and rehabilitation fields
    C. after an offender has been found guilty in court, the decision as to the place and method of treatment should be decided by specialists in the correction field
    D. after an offender has been found guilty in court, immediate psychiatric examination should determine the inmate's attitude toward work and his future vocational program

16. The key to the successful operation of a classification program in a prison institution is the

    A. professional qualifications of the psychiatrist and social worker
    B. support and leadership given by the head of the institution
    C. careful application of the techniques and purposes of scientific classification
    D. willing participation of the hardened inmates

17. Classification, as the term is generally used in correctional work, is PRIMARILY

    A. a method that will assure coordination in diagnosis, training, and treatment of prison inmates
    B. in itself diagnosis, training, and treatment of prison inmates
    C. integration of like or similar groups of offenders into the general inmate population
    D. the labeling of prison inmates in different mental or attitudinal categories or types and the measurement of willingness to work

18. A study of the Federal prison system has compared the yearly average number of escapes per thousand inmates for the four years BEFORE and AFTER their classification program was established.
This comparison shows that the rate of escapes per year

    A. was much higher before classification
    B. is unknown because no such study has ever been officially approved
    C. was much lower after classification
    D. was about the same before and after classification

19. All studies of parole failures have shown that, of the following, the highest percentage of violations occur after the inmate has been released

    A. six months
    B. one month
    C. one week
    D. 12-14 months

20. Many correctional administrators believe that any institution operating as a single unit becomes increasingly inefficient and unsafe as its inmate population exceeds a critical figure. This critical figure can be enlarged by breaking up the institution into several smaller units, but still operating as a single administrative unit, or by locating two or more separate institutions on the same site.
    In building new facilities or splitting older institutions into more manageable small units, it is considered unwise for the number of inmates to be included in any one unit to exceed

    A. 1200   B. 1000   C. 50   D. 600

21. As a group, youthful offenders are _____ susceptible to positive treatment efforts than juvenile delinquents _____.

    A. *less;* or adult criminals
    B. *more;* or adult criminals
    C. *more;* but they are not as susceptible to positive treatment efforts as adult criminals
    D. *less;* but they are more susceptible to positive treatment efforts than adult criminals

22. Perhaps the young person who becomes legally defined as an offender has developed and become *socialized* in a milieu more characterized by anti-social than social customs and standards. His inability to control himself according to the requirements of the larger social order then signifies commitment to an unacceptable code of conduct rather than psychological aberration.
    An implication of the foregoing is that

    A. a young offender in an institutional setting will accept the guidance of fellow inmates and not that of treatment or custodial personnel
    B. where a youthful offender lacks self-control his behavior toward his associates is bound to be assaultive
    C. the use of narcotics or *hard* drugs may assist the individual to escape from people and problems
    D. the young offender may behave according to the standards of his friends and neighbors

23. There are three major means by which a conviction may be set aside after the ordinary statutory channels of appeal are closed.
    Which one of the following is NOT such a major means?

    A. Parole
    B. Habeas corpus
    C. Pardon
    D. Coram nobis

24. Which of the following types of housing is deemed preferable for female inmates?

    A. Cottage type
    B. Dormitory type
    C. One inmate per cell
    D. Three inmates per cell

25. Regarding library services, which of the following is recommended?

    A. Inmates should be encouraged to ask friends, relatives, and charitable organizations to contribute funds for the operation of the institutional library.
    B. Since most inmates are functional illiterates, at least ten comic books per inmate should be purchased for the institutional library.
    C. The requirement of a male librarian in all-male institutions should be waived since experience has proved that women are highly efficient and effective serving as librarians in all-male institutions.
    D. To discourage the planning of disturbances, inmates should not be permitted to read books in the library.

26. Which of the following measures is deemed to be advisable in establishing property control standards for inmates entering prison?

    A. An inmate's valuables should be itemized and sealed in a clear plastic bag.
    B. Inmates should be permitted to retain on their persons their social security cards, watches, and small quantities of postage stamps.
    C. Inmates who handle inmates' personal property should be carefully selected for their qualities of trustworthiness.
    D. Jewelry taken from inmates at time of incarceration should be carefully described with such words as gold, silver, diamond, or ruby to avoid the possibility of substitution.

27. Emergency doors must be provided into housing and to the areas where prisoners are congregated.
    All housing units should have an emergency entrance door with a lock opening on the _____ only and the door made to swing _____ only.

    A. inside; inward   B. inside; outward
    C. outside; inward   D. outside; outward

28. Which of the following does NOT represent the view of authorities regarding the use of tear gas?

    A. A limitation on using gas inside a building is the danger of getting a concentration which is too dense.
    B. It is economically sound to keep large quantities of gas munitions on hand due to the economies of large scale purchasing.
    C. The threat and availability of gas at the scene of a disturbance has probably halted more incipient disorders than its actual use.
    D. The use of tear gas in suppressing disturbances is more humane than bullets.

29. To schedule an official count at or near the time of officer shift changes is USUALLY found to be a

    A. *bad* practice since officers coming on duty resent being held up while a previous shift makes its count
    B. *bad* practice since officers responsible for the count are too easily distracted
    C. *good* practice since accuracy in the count is assured and interference with inmate activities is avoided
    D. *good* practice since a large number of officers will be on hand if discrepancies in the count are found

30. More disturbances have originated or culminated in the _____ areas than any other area.
Which of the following words, when inserted in the blank space, would MOST accurately complete the statement?

   A. dining
   B. housing
   C. recreational
   D. work

30._____

31. According to a recent handbook on how to recognize and handle abnormal people, the BEST way, generally, to handle a disturbed, potentially violent person is to

   A. display any physical restraint that is readily available and calmly but firmly tell the inmate that the restraint will be employed unless he apologizes for his behavior
   B. try to talk to him and find out what is bothering him, since this tends to gain his confidence
   C. tell him whatever he wants to hear since the deception of an abnormal individual is necessary for his own protection
   D. be as self-confident and assured as possible since an easy approach will appear as a sign of weakness to a deranged mind

31._____

32. Assume that you are explaining a procedure to a visitor to an inmate in an institution, but the visitor does not seem to quite understand what you are saying. This lack of understanding has occurred occasionally in the past with other visitors. A language barrier does not appear to be the problem.
According to a training bulletin issued by the City Department of Correction, the BEST way, generally, to handle this type of situation is to

   A. carefully use appropriately colorful language, since the display of colorful words will likely stimulate the visitor to an understanding of your instructions
   B. gently question the visitor's inborn communications capacity, since a little kidding often goes a long way to bridge a communications gap
   C. slowly increase a show of legitimate authority, since a little authority goes a long way in expediting matters with insecure persons
   D. find out what the visitor does not understand, since this may provide a clue as to improvements in your explanation

32._____

Questions 33-42.

DIRECTIONS: Questions 33 through 42 consist of two statements, based on the current Rules and Regulations and Manual of Procedure, Department of Correction.
If BOTH statements are correct, mark your answer A.
If NEITHER statement is correct, mark your answer B.
If Statement I ONLY is correct, but NOT Statement II, mark your answer C.
If Statement II ONLY is correct, but NOT Statement I, mark your answer D.

33. I. In the event of an inmate's death in any institution of the Correction Department, four people only shall be immediately notified in the following order: the institutional physician, the police precinct having jurisdiction, the Commissioner of Correction, and the Director of Operations.

    II. In the event of an attempted suicide by an inmate in his cell, the correction officer who first observes the incident shall immediately administer first aid. In the event that the inmate does not respond to first aid, the correction officer shall notify a superior officer or another correction officer in the vicinity to assist in the administration of first aid.

34. I. Upon the escape of an inmate, if the escapee is a member of a work gang, the officer in charge shall immediately line up all the inmates and, as expeditiously as possible, communicate with his superior officer.

    II. A correction officer shall be constantly alert while on duty, observing everything that takes place on his post within his sight or hearing, and shall periodically patrol his post during his tour of duty.

35. I. Whenever an inmate receives a written communication from a duly accredited reporter requesting permission to interview him, the inmate, if he wishes to be interviewed, shall submit such information in writing to the head of the institution.

    II. The following shall be the only types of punishment administered: reprimand; loss of one or more privileges, temporarily or permanently; loss of part or all good time; punitive segregation; restricted diets.

36. I. A correction officer in charge of any area within an institution shall check all bars, locks, windows, doors, and other security facilities on his post at least twice during his tour of duty for evidence that they are in good condition and have not been tampered with.

    II. When it is deemed necessary at any time to search the person of any employee on duty, such search shall be made by a captain or other superior officer. Refusal of any employee to be searched shall constitute grounds for disciplinary action.

37. I. Whenever prisoners are received from departmental and police vans, they must be searched and counted as soon as possible.

    II. The following categories of inmates shall not be assigned as sentenced help:
    a. Drug Addicts or Drug Offenders
    b. Gambling Law Violators

38. I. A correction officer assigned to court detention pens shall each day check the court calendar with the names of the prisoners sent from the various institutions.

    II. A captain shall call the attention of the assistant deputy warden to all matters of importance within the institution. The assistant deputy warden shall, in turn, call these matters of importance to the attention of the head of institution, the relieving assistant deputy warden, and the relieving captain.

39. I. In the event that any employee is made captive by prisoners, all orders issued by him during his captivity shall have full force and effect, except as pertaining to inmates.

    II. There shall be no restrictions as to correspondents, nor to the number of letters an inmate of any institution may receive as incoming mail or send out as outgoing mail.

40. I. No cell, tier, floor, or dormitory assignment of inmates, or changes in such assignments, shall be made without the authorization of a captain or superior officer.
    II. Whenever a correction officer receives information from any source which directly or indirectly involves the security of any institution, he shall immediately notify the head of his institution or division.

41. I. A designated captain shall be responsible for the daily accounting of all firearms and protective equipment assigned to an institution or division.
    II. Whenever an inmate commits an infraction of discipline important enough to necessitate action, the captain or other superior officer on duty in the institution shall, as soon as practicable, but no later than the same day, investigate the complaint and, if in his judgment the facts warrant, he will place the inmate in punishment status.

42. I. The correction officer assuming the duties of a post requiring the supervision of inmates shall examine the entire area of his post for its security and good order only if the correction officer who was just relieved of this post had not reported all secure and in good order within the previous three hours.
    II. A member of the department shall not indulge in any undue familiarity with inmates nor shall he permit any familiarity, on the part of inmates, toward him.

43. When time is NOT a factor, a supervisor enhances both initiative and cooperation by using which one of the following orders?

    A. Command
    B. Plea
    C. Detailed written instructions
    D. Suggestion

44. The development of a *grapevine* or a *rumor clinic* in an institution is USUALLY the result of

    A. the constant provocation of gossip by a few problem individuals
    B. unofficial approval of this employee activity
    C. lack of adequate communication through official channels
    D. employees' disapproval of the administration

45. Appraisal of an employee during his probationary period by an immediate supervisor who happens to be a personal friend of the employee is

    A. *unacceptable* because familiarity results in favoritism
    B. *unacceptable* because people on probation should not be evaluated by immediate supervisors
    C. *acceptable* because it encourages other employees to perform their duties in a manner satisfactory to the appraiser
    D. *acceptable* because the familiarity of the appraiser helps in a complete evaluation

46. In planning the weekly work routine, it is MOST important for a supervisor to

    A. ask employees which assignments they would prefer
    B. ask for volunteers to perform routine tasks
    C. indicate the daily anticipated attendance
    D. list areas of priority interest

47. Of the following, which is NOT a recommended practice of a supervisor?

    A. Giving reasons for emergency assignments or overtime work
    B. Attempting to detect a deep neurosis by examination of work habits or observation of behavior
    C. Taking corrective disciplinary action when an employee fails to improve his attendance following a corrective interview
    D. Consulting with employees as to the best way of getting a job done

48. If a correction officer attended a preparatory class on supervisory techniques, he would MOST likely be instructed that a good supervisor is one who

    A. believes in strong and centralized administrative control
    B. is extremely ambitious
    C. maintains a favorable attitude towards those he encounters
    D. maintains his own method of handling problems

49. Of the following, the MOST important consideration for recommending a provisional promotion to captain should be the correction officer's

    A. capacity to take disciplinary action
    B. ability to control inmate movement
    C. detailed knowledge of departmental rules and regulations
    D. seniority

50. The parts of the decision-making process are GENERALLY the
    I. research of background material
    II. development of details of alternative plans of action
    III. study and interpretation of collected data
    IV. selection of the best course of action
    V. statement of purpose or need

    The CORRECT answer is:

    A. I, II
    B. I, III, V
    C. I, III, IV, V
    D. All of the above

KEY (CORRECT ANSWERS)

1. D	11. D	21. B	31. B	41. A
2. B	12. A	22. D	32. D	42. C
3. A	13. D	23. A	33. B	43. D
4. C	14. C	24. A	34. C	44. C
5. B	15. C	25. C	35. B	45. A
6. D	16. B	26. A	36. A	46. D
7. B	17. A	27. D	37. D	47. B
8. C	18. C	28. B	38. C	48. C
9. B	19. A	29. D	39. C	49. A
10. C	20. D	30. A	40. D	50. D

TEST 2

DIRECTIONS: Each question or incomplete statement is followed by several suggested answers or completions. Select the one that BEST answers the question or completes the statement. *PRINT THE LETTER OF THE CORRECT ANSWER IN THE SPACE AT THE RIGHT.*

1. A threat to institutional order arises from the behavior of the *resister,* the inmate who flagrantly refuses to cooperate with staff. One study has shown that the *resister* exhibits certain characteristics.
   A characteristic NOT exhibited by *resisters* is

   A. a lower average intelligence than other prisoners
   B. a greater tendency toward sadism
   C. poorer preprison employment records
   D. fewer contacts with families while in prison

   1.____

2. Which of the following is NOT a correct reason for the persistence of the inmate social system?

   A. Conformity with inmate values, beliefs, and behavior provides prestige for the inmate.
   B. Inmates frequently complain of being forced to live with other inmates who are inferior and vicious; consequently, they seek acceptance by like inmates as a way of protection against the physical aggression of inferior inmates.
   C. Confinement threatens the masculinity of the inmate; inmates are motivated to overreact to confinement and loss of the masculine self-image by open support of the masculine values of aggressiveness.
   D. At least one-third of all inmates possess the inborn, hostile instincts of primitive humanity and, since this is a high percentage, inmate social systems tend to reflect the patterns of behavior of this aggressive population.

   2.____

3. According to recognized authorities, the population in a prison is together sufficiently large to create regularities in behavior.
   This means that

   A. the regularities require a de-emphasis of coercion and an emphasis on counseling and psychiatric therapy
   B. confinement is an experience requiring major continuous readjustments
   C. the regularities reflect the efforts of employees and inmates to achieve goals and meet problems
   D. the regularities in a prison imply the systematic lack of concern for the dignity of the individual

   3.____

4. The concept of occupation is useful for differentiating criminal behavior systems according to the degree of commitment to criminal values and to the degree to which it qualifies as a career.
   This statement implies that

   A. a person is less intensively committed to criminality when his feelings about himself and his behavior reflect the criminal group's attitudes toward him
   B. when an individual is strongly committed to a criminal culture, the consistency of his crime-oriented behavior is difficult to redirect through rehabilitative programs

   4.____

C. to *go straight* would cause the inmate to appear *honest* in the sense that his previous personal adjustment to daily recurring events would no longer appear consistent
D. professional career criminals regard violence and use of weapons as a mark of resourcefulness not possessed by ordinary career criminals

5. The statement below which most contemporary criminologists would find MOST accurate is that

   A. criminal behavior is explained by the lack of freedom in a materialistic society
   B. although criminal behavior is learned, it is not learned like most social behavior
   C. the process of becoming a criminal is regarded as the same as all personality development
   D. although criminal techniques are learned, the basic origin of criminality lies in inborn defects

6. Central to the association between urbanization and deviant behavior in American society is the problem neighborhood. Such neighborhoods are generally characterized by all of the following factors EXCEPT

   A. great cultural diversity
   B. total community disorganization
   C. general social instability
   D. high population turnover

7. An authority states that, although urbanization and industrialization have tended to standardize behavior, they have also increased the possibility of deviant behavior.
   This means MOST NEARLY that

   A. crime statistics tend to underestimate crimes in rural areas
   B. population density in industrialized cities favors the criminal because sheer numbers, coupled with the close personal relationship characteristic of city life, provides a great many customers for organized crime per 1,000 population
   C. urbanized areas have higher rates for all major crimes because city police systems are understaffed and lack public support
   D. the city-dweller is forced into mechanical conformity but has also been released from traditional constraints

8. Based on authority, the MOST accurate statement concerning the relationship between intelligence and criminality is that

   A. general intelligence as measured by I.Q. tests is unaffected by the individual's cultural background
   B. mental deficiency, by itself, can result in crime
   C. persons at the highest mental levels do not become criminals
   D. mental deficiency may reduce criminality by insulating the individual from frustrations

9. The basic distinction between the professional and non-professional criminal is that the professional criminal

   A. breaks the law more often than the nonprofessional
   B. sees himself as a criminal with a definite means of livelihood, whereas the nonprofessional still retains the basic morals of the dominant society
   C. is part of the larger society, whereas the nonprofessional is isolated from the dominant society
   D. has pride in his criminal techniques, but feels a sense of compassion for his victims, whereas the nonprofessional has neither pride in his techniques nor does he have any sense of guilt

10. Based on objective discussion of the general theory of *white-collar crime*, this type of crime can BEST be defined as any crime committed by a person of respectability and high social _____.

    A. status in the course of his occupation
    B. status in the course of his occupation, excluding crimes of the medical and legal professions, which are generally handled by administrative rather than judicial agencies
    C. status in the course of his occupation, excluding crimes not part of his occupational procedures
    D. status

11. The THREE major ideologies, or systems of belief, affecting law enforcement, court, and correctional activities are the punitive, therapeutic, and preventive ideologies.
    Of the following, the MOST correct statement is that the

    A. therapeutic ideology rather than the punitive or preventive ideology is recognized as offering the ultimate promise for reducing crime
    B. preventive ideology seeks to promote healthy personality development by means of immediate and drastic social changes so that criminals will engage in socially approved conduct
    C. therapeutic ideology considers the criminal to be a victim of defective conditioning of his personality and, consequently, generally seeks a lifetime clinical treatment approach by specially trained psychiatrists
    D. punitive ideology affords the most immediate relief for the requirements of the offended society

12. Group therapy commonly used in the treatment of offenders is intended to have each of the following benefits EXCEPT

    A. creation of a model inmate not demonstrating any potentiality for behavioral change
    B. encouragement of members of the group to see meanings they previously failed to recognize
    C. modification of staff and inmate cultures which are barriers to rehabilitation programs
    D. changing of attitudes in such areas as discipline and authority relationships

13. Crime rates vary with the age of the offender. American data show that the age range which has the highest ARREST RATE is

    A. ages 36 to 45
    B. ages 26 to 35
    C. ages 15 to 25
    D. a figure which cannot be estimated because of the great variations in different kinds of crimes committed by different age groups

14. Prisoners differ in their escape-proneness.
    The following sets of factors are generally associated with the escape behavior of prison inmates EXCEPT set

    A. mental stability and superior intelligence
       cooperative attitude
       mature when first arrested
    B. poor employment record
       uncooperative attitude
       daring and aggressive personality
    C. weak home ties
       habitual offender
       age less than 30 years
    D. poor employment record
       mental instability and inferior intelligence
       served less than 40 percent of his term

15. The correctional agency is an element in the system of criminal justice, which in turn is subject to the social-cultural environment of which it is a product and for which it is a social control instrumentality.
    This statement MOST NEARLY means that

    A. prisons very rarely change
    B. prisons must change if society is to reform
    C. prisons, courts, and police are part of society
    D. the police and courts have a negative impact on prisons

16. Which one of the following statements regarding probation and parole is MOST correct?

    A. Both probation and parole have similarities in objectives, in the use of casework, and in promotion of rehabilitation.
    B. Both probation and parole have similarities in the use of casework and in promotion of rehabilitation, but are dissimilar in their social objectives.
    C. Parole tries to promote change within the offender, whereas probation stresses that punishments should be standardized on the basis of the crime.
    D. Probation generally involves the more serious, criminalistic offender.

17. Walled prisons have been criticized for depriving inmates of normal contact with the outside community and for imposing a daily regime of frustration and aimlessness. The *open institution* has been advocated as an answer to such criticism.
Of the following pairs of statements, the pair which is TRUE is:

    A. I. Penologists generally agree that the open institution will replace the closed prison.
       II. To obtain properly selected inmates, the open institution requires the outside community as the source of its population.
    B. I. Penologists generally agree that the open institution requires the closed prison as the source of its population.
       II. To obtain properly selected inmates, the open institution requires the closed prison as the source of its population.
    C. I. Penologists generally agree that the open institution will replace the closed prison.
       II. Psychological controls are substituted for physical barriers against escape from the open institution.
    D. I. Penologists generally agree that the open institution will not replace the closed prison.
       II. The open institution is far less expensive to construct and to operate than the closed prison.

18. Prison industrial supervisors in this country have generally been accustomed to using excessive numbers of prisoners because

    A. the inmates' qualities as workers usually depress productivity
    B. it is difficult to strike a proper balance between vocational training for prisoner rehabilitation and the achievement of high production for its own sake
    C. prison industrial work is a real asset to vocational training
    D. of the stigma attached to prison-made goods

19. Increases in recidivist rates can result from

    A. more liberal enforcement of parole supervision
    B. increased use of probation by the courts
    C. stricter enforcement of probation supervision
    D. more liberal law enforcement

20. In recent developments in crime prevention, a basic theme has been *reaching the unreached.*
A disproportionate share of the *unreached* consists of

    A. college students arrested for campus demonstrations
    B. multi-problem families
    C. children of affluent suburbia who have been arrested for marijuana possession
    D. highly literate individuals who have been sentenced to correctional institutions for violation of the draft laws

21. Which one of the following statements is correct according to William D. Teeke's article, *Collective Violence in Correctional Institutions,* in a memorable issue of the AMERICAN JOURNAL OF CORRECTION?
    Riots are MORE likely to occur in the

    A. January-June period; the beginning of a new calendar year brings hope for a change in the correctional system in general
    B. January-June period; the densely populated Eastern coastal region is usually in the grip of a cold wave and this, coupled with defective heating systems in old institutions, creates many grievances
    C. July-December period; there is no definite evidence as to why this is the most probable time
    D. July-December period; people are hot and most troubled, and, living in dirty and cramped quarters, under close restraint, seek to rebel

Questions 22-26.

DIRECTIONS: Questions 22 through 26 consist of passages of one or more sentences. Each of the passages contains an incorrectly used word. First, decide which is the incorrectly used word. Then, from among the options given, decide which word, when substituted for the incorrectly used word, makes the meaning of the passage clear.

SAMPLE QUESTION

Prisoners frequently bring hazards to compel prison officials to allow them more medical care of different medical care than has been provided by the prison physician.
They rarely succeed.
   A. negligence   B. mistreatment
   C. actions   D. evaluations
The word *hazards* in the passage does not convey the meaning the passage is evidently intended to convey. The word *actions* (answer C), when substituted for the word *hazards,* makes the meaning of the passage clear. Accordingly, the answer to the question is C.

22. In the years since passage of the Harrison Narcotic Act of 1914, making the possession of opium amphetamines illegal in most circumstances, drug use has become a subject of considerable scientific interest and investigation.
    There is at present a voluminous literature on drug use of various kinds.

    A. Ingestion   B. Derivatives
    C. Addiction   D. Opiates

23. Of course, the fact that criminal laws are extremely patterned in definition does not mean that the majority of persons who violate them are dealt with as criminals. Quite the contrary, for a great many forbidden acts are voluntarily engaged in within situations of privacy and go unobserved and unreported.

    A. Symbolic   B. Casual
    C. Scientific   D. Broad-gauged

24. The most punitive way to study punishment is to focus attention on the pattern of punitive action: to study how a penalty is applied, to study what is done to or taken from an offender.

    A. Characteristic   B. Degrading
    C. Objective   D. Distinguished

25. The most common forms of punishment in times past have been death, physical torture, mutilation, branding, public humiliation, fines, forfeits of property, banishment, transportation, and imprisonment.
Although this list is by no means _____ differentiated, practically every form of punishment has had several variations and applications.

    A. Specific
    B. Simple
    C. Exhaustive
    D. Characteristic

26. There is another important line of inference between ordinary and professional criminals, and that is the source from which they are recruited.
The professional criminal seems to be drawn from legitimate employment and, in many instances, from parallel vocations or pursuits.

    A. Demarcation
    B. Justification
    C. Superiority
    D. Reference

27. Of the following, what should generally be the MAJOR objective of the institution in dealing with a prisoner?
Focus on

    A. helping him adjust to institutional life
    B. helping him develop his latent talents
    C. helping him prepare for a new career once out of prison
    D. his adjustment to freedom in the community

28. Of the following, the reason which BEST explains why outstanding authorities on penology believe that one city prison may not always be the BEST location for all inmates is that

    A. incarcerating second time offenders in city institutions increases their exposure to the bad influences of their criminal acquaintances
    B. some offenders may have problems which require treatment away from their local environment
    C. incarcerated individuals would be less prone to recidivism in a rural environment
    D. penal institutions on islands have a tendency to increase inmate tensions

29. Under the criminal treatment system, the justification for treating the condition of the individual is the fact that he has engaged in criminal conduct.
In the civil treatment system, the justification for treating the condition is

    A. always related to the crime
    B. given by the courts
    C. never related to the crime
    D. may or may not be related to the crime

30. On the basis of recent trends, which of the following statements would be INCORRECT?

    A. Less than one-quarter of the sentenced prisoners incarcerated in locally operated institutions can be considered civil prisoners.
    B. Many of the persons sentenced to local institutions have either been incarcerated in, or are destined to be incarcerated in, institutions administered by the state.
    C. Most of the persons incarcerated under sentence throughout the state today are first offenders.
    D. There is no reliable evidence to show that education or vocational training applied on a general basis has any effect in reducing recidivism.

31. There are two basic rationales for subjecting persons to treatment: one is called the *civil* system; and the other is called the *criminal* system.
    Of the following, the BASIC difference between these two systems is

    A. that the civil system is used to administer justice to those first time offenders who have committed a mild crime
    B. that the civil system usually requires facilities or institutions separate from those of the criminal system
    C. the criminal institution's employment of more highly skilled personnel
    D. the degree of exposure to community life

31.____

32. The MAJOR purpose of the recreational facilities located atop a major house of detention for men is to

    A. allow inmates a greater opportunity to socialize and expose themselves to sunshine
    B. enable fewer guards to watch inmates so the cost of institutional operations can be decreased
    C. allow greater freedom of movement of inmates within the confines of the institution
    D. provide relaxing and exhausting activities which will remove tension

32.____

33. A group of 50 youths is currently commuting from a local prison to an experimental training program in group counseling.
    The purpose of this program is

    A. basically to enable the inmates to serve as counselors for their fellow inmates
    B. chiefly to stimulate inmates and prepare them for future college training
    C. to expose inmates who have almost completed their sentence to civilian community life
    D. chiefly to prepare them for employment at the completion of their incarceration

33.____

34. A recent ruling by the courts held that no citizen awaiting trial be held in detention for more than _____ days.

    A. 90   B. 60   C. 30   D. 120

34.____

Questions 35-39.

DIRECTIONS: Questions 35 through 39 are based on the following tables.

Forest City, an imaginary jurisdiction, classifies its offenders as juvenile delinquents, youthful offenders, or adult offenders. There are two institutions for female offenders and five institutions for male offenders. Table A shows the average daily number of inmates for the years shown. Table B shows what percentage of average daily number of male inmates for the years shown were juvenile delinquents, youthful offenders, or adult offenders.

TABLE A - FOREST CITY INMATES

	1990	2000	2001 (estimate)
Institutions for Female Offenders:			
(1) Pleasantdale	70	105	120
(2) Shady Valley	W	190	210
TOTAL	195	295	330
Institutions for Male Offenders:			
(1) Leadurney	260	320	310
(2) Sherman	110	130	Y
(3) Riveredge	1700	1800	1850
(4) Thompson	650	800	Z
(5) Maxim	1200	1625	1700
TOTAL	3920	4675	5030
TOTAL MALE & FEMALE	X	4970	5360

TABLE B - FOREST CITY OFFENDERS
PERCENTAGE OF AVERAGE DAILY NUMBER OF INMATES CLASSIFIED AS JUVENILE DELINQUENTS, YOUTHFUL OFFENDERS, OR ADULT OFFENDERS
(See Code Below)

	1990 A	1990 B	1990 C	2000 A	2000 B	2000 C
Institutions for Female Offenders:						
(1) Pleasantdale	20%	60%	20%	25%	75%	-
(2) Shady Valley	15%	30%	55%	-	35%	65%
Institutions for Male Offenders:						
(1) Leadurney	5%	95%	-	80%	20%	-
(2) Sherman	10%	35%	55%	10%	35%	55%
(3) Riveredge	90%	10%	-	85%	15%	-
(4) Thompson	-	40%	60%	-	35%	65%
(5) Maxim	-	20%	80%	-	5%	95%

CODE
A - JUVENILE OFFENDERS
B - YOUTHFUL OFFENDERS
C - ADULT OFFENDERS

35. From 1990 to 2000, the average daily number of female youthful offenders in the Pleasantdale institution increased MOST NEARLY by

    A. 20
    B. 29
    C. 37
    D. a figure greater than 40

36. One of the following sets of figures belongs in the circled spaces marked Y and Z. Which one of the following sets of figures LOGICALLY belongs in these spaces?

    A. 115 and 990
    B. 115 and 1050
    C. 120 and 990
    D. 120 and 1050

37. The figures which LOGICALLY belong in the circled spaces marked W and X are

    A. 125 and 4115
    B. 125 and 4215
    C. 175 and 4115
    D. 175 and 4215

38. In 2000, of the average daily number of Forest City male and female inmates, the percentage to be found in Maxim was MOST NEARLY

    A. 27%   B. 30%   C. 33%   D. 36%

39. In 1990, the average daily number of adult male offenders was MOST NEARLY   39.____

    A. 60 in Sherman and 390 in Thompson
    B. 110 in Sherman and 650 in Thompson
    C. 390 in Thompson and 1300 in Maxim
    D. 800 in Thompson and 1625 in Maxim

Questions 40-43.

DIRECTIONS: Questions 40 through 43 are based on the following passage.

Female criminality is very much under-reported, especially if one considers offenses such as shoplifting, thefts by prostitutes, offenses against children, and homicide. There are even certain offenses such as homosexuality and exhibitionism that go practically unprosecuted if committed by women. Female offenders are really protected by men, even by victims, who are usually disinclined to complain to authorities. Since women play much less active roles in society than men do, one must be prepared for the fact that women are often the instigators of crimes committed by men and, as instigators, they are hard to detect. There are several crimes that are ordinarily highly detectable in men but have very low detectability in women. Her roles as homemaker, mother, nurse, wife, and so forth, permit the female to commit a crime and yet screen that crime from public view—for example, slowly poisoning her husband or treating her children abusively. In addition, law enforcement officers, judges, and juries are much more lenient toward women than toward men. Such considerations lead to the conclusion that criminality of women is largely masked criminality. Consequently, official statistics and records of criminality should be expected to under-report female offenses. The true measure of female crime must be sought from unofficial sources. The masked character of female crime and its gross under-reporting are consistent with the official view that the female is a very low risk for crime.

40. What has the writer inferred about the incidence of female offenses?   40.____

    A. It gives an adequate representation of the number of crimes committed by men but instigated by women.
    B. It is not to be considered an important area of criminality.
    C. It is understated because the classic female role makes her less visible to social scrutiny.
    D. In every crime the incidence of male offenses is more difficult to detect than that of women.

41. Judges are inclined to be lenient toward female offenders because   41.____

    A. the role of the woman in society has stereotyped her as maternal and non-hostile
    B. the majority of their crimes do not physically harm others
    C. they commit crimes which are difficult to detect
    D. official statistics report them as less likely to commit crimes

42. Of the following, the title MOST suitable for this passage is   42.____

    A. Male Criminality
    B. The Petty Offender
    C. The Female Murderer
    D. Exposing Female Criminality

43. According to the passage, which of the following crimes is LEAST likely to be prosecuted against a woman?

   A. Child abuse
   B. Exhibitionism
   C. Homicide
   D. Prostitution

Questions 44-47.

DIRECTIONS: Questions 44 through 47 are based on the following passage.

The usual explanation for drunken behavior is that alcohol, which is a physiological depressant impairs reasoning and inhibition powers before it depresses the ability to act and to express emotion.

The purely physiological effects of alcohol are very much like those of fatigue. Individual personality and social and cultural influences apparently greatly determine how these effects are reflected in changed behavior as alcohol is consumed. Therefore, one can assert that alcohol alone does not cause drunken behavior; rather, drunken behavior expresses personal character, cultural traditions, and social circumstances, as they influence a person's reactions to the physiological effects of alcohol on his body.

For some people, and in some circumstances, these personal, cultural, and social factors may readily express themselves as criminal behavior. The most obvious case, of course, is public drunkenness.

The exact relationship between various crimes and various stages of intoxication is not completely known. G.M. Scott believes that the moderate stages of intoxication are the ones usually associated with crime, since the latter states of intoxication make performance of crime impossible. Dr. Banay found that many drunks are drawn into crime not only by the need of money to replace wages that drinking prevents them from earning, but also by their increased irritability and pugnacity.... He discovered that most of the sex offenses for which offenders are committed to state prisons show a relation between alcohol and the crime and that the average sex case is a clear-cut illustration of the hypothesis that alcohol covers up an underlying condition and that some dormant tendency is either brought to the surface or aggravated by alcohol.

In addition to drunken behavior resulting in criminal acts, it is also connected to several other important social problems. Reference can be made particularly to dependency, unemployment, desertion, divorce, vagrancy, and suicide. For all of these social ills, alcohol acts as the physiological depressing agent which influences one's deviation from normative behavior.

44. Discussions of intoxication customarily state that alcohol

   A. initially affects the analytic faculty
   B. initially affects the ability to express feelings
   C. reduces the desire for money
   D. stimulates perception of the true nature of one's condition

45. Which one of the following hypotheses would Dr. Banay MOST likely support? 45._____

    A. The casual drinker is less likely to commit a crime than the chronic drinker.
    B. An aggressive drunk is likely to have aggressive tendencies when not under the influence of alcohol.
    C. The underlying cause of most sex offenses is excessive drinking.
    D. There is no connection between cultural background and drunken behavior.

46. The title BEST suited for this passage is: 46._____

    A. How Alcohol Influences Potential Sexual Offenders
    B. Stages of Intoxication
    C. The Role of Alcoholic Consumption in Human Behavior
    D. The Relationship Between Alcohol and Emotion

47. The writer implies that 47._____

    A. a desire to destroy oneself is a frequent side effect of drinking intoxicating liquors
    B. a person who is drunk may find it easier to kill himself
    C. there is a pattern of drinking behavior in the background of most suicides
    D. there is no relationship between the problems of drinking and suicide

Questions 48-50.

DIRECTIONS: Questions 48 through 50 are based on the following passage.

A survey of the drinking behavior of 1,185 persons representing the adult population of Iowa in 2008 aged 21 years and older revealed that approximately 40 percent were abstainers. Of the nearly 1 million drinkers in the State, 47 percent were classed as light drinkers, 37 percent as moderate, and 16 percent as heavy drinkers. Twenty-two percent of the men drinkers were classed as heavy drinkers but only 8 percent of the women drinkers. The proportion of heavy drinkers increased with level of education among drinkers residing in the city –from 15 percent of the least educated to 22 percent of the most educated but decreased among farm residents from 17 percent of the least educated to 4 percent of the most educated. Age differences in the extent of drinking were not pronounced. The age class of 36-45 had the lowest proportions of light drinkers while the age class 61 and over had the lowest proportion of heavy drinkers.

48. Of the total drinking population in Iowa, how many were moderate drinkers? 48._____

    A. 370,000   B. 438   C. 370   D. 438,150

49. What percent of the men drinkers surveyed were NOT heavy drinkers? 49._____

    A. 60%   B. 84%
    C. 78%   D. Cannot be determined

50. According to the passage, which one of the following statements concerning heavy drinking would be CORRECT? 50._____

    A. Experts are in sharp conflict regarding the reason for heavy drinking.
    B. The amount of heavy drinking in the city is directly proportional to the amount of education.
    C. The degree of heavy drinking is directly proportional to the age class of the drinkers.
    D. The degree of heavy drinking is inversely to the number of light drinkers.

KEY (CORRECT ANSWERS)

1. A	11. D	21. C	31. B	41. A
2. D	12. A	22. B	32. D	42. D
3. C	13. C	23. D	33. D	43. B
4. B	14. A	24. C	34. A	44. A
5. C	15. C	25. C	35. C	45. B
6. B	16. A	26. A	36. D	46. C
7. D	17. B	27. D	37. A	47. B
8. D	18. A	28. B	38. C	48. A
9. B	19. C	29. D	39. A	49. C
10. C	20. B	30. C	40. C	50. B

EXAMINATION SECTION
TEST 1

DIRECTIONS: Each question or incomplete statement is followed by several suggested answers or completions. Select the one that BEST answers the question or completes the statement. *PRINT THE LETTER OF THE CORRECT ANSWER IN THE SPACE AT THE RIGHT.*

1. In the ten years from 1970 to 1980, in the nation as a whole, the

    A. number of major crimes remained constant but the number of lesser offenses increased markedly
    B. percentage increase in population was greater than the percentage increase in major crimes
    C. percentage increase in population was smaller than the percentage increase in major crimes
    D. percentage increase in population equaled the percentage increase in major crimes

    1.____

2. According to figures released, major crimes in the period of 1980-1985, compared with the period of 1975-1980,

    A. decreased slightly
    B. remained steady
    C. showed an increase of less than one quarter
    D. showed an increase of more than one third

    2.____

3. During the late 60's, major prison riots occurred in the states of

    A. New York and New Jersey
    B. Michigan and Ohio
    C. New Jersey and Washington
    D. Washington and Michigan

    3.____

4. The Annual Congress of Correction is held every year in a

    A. city   B. town   C. village   D. seaport

    4.____

5. The book MY SIX CONVICTS

    A. has its setting in a state prison
    B. is a completely factual autobiography
    C. was unfavorably received by penologists
    D. was written by a former warden

    5.____

Questions 6-10.

DIRECTIONS: For each book in Column I, select the author of the book from Column II; then write the letter preceding the author's name in the appropriate space at the right.

63

COLUMN I	COLUMN II
6. Jails - Care and Treatment of Misdemeanant Prisoners in the United States	A. Barnes, Harry E. and Teeters, Negley K.
7. New Horizons in Criminology	B. Glueck, Sheldon and Eleanor
8. Probation and Parole	C. Harris, Mary B
9. The Training of Prison Guards in the State of New York	D. Monahan, Florence
	E. Pigeon, Helen D.
10. Women in Crime	F. Robinson, Louis N.
	G. Wallack, Walter M.

11. A person with a *psychopathic personality* is

    A. consistently abnormal in his behavior
    B. feebleminded
    C. insane and has criminal tendencies
    D. psychotic

12. A person is considered to be of normal intelligence if his IQ or intelligence quotient falls within the range of

    A. 60-80   B. 70-90   C. 80-100   D. 90-110

13. The term *malingerer* is MOST correctly applied to an inmate wh

    A. bears an officer a grudge for a long time
    B. is a habitual liar
    C. pretends to be ill in order to avoid working
    D. takes a long time to recover from an illness

14. The MOST accurate of the following statements about the County Grand Jury is:

    A. Considers evidence to determine if a crime has been committed
    B. Is composed of 12 persons
    C. Is sworn in for an indefinite period of service
    D. Serves at the call of the Chief Magistrate and the District Attorney

15. The one of the following which is NOT a function of the Criminal Courts in the city is

    A. holding a defendant charged with a misdemeanor for the Court of Special Sessions if the evidence indicates that he has committed the crime charged
    B. sitting as a Court of Special Sessions in certain misdemeanor cases
    C. trying defendants charged with felonies
    D. trying defendants charged with minor traffic violations

16. In the city, the Night Court is a branch of

    A. County Court   B. Supreme Court
    C. Civil Court   D. Criminal Court

17. Members of the uniformed force of the Department of Correction are designated as peace officers by the

    A. Administrative Code
    B. City Charter
    C. Code of Criminal Procedure
    D. Penal Law

17._____

18. In the city, jurisdiction over court detention pens is vested in the Department of Correction by the

    A. Administrative Code   B. City Charter
    C. Correction Law   D. Penal Law

18._____

19. Of the following State institutions, the one which houses MAINLY female defective delinquents is the

    A. Albion State Training School
    B. Institution for Defective Delinquents at Napanoch
    C. Westfield State Farm
    D. Woodbourne Institution for Defective Delinquents

19._____

20. According to the Penal Law, escape from lawful imprisonment is always a

    A. felony
    B. felony if the imprisonment was for a felony
    C. misdemeanor
    D. misdemeanor if the imprisonment was for a felony

20._____

21. A writ or order by a Magistrate, Justice or other competent authority and addressed to an officer requiring him to arrest the person named therein and bring him before the Court to be examined regarding the offense with which he is charged. The preceding definition refers MOST directly to a

    A. certificate of reasonable doubt
    B. mandamus
    C. warrant
    D. writ of habeas corpus

21._____

22. From 2000 to 2005, inclusive, the inmate census in the Department

    A. decreased steadily   B. fluctuated up and down
    C. increased steadily   D. remained almost constant

22._____

23. In 2005, the average daily inmate census in the Department was between

    A. 5,500 and 10,000   B. 4,500 and 5,500
    C. 3,500 and 4,500   D. 2,500 and 3,500

23._____

24. The MOST accurate of the following statements about the offenses for which prisoners were sentenced to the institutions of the Department last year is that the

    A. largest number of male commitments was for disorderly conduct whereas the largest number of female commitments was for vagrancy (prostitution)
    B. largest number of male commitments was for vagrancy whereas the largest number of female commitments was for disorderly conduct

24._____

C. number of women committed for drug offenses was about 50% of the number of men committed for drug offenses
D. second largest number of male commitments was for gambling whereas the second largest number of female commitments was for petty larceny

25. Of the inmates committed to the Department last year, the average age of the inmates committed to the workhouse as compared to the average age of the inmates committed to the penitentiary was

A. higher
B. higher for male commitments but lower for female commitments
C. lower
D. neither higher nor lower

26. Of all the inmates sentenced to the institutions of the Department last year, those who had any education beyond the elementary school constituted between

A. 15% and 20%   B. 10% and 15%
C. 5% and 10%   D. 0% and 5%

27. Last year, the average rate of recidivism among workhouse and penitentiary inmates (men and women) in the institutions of the Department was

A. between 50% and 60%
B. less than 30%
C. more than 30% but less than 55%
D. more than 60% but less than 75%

28. Of all workhouse sentences to the Department in 1985, definite workhouse sentences of 6 months or less (men and women) constituted

A. between 75% and 80%   B. between 80% and 90%
C. less than 75%   D. more than 95%

29. During the fiscal year 1984-1985, the average daily food cost per prisoner in the institutions of the Department was between

A. 50? and $1.00   B. $1.00 and $2.00
C. $2.00 and $3.00   D. $3.00 and $4.00

30. In the detention prisons of the Department, persons charged with felonies GENERALLY constitute

A. about half of the inmate population
B. a majority of the inmate population
C. a minority of the inmate population
D. less of a discipline problem than persons charged with misdemeanors

31. A uniformed member of the city police department may interview a trial inmate in a Department of Correction institution if he presents a

A. police department form properly filled out and a special Department of Correction pass
B. police department form properly filled out and signs a consent form which is also signed by the inmate

C. special Department of Correction pass and a consent form signed by himself and the inmate
D. special Department of Correction pass and a letter of authorization signed by the police commissioner or his authorized representative

32. When an inmate enters the custody of the Department, certain forms are filled out. Of these forms, the ones which must always accompany the inmate while he is in the custody of the Department are the _____ card and _____ card.

   A. commitment; accompanying
   B. commitment; pedigree
   C. registration; accompanying
   D. registration card, accompanying; commitment

33. A correction officer in charge of a court detention pen should be instructed by the captain that when a police officer delivers a prisoner to the court pen, the correction officer should

   A. enter in the *police blotter* the name, shield number, command and time of arrival of the police officer and the prisoner's name and sex
   B. fill out an arraignment card and complaint form
   C. require the police officer to present a valid commitment signed by a Magistrate
   D. search the prisoner and turn over to the police officer any articles of contraband

34. In the Department, *jail time* is

   A. figured from the day of admission on a charge to and including the day of sentence
   B. not considered in determining the length of custody under an indefinite sentence
   C. not deducted from the time to be served if the sentence includes an alternative fine
   D. the amount of time in days that an inmate has been confined in the custody of the Department

35. The LEAST accurate of the following statements is that a

   A. commitment under an alternate sentence of a fine or a definite term can be made both to the workhouse and to the penitentiary
   B. maximum workhouse definite sentence is for a longer period than a maximum penitentiary definite sentence
   C. maximum workhouse indefinite sentence is for a shorter period than a maximum penitentiary indefinite sentence
   D. minimum penitentiary definite sentence is for a longer period than a minimum workhouse definite sentence

36. The LEAST accurate of the following statements about time off for good behavior in the institutions of the Department is that

   A. penitentiary definite sentences of 3 months or more are allowed 5 days good time per month
   B. penitentiary indefinite sentences are allowed 5 days good time per month
   C. workhouse definite sentences of 30 days or more, where no alternative fine is imposed, are allowed 5 days good time per month
   D. workhouse indefinite sentences are allowed 5 days good time per month

37. If an inmate is committed to the Department by a judge for more than one charge,

    A. all charges must be stated on the one commitment
    B. duplicate records must be kept at the institution for each charge
    C. separate commitments are always required for each charge
    D. separate commitments are required only if the inmate must answer to each charge in a different court

38. A *short commitment* is a commitment issued by a judge wherein the defendant is

    A. held for future action in the Criminal Courts
    B. held for the Court of Special Sessions
    C. held for the Grand Jury
    D. sentenced by the judge for the offense committed

39. A defendant was committed to the Department by a judge for a future hearing. After the hearing, the defendant was re-committed for another hearing by a judge. In this case,

    A. a new commitment must be issued by the judge
    B. the issuance of a new commitment is at the discretion of the judge
    C. the original commitment is designated as the superseding commitment
    D. the original commitment is still valid

40. When the arresting officer calls for an inmate to produce the inmate in court to answer to the charge, it is important that he be informed by the pen officer of any warrants against the inmate MAINLY because

    A. it may be necessary to produce the warrants in court together with the inmate
    B. the inmate may be released on the original charge
    C. the warrants may be for more serious offenses than the present arrest
    D. this information will help to identify the inmate

41. When a prisoner is committed on a direct admission, the officer at the detention pen is required to note on the back of the commitment the condition of the inmate at the time when taken into custody by the Department. Of the following, the PRINCIPAL reason why this information is important is that

    A. a comparison can be made at the time of release to see if any improvement has been made
    B. drug addicts and alcoholics can be noted and segregated
    C. it may influence the determination as to which institution the inmate is to be transferred
    D. subsequent charges that an inmate was mistreated while in the Department's custody can be refuted

42. The pen officer shall make a thorough inspection of the court pens at the beginning of the tour every day. In the court pens operated by the Department, this thorough inspection is very important MAINLY because the pens are

    A. directly accessible from the street
    B. not escape-proof
    C. not under the supervision of Department of Correction personnel at all times
    D. very antiquated for the most part compared with other facilities for housing prisoners

43. When opening or closing a mechanically operated cell door, the officer should, after setting the door in motion, stop such motion for a fraction of a second and then complete the movement of the door. Of the following, the BEST reason for operating a mechanical cell door in the manner described in the statement is that the

    A. door will not function properly unless it is operated in this way
    B. obstructions in the path of the door can be removed in time
    C. officer can observe if the door is operating properly
    D. fast inmate is warned to get in or out of the cell immediately

44. Detention prisons house mainly prisoners awaiting trial, A house gang of sentenced inmates is often transferred to a detention prison to do maintenance work throughout the institution. Of the following, the GREATEST potential danger from such a house gang is that its members will

    A. gain control over inmates awaiting trial by claiming to be *in the know*
    B. have too many opportunities for escape
    C. pass contraband to inmates awaiting trial
    D. upset prison discipline by fighting with inmates awaiting trial

45. It is important that the tier officer be notified as soon as possible of any change in an inmate's court status MAINLY because

    A. a change in an inmate's court status may necessitate a change in custodial supervision
    B. prison records to be of value must be accurate and up-to-date
    C. subordinates should not be able to justify errors
    D. of judgment on the grounds of ignorance of the facts
    E. the tier officer, who supervises many inmates, may find it difficult to remember every detail of each inmate's status

46. The importance of full and complete fact-finding by the correction officer assigned to getting the newly admitted prisoner's pedigree cannot be too greatly stressed. Of the following, the BEST justification for this statement is that

    A. a job worth doing at all is worth doing well
    B. the correction officer will be held responsible for the completeness and correctness of the information obtained
    C. the information so obtained will be used to identify the inmate in the future
    D. incomplete information is of little value

47. Department procedure requires the keeping of complete and permanent records of all telephone calls made by inmates. Of the following, the BEST justification for this requirement is that

    A. an excessive number of calls by any inmate will be revealed and can be investigated
    B. attempts by inmates to communicate illegally with outside persons can be controlled
    C. the records can be used to refute charges by an inmate that the privilege of making telephone calls was denied
    D. while an inmate may make only one free call, other calls paid for by the inmate are not limited to number

48. When a police line-up is conducted for the purpose of identification of an inmate by a witness, it is MOST desirable that the

   A. inmates selected for the line-up be informed of the reason for their selection
   B. inmate to be identified be dressed in the clothes worn on admission to the institution
   C. other inmates in the line-up be of a different general appearance than the inmate to be identified
   D. police officer who brought the witness to the institution be present at the line-up at the time the identification is made

49. The presence of any sanitation equipment, such as mops and buckets, in the cells of inmates is prohibited. Of the following, the BEST justification for this rule is that

   A. many inmates are not concerned about taking good care of prison equipment
   B. such equipment should be available for use by all inmates
   C. the presence of such equipment in cells detracts from the neat appearance of the institution
   D. the ready availability of such equipment may tempt an inmate to use it in an attack

50. The newly sentenced inmate in the institutions of the Department is usually more relaxed mentally than the inmate awaiting trial. Of the following, the MAJOR reason for this is that the newly sentenced inmate

   A. has formed friendships with other inmates in similar circumstances
   B. is able to receive regular visits from family members
   C. is no longer uncertain as to the immediate future
   D. realizes that good behavior may earn a reduction in time

KEY (CORRECT ANSWERS)

1. C	11. A	21. C	31. B	41. D
2. D	12. D	22. C	32. D	42. C
3. A	13. C	23. A	33. D	43. B
4. A	14. A	24. A	34. C	44. C
5. C	15. C	25. A	35. B	45. A
6. F	16. D	26. D	36. A	46. C
7. A	17. C	27. C	37. C	47. C
8. E	18. B	28. D	38. A	48. B
9. G	19. A	29. D	39. A	49. D
10. D	20. B	30. B	40. B	50. C

TEST 2

DIRECTIONS: Each question or incomplete statement is followed by several suggested answers or completions. Select the one that BEST answers the question or completes the statement. *PRINT THE LETTER OF THE CORRECT ANSWER IN THE SPACE AT THE RIGHT.*

1. Of the following, the PRIMARY factor governing the assignment of an inmate to work in a penitentiary should be

    A. his intelligence
    B. his previous work experience
    C. his vocational plans after release
    D. the special training he requires
    E. the degree of custody required

    1.____

2. Shackles, the lock step, prison stripes, and enforced silence are almost entirely out of vogue. Of the following, the CHIEF objection to such correctional procedures is that they

    A. are difficult to enforce
    B. are detrimental to the inmate after release from prison
    C. make prison discipline more difficult to control
    D. require a large and well trained staff if they are to be utilized effectively
    E. are very unpopular with inmates

    2.____

3. The releasing officer questioned the prisoner about to be released concerning such personal details as the address of his mother and his father's first name. Of the following, the BEST explanation of the releasing officer's behavior is that

    A. there were probably errors in the prison records
    B. prisoners often change their stories after a period of time
    C. it sometimes happens that the wrong prisoner is released
    D. rehabilitation of an inmate requires personal attention at every stage of the correctional process
    E. prisoners are occasionally not sufficiently well oriented to be released

    3.____

4. Frequently, the man who makes an ideal inmate in the penitentiary does not make an ideal parolee when released. Of the following, the BEST justification for this statement is that

    A. adjustment to prison life is in many respects more complex than adjustment to civilian life
    B. high moral standards tend to remain well established once they have been developed
    C. prison-wise inmates are often on their best behavior while they remain in prison
    D. prison constitutes an acid test and no man is ordinarily paroled unless he passes this test
    E. there is no such thing as an ideal inmate, each inmate is an individual

    4.____

5. Suppose that a judge, on the basis of the chief medical officer's petition and the examiner's certificate of lunacy, signs an order for the transfer of an inmate to a state hospital for the criminally insane. The inmate must be transferred within

    5.____

A. 24 hours after receipt of the order
B. 15 days after the signing of the order
C. 48 hours after receipt of the order
D. 10 days after the signing of the order
E. a reasonable period of time fixed at the discretion of the warden

6. The one of the following items of information concerning an inmate which is NOT recorded on the BACK of the commitment when the inmate is received at a correctional institution is the

    A. name of the committing judge
    B. age of the inmate
    C. religion of the inmate
    D. name of the nearest relative of the inmate
    E. apparent physical condition of the prisoner

7. Of the following, the MOST accurate statement concerning bonds, notes, or certificates accepted for bail at a city prison is that

    A. one bond, note, or certificate may be accepted for two or more cases
    B. registered bonds may be accepted
    C. part cash and part securities may be accepted
    D. bonds, notes, or certificates may be accepted only in such denominations as to make the sum of the bail in each case
    E. securities must be in coupon or bearer form only, with all coupons detached

8. The one of the following cases in which probation is likely to be MOST effective is the case of the

    A. sex pervert
    B. elderly recidivist
    C. chronic alcoholic
    D. young first offender
    E. young hardened criminal

9. The common age limits for reformatories are USUALLY

    A. 16 to 30   B. 12 to 18   C. 19 to 25
    D. 12 to 40   E. 19 to 21

10. The one of the following which is NOT a type of commitment received at city prisons is

    A. Short Form
    B. Magistrates' General
    C. Mental Observation
    D. Material Witness
    E. Bail Surrender

11. MOST of the writs of Habeas Corpus served upon the warden of Riker's Island are returnable in

    A. Felony Court
    B. the Court of Appeals
    C. Criminal Court
    D. the Appellate Division
    E. the Supreme Court, Bronx County

12. Henry Doe is sentenced on April 4, 2008 in the Supreme Court for the crime of second degree assault, to serve 6 months in the penitentiary. He is received at the penitentiary on April 6, when the sentence begins. He has spent twenty days in jail awaiting trial. The length of time on which commutation is allowed is _____ months _____ days.

    A. 5; 9   B. 5; 28   C. 6; 0   D. 6; 2   E. 6; 20

13. Suppose that John Doe is sentenced on June 16, 2008 on a paternity charge to serve one year in the workhouse, or place a bond of $500. Of the following, the MOST accurate statement under these circumstances is that

    A. he will be discharged on June 17, 2008 if no bond is placed
    B. he will be allowed 5 days off for each month of good behavior
    C. he will be allowed 2 days a month good time for good behavior
    D. a minimum of at least 30 days must be served even if bond is placed
    E. the institution is not empowered to accept a cash bond in this type of case

14. Henry Doe is sentenced on September 1 to serve 5 months and 29 days in the workhouse for disorderly conduct. With full time off for good behavior, his time will be up on _____ of the following year.

    A. January 28   B. February 4   C. February 9
    D. February 20   E. March 1

15. Of the following, the LEAST accurate statement concerning the time served by an inmate is that

    A. should the day of discharge fall on a Sunday, the inmate is discharged the day before
    B. should the day of discharge fall on a holiday, the inmate is discharged the day before
    C. no credit is allowed for time awaiting trial in any fine case
    D. time served in a fine case may be prorated on the basis of the amount of fine paid
    E. good time is allowed only on a sentence of 30 days or more

16. Of the following, the MOST accurate statement concerning the time to be served before an inmate may be released on parole is that in the case of

    A. penitentiary indefinite sentences, the date of discharge is fixed by the committing judge
    B. workhouse indefinite sentences, the date of discharge is fixed by the committing judge
    C. penitentiary indefinite sentences the time to be served is fixed by the Parole Commission with the written consent of the committing judge
    D. reformatory cases, the time to be served is fixed by the committing judge
    E. penitentiary definite sentences, the time to be served is fixed by the Parole Commission

17. The approval of the Governor of the State must be received before release or discharge, with commutation for good time, of _____ cases.

    A. penitentiary definite   B. penitentiary indefinite
    C. workhouse definite   D. workhouse indefinite
    E. both penitentiary indefinite and workhouse indefinite

18. The *Auburn System* refers MOST accurately to the practice of 18.____

    A. having inmates work in shops during the day and keeping them in individual cells at night
    B. keeping prisoners in solitary confinement most of the time
    C. classifying and segregating prisoners according to their needs
    D. establishing inmate councils elected by the inmates themselves
    E. establishing minimum security institutions without walls

19. The indeterminate sentence applies to the vast majority of penitentiary commitments and to a relatively small number of workhouse sentences. Penitentiary indeterminate sentences are for a maximum of _____ years. 19.____

    A. 1   B. 2   C. 3   D. 4   E. 5

20. The *Bertillon record,* in connection with a newly received inmate, refers MOST accurately to his 20.____

    A. medical history   B. court record
    C. commitment papers   D. physical measurements
    E. fingerprints

21. Of the following, the MOST accurate statement concerning sentences in the city is that _____ sentences are _____ only. 21.____

    A. workhouse; definite   B. penitentiary; indefinite
    C. workhouse; indefinite   D. penitentiary; definite
    E. reformatory; indefinite

22. Walkill is BEST described as a(n) 22.____

    A. major receiving institution for the western part of the state
    B. institution for mental defectives
    C. institution for the criminally insane
    D. centralized prison hospital
    E. institution for the re-training of men about to be released

23. The State *Use* Plan refers MOST accurately to 23.____

    A. vocational guidance for juvenile delinquents
    B. inspection of local correctional institutions by the State
    C. disposal of goods manufactured by prison labor
    D. a method of classifying prisoners
    E. determination of the actual length of indeterminate sentences

24. The non-self-contained gas mask used in the Department of Correction is LEAST effective 24.____

    A. against phosgene gas
    B. against chlorine gas
    C. against carbon monoxide gas
    D. in an atmosphere containing less than 16% oxygen
    E. in an atmosphere containing more than 50% of combined poisonous gases

25. Suppose that a correction officer has been exposed to tear gas. As his superior officer, you should recommend that he bathe his eyes with a solution of

   A. baking soda
   B. gentian violet
   C. boric acid
   D. tannic acid
   E. epsom salts

26. The use of the liquid type of tear gas has been discontinued in the Department of Correction in favor of the crystal type CHIEFLY because the liquid type

   A. will not rise more than 12 or 15 feet above the ground
   B. forms a vapor which is heavier than air
   C. is too mild to be greatly effective
   D. deteriorates rapidly in storage
   E. is too heavily concentrated

27. Prison officers must constantly exercise vigilance that poisonous insecticides are not stored, even temporarily, near foodstuffs. The one of the following insecticides to which the above statement is ESPECIALLY pertinent is

   A. sodium fluoride
   B. red squill
   C. finely powdered borax
   D. a spray made with odorless kerosene
   E. a spray made with pyrethrum

28. In the city, a self-committed drug addict MOST usually serves a term of

   A. 30 days
   B. 60 days
   C. 100 days
   D. 6 months
   E. 8 months

29. The number of days per month commutation for good behavior allowed by law to penitentiary definite cases in the State is

   A. 1
   B. 3
   C. 5
   D. 7
   E. 10

30. It is desirable that courts have discretion in determining penalties in criminal cases MAINLY in order to

   A. make the punishment fit the gravity of the crime
   B. deter possible offenders
   C. curb interference from the courts
   D. encourage more widespread use of probation
   E. adjust the punishment to the crime, the offender, and the circumstances

31. Inmate John Jones is aged 45. He has had only two years of elementary school and is unable to read or write. Because of this disability, he is shy and lacks confidence in himself. For the correction officer assigned to classification to recommend that this inmate be given additional schooling would be

   A. *foolish*; he is obviously too old
   B. *wise*; he has insufficient education to make a good moral adjustment
   C. *foolish*; his intelligence is obviously too low
   D. *wise*; his confidence in himself would be increased
   E. *foolish*; he has already had more years of education than he can expect to obtain in prison

32. The correction officer will usually find correlation of human traits rather than compensation. On the basis of this statement, the correction officer should expect a mentally defective prisoner to be

    A. talented in some single respect
    B. able to learn a skilled trade in prison more easily than a highly intelligent prisoner
    C. less adept at manual skill than a highly intelligent prisoner
    D. well adjusted from a personality viewpoint
    E. equally competent in all respects

33. A representative group of young criminals in a certain state were found to be normal in intelligence, but 86% were retarded from one to six grades in school. Of the following, the BEST inference from these data is that

    A. lack of intelligence is highly correlated with delinquency
    B. criminals should be removed from the school system as soon as possible
    C. educational maladjustments are closely associated with delinquency
    D. the usual rate at which criminals progress educationally represents the limit of their learning powers
    E. in virtually any group of young persons there is little relationship between intellectual capacity and scholastic achievement

34. Many years ago, the establishment of the Children's Court was hailed as the solution to juvenile delinquency. And yet, the rate of juvenile delinquency has continued to increase. The one of the following which is LEAST valid as a possible explanation of the apparent failure of Children's Courts to reduce the rate of juvenile delinquency is that

    A. the emphasis has been chiefly on correction after the crime rather than on crime prevention
    B. inadequate funds and facilities have been provided for these courts
    C. the number of children in the population has increased in proportion to the population increase
    D. there has been a general crime increase over a period of years due to general social insecurity
    E. insufficient attention has been given to the remedying of environmental and family conditions leading to crime

35. To base a generalization regarding the causation of criminal behavior on a comparison of prison inmates with a civilian group is defective MAINLY because

    A. prison inmates comprise those criminals who have been convicted
    B. quantitative analysis is a misleading type of approach
    C. prison inmates do not include misdemeanants
    D. generalizations tend to be meaningless abstractions
    E. causation of criminal behavior is an individual matter

36. The purpose of a prison is the keeping in custody of individuals who may, because of their criminal behavior, be a menace to the persons and property of free citizens. This function of the correctional institution, however, is only half the job. Of the following, the CHIEF implication of the above statement is that

A. individuals may be expected to show criminal behavior even in prison
B. criminal behavior is a menace to the person and property of free citizens
C. the chief purpose of a prison is accomplished when the prisoner is removed from society
D. persons who are truly a menace to society have little chance for rehabilitation
E. influences must be brought to bear on the prisoner which will tend to prevent him from resorting again to criminal behavior when released

37. The one of the following parole procedures which has proven MOST effective in preventing recidivism is that

    A. no person is paroled unless he has served at least half his sentence
    B. every person paroled is required to write his parole officer at least once every three months
    C. no person is paroled unless he has a job waiting for him
    D. no person is paroled who has a record of a previous conviction
    E. a juvenile delinquent is paroled only in the custody of his parent or guardian

38. One can only see what one observes, and one observes only things which are already in the mind. Of the following, the CHIEF implication of this statement for the correction officer is that

    A. observation, to be effective, should be directed and conscious
    B. all aspects of a situation, unless the correction officer exercises caution, are likely to strike him with equal forcefulness
    C. memory is essentially perception one step removed from observation
    D. observation should be essentially indirect if it is to be accurate
    E. the mind observes and remembers each object seen, whether consciously or not

39. A promise to a subordinate is more important in a system of discipline than a promise to a superior. Of the following, the BEST justification for the above statement is that

    A. subordinates are generally in no position to make promises to superiors
    B. there is no obligation to make promises to subordinates
    C. discipline cannot be maintained if promises are broken
    D. discipline rests essentially on the respect of subordinates for their superior
    E. superiors are in a position to order whatever action is required

40. Suppose that you are a supervisor. A correction officer under your supervision submits to you a written recommendation concerning administrative procedure. You believe that the objective is worthwhile, but that certain precautions are necessary. Of the following, the BEST action for you to take is to

    A. submit the correction officer's memorandum to the warden, along with a statement of your own opinion
    B. submit the correction officer's memorandum to the warden without additional comment
    C. advise the correction officer to submit his memorandum to the warden directly
    D. advise the correction officer to withdraw his memorandum
    E. rewrite the correction officer's memorandum to include the necessary precautions and submit it to the warden as your own recommendation

KEY (CORRECT ANSWERS)

1. E	11. E	21. E	31. D
2. B	12. A	22. E	32. C
3. C	13. E	23. C	33. C
4. C	14. B	24. D	34. C
5. D	15. D	25. C	35. A
6. A	16. C	26. D	36. E
7. D	17. A	27. A	37. C
8. D	18. A	28. C	38. A
9. A	19. C	29. E	39. D
10. E	20. D	30. E	40. A

TEST 3

DIRECTIONS: Each question or incomplete statement is followed by several suggested answers or completions. Select the one that BEST answers the question or completes the statement. *PRINT THE LETTER OF THE CORRECT ANSWER IN THE SPACE AT THE RIGHT.*

1. While delegation of responsibility is undesirable, delegation of authority is wise. The supervisor who is a competent officer should realize that this statement is essentially

    A. *false,* because neither authority nor responsibility should be delegated by a supervisor
    B. *true,* because a supervisor should be responsible for his men but cannot be on hand to make all decisions
    C. *false,* because only the person ultimately responsible for an action should be expected to make decisions
    D. *true,* because the authority of a supervisor is specifically set forth in the Rules and Regulations
    E. *true,* because each supervisor is ultimately responsible for the work of the correction officers he supervises

2. Of the following, the LEAST accurate statement concerning the supervision of correction officers is that

    A. mistakes should generally be corrected as soon as detected
    B. it can be assumed that nearly all correction officers can analyze their own weaknesses
    C. misunderstandings are often due to the failure of superior officers to explain instructions properly
    D. repetition of a wrong procedure serves to fixate the habit
    E. it is good practice not only to call the attention of a correction officer to his mistakes, but to show him how to correct them

3. A correction officer, it is true, must obey orders implicitly, but this fact places a definite responsibility upon the supervisor. Of the following, the MOST accurate statement of the responsibility referred to in the above quotation is that a supervisor should

    A. issue orders in a manner commanding obedience
    B. demonstrate immediately to the correction officers the reasonableness of every command he issues
    C. issue direct commands only as a last resort
    D. be on hand to assist in carrying out every order he issues
    E. issue only orders which can be justified by him

4. Suppose that a correction officer newly assigned under your command appears to lack confidence in the performance of his duties. Of the following, the BEST action for you as a supervisor to take is to

    A. warn him that he is being observed constantly and that the poor quality of his work is being given special consideration
    B. give him an assignment which you believe he will be able to perform well
    C. assign him to exceptionally difficult tasks which you believe will constitute a definite challenge to him

D. have him observe the other correction officers at their work for a few months until his confidence improves
E. assign him to tasks on which he will be required to work alone

5. Of the following, the LEAST effective method that can be employed by a supervisor instructing the correction officers under his command in the proper discharge of their duties is to

    A. observe the mistakes a correction officer makes during his tour of duty and then discuss these mistakes with him individually
    B. discuss with the correction officers hypothetical situations which may occur in their work
    C. question the correction officers frequently on provisions of the Rules and Regulations relating to their work
    D. refer a correction officer to the proper provisions of the Rules and Regulations whenever it appears that the situation requires their application
    E. discuss the mistakes made by a correction officer with the other correction officers under your supervision, emphasizing both the kind of mistakes made and the person making them

6. Assume that you are a supervisor and that a correction officer with a long and excellent record has recently begun to exhibit laziness and lack of interest in his work. Of the following, the BEST course of action for you as his superior officer to follow is to

    A. call the attention of the other men specifically to this case to demonstrate that good work requires constant, diligent application
    B. start disciplinary action immediately against this correction officer as you would against any other
    C. overlook the matter until the correction officer again demonstrates his usual high quality of work
    D. interview the correction officer and attempt to determine the reason for his unusual behavior
    E. point out to the correction officer at the earliest opportunity that his excellent record is no excuse for incompetence and threaten disciplinary action unless he improves

7. The correction supervisor should realize that the best correction officer is not necessarily the one who leaps most quickly to execute an order, nor even the one who executes an order most efficiently. Of the following, the BEST justification for the above statement is that

    A. on many occasions, correction officers must show initiative in working without orders
    B. some correction officers work faster than others
    C. on some occasions, an order is executed rapidly, but inefficiently
    D. the correction officer who is really competent, when given an order, is cautious to think carefully before performing hasty action
    E. the correction officer who acts first may not be the one to finish first or to do the best job

8. A few men may be born leaders, but all of you new correction supervisors will soon find that command is essentially a habit. Of the following, the CHIEF implication of this statement is that

   A. relatively few men have the ability to become outstanding leaders and commanders
   B. the respect and confidence of his men can be developed by conscious effort on the part of a correction supervisor
   C. discipline is so well developed in a prison force that correction officers will obey the command of a supervisor as a matter of habit
   D. the correction officers who have been longer on the job and have more firmly fixed habits will probably make the better supervisors
   E. a new supervisor will probably make a better adjustment if placed with an older group of correction officers whose habits are more firmly fixed

9. Correction officers will rarely bear a grievance about a competent supervisor but something can be learned from every grievance situation that does occur if the supervisor is sufficiently alert and open-minded to accept responsibility for his own mistakes and to see the viewpoint of the men who bring up the grievance. Of the following, the MOST accurate statement on the basis of the above quotation is that

   A. grievances can usually be avoided by open-mindedness concerning the duties of the men
   B. satisfactory handling of grievances is essentially a matter of allocating responsibility between superiors and subordinates
   C. a supervisor should always attempt to understand the reason for every grievance brought to him by his men
   D. grievances can always be settled to the satisfaction of the men if the supervisor merely takes the trouble to see their viewpoint
   E. a supervisor should accept responsibility for his own mistakes but not for the mistakes of his men

10. Of the following, the BEST justification for having the limits of authority and responsibility clearly defined in an organization such as the Department of Correction is that

    A. responsibility is most properly mutual and interrelated
    B. every correction supervisor should probably be given some training in supervisory techniques
    C. some correction supervisors may be more competent than others
    D. every organization will probably benefit by exchange of viewpoints at parallel levels of authority
    E. overlapping authority will probably lead to conflicts

11. It is impossible to draw up a list of qualifications and maintain that the person who has these qualifications will make a successful correction supervisor. Of the following, the CHIEF justification for this statement is that

    A. the qualifications contributing to competence as a correction supervisor are probably independent in nature
    B. success as an officer is a temporary rather than a universal trait
    C. leadership is a habit rather than an acquirable skill

D. the qualities of a competent officer are often intangible and difficult to define
E. the qualifications necessary for competence in a correction supervisor are easily detected but difficult to substantiate

12. It has been suggested that the Rules and Regulations, when describing a recommended procedure, should state the reason for the recommendation. Of the following, the BEST justification for this suggestion is that

    A. correction officers should be sufficiently intelligent to understand the significance of their actions
    B. the Rules and Regulations are most accurately viewed as an official training document
    C. performance on the job is most likely to be efficient if based on understanding
    D. varied associations improve the recall of information
    E. discipline is improved if recommended procedures are specific and definite

13. Suppose that you are a correction supervisor. A newly appointed correction officer reports to you for duty. Of the following, the BEST procedure for you to follow to assure rapid orientation of this correction officer to his work is to

    A. ask him to give a brief survey of his qualifications for the job
    B. observe him carefully as he performs the routine aspects of his duties
    C. make a careful study of his previous work record before coming to the Department
    D. review with him the important elements of the job he will be required to perform
    E. question him at length concerning his knowledge of the inmates under his supervision

14. A newly appointed correction supervisor should be cautioned to avoid close familiarity with one of the correction officers under his command CHIEFLY because

    A. good discipline requires prompt obedience to commands
    B. respect for a superior officer must be implicit
    C. familiarity creates the impression of special favors
    D. the relationship between correction supervisors and correction officers is necessarily a close one
    E. a new correction supervisor can hardly be expected to be fully acquainted with the capabilities of his men

15. Assume that you are a correction supervisor. The CHIEF objection to allowing newly appointed correction officers under your supervision to learn how to perform their duties properly on the basis of their own experience is that a correction officer

    A. is likely to learn best when he is allowed to exercise originality
    B. will rarely forget a lesson learned through hard experience
    C. will learn more quickly when he is guided
    D. will be assigned only relatively routine jobs during his initial training period
    E. is likely to remember best what he learns first

16. The correction supervisor must enforce strict discipline, but he must not be devoid of personal sympathy or understanding. This statement is BEST illustrated by the correction supervisor who

    A. issues commands that are clear and understandable
    B. treats all correction officers equally regardless of personal sympathy
    C. defends impartially the actions of those men who are loyal to him
    D. understands the necessity of being military and commanding in bearing
    E. investigates the reasons for a correction officer's infractions of regulations

17. If the medical examiner's report on an inmate indicates that the inmate has *schizoid* tendencies, the one of the following types of behavior which the supervisor may MOST reasonably expect the inmate to demonstrate 'is

    A. epileptic fits
    B. withdrawal from reality
    C. sleepwalking
    D. incontinence
    E. constant aggressiveness

18. Of the following, the CHIEF distinction between a psycho-neurotic and a psychotic is that a psychoneurotic usually

    A. is suspicious and unfriendly whereas a psychotic is genial and happy
    B. has high intelligence whereas a psychotic has low intelligence
    C. requires the attention of a psychiatrist whereas a psychotic should be treated by a doctor
    D. suffers delusions whereas a psychotic does not suffer delusions
    E. is well-oriented to his surroundings whereas a psychotic lacks orientation

19. Of the following, the MOST accurate statement concerning the riot gun stocked by the city Department of Correction is that it

    A. is about 45" in length
    B. fires a .45 inch calibre cartridge
    C. is single action in type
    D. weighs about 7 1/2 pounds
    E. has an automatic device which ejects the cartridge case after each shot

20. Always use a brass rod when cleaning a revolver. Of the following, the BEST justification for the above statement is that

    A. a brass rod will not wear the bore around the muzzle
    B. brass rods are rigid and inflexible
    C. revolvers are rarely cleaned from the muzzle end
    D. brass can be tooled with great accuracy
    E. brass is a very hard alloy

21. The correction officer should know that the term *double action,* with reference to a revolver, means MOST NEARLY that

    A. the shell of a fired shot is ejected and a fresh cartridge is pushed from the magazine at the same time
    B. pulling the trigger cocks the hammer and presents a fresh cartridge for firing
    C. the revolver has both safety and automatic firing action
    D. the revolver can fire with or without automatic shell ejection
    E. pulling the trigger ejects the empty cartridge

22. A tourniquet is always a dangerous instrument and should be used with caution. Of the following, the CHIEF danger in the use of a tourniquet is

    A. shock
    B. increased venous bleeding
    C. blood clotting
    D. uninterrupted arterial bleeding
    E. gangrene

23. The correction officer must be able to detect the difference between sunstroke and heat exhaustion because different treatment is required. The one of the following symptoms which is MOST usually found in heat exhaustion rather than sunstroke is

    A. red face
    B. hot skin
    C. strong pulse
    D. very high temperature
    E. profuse sweating

24. All court pens in the city are under the jurisdiction of the Department of Correction. The jurisdiction cited in the above quotation is provided by

    A. an ordinance of the city
    B. the Rules and Regulations of the Department of Correction
    C. the charter of the city
    D. the Penal Law of the State
    E. a ruling of the Chief Magistrate of the city

25. The one of the following which is NOT a provision of the Constitution of the State regarding the administration of correctional institutions in the city is that

    A. no person may lose a residence by being held in a correctional institution
    B. a city may maintain a correctional institution
    C. a prisoner may be assigned work while he is in prison
    D. contract labor in prisons is forbidden
    E. wardens of correctional institutions are required to make weekly reports concerning the condition of their prisons

26. The one of the following which provides SPECIFICALLY for a Commissioner of Correction in the city and assigns duties to that office is the

    A. State Penal Law
    B. Criminal Procedure Law
    C. Constitution of the State
    D. Charter of the city
    E. Administrative Code of the city

27. The Criminal Procedure Law should be of interest to correction supervisors CHIEFLY because it

    A. describes unlawful procedures frequently employed by criminals
    B. establishes parole and probation procedures
    C. indicates whether imprisonment should be in a state or local prison
    D. fixes the legal definition of each crime and the appropriate penalty
    E. describes the conditions under which bail may be accepted and the procedures to be followed

28. The one of the following which is considered a court of general jurisdiction rather than a criminal or civil court is the

   A. Appellate Division
   B. Civil Court
   C. Criminal Court
   D. Family Court
   E. Surrogate's Court

29. The one of the following which is a Federal Court is the

   A. Appellate Division
   B. Court of General Sessions
   C. Circuit Court of Appeals
   D. Supreme Court (Criminal Term)
   E. Family Court

30. An order issued by the Supreme Court or Appellate Division to compel a person or body to do or refrain from doing something. This definition applies MOST accurately and completely to

   A. warrant
   B. mandamus
   C. certiorari
   D. writ of habeas corpus
   E. subpoena duces tecum

31. A child less than 16 years of age cannot be convicted of a crime UNLESS

   A. the offense committed is punishable by death or life imprisonment
   B. the offense committed is a felony
   C. negligence was a factor in the crime
   D. violation of a Federal law is involved
   E. it can be demonstrated that the crime was committed with motive and intent

32. A list, prepared by the clerk of the court, of all defendants then at the city prisons whose cases will be heard the following day is called a

   A. court calendar
   B. writ
   C. court probate
   D. daily roster
   E. court recall

33. There is a limitation of time within which prosecution of certain crimes must be commenced. Of the following, the MOST accurate statement is that prosecution for a _____ must be commenced within _____ years.

   A. murder; 5
   B. felony; 5
   C. misdemeanor; 7
   D. felony; 2
   E. murder; 2

34. In order to be adjudged a youthful offender, a defendant MUST be _____ years of age.

   A. under 16
   B. over 16 but under 21
   C. over 16 but under 18
   D. over 15 but under 19
   E. over 18 but under 21

35. The one of the following organizations which publishes the UNIFORM CRIME REPORTS is the   35._____

    A. American Prison Association
    B. New York City Police Department
    C. American Institute of Criminology and Penology
    D. Federal Bureau of Investigation
    E. National Crime Prevention Institute

Questions 36-40.

DIRECTIONS: Column I below lists five books in the field of penology and criminology. In the space at the right, alongside the number of each of the books in Column I, write the letter preceding the author as listed in Column II.

COLUMN I

36. Education of Adult Prisoners
37. Prisons and Beyond
38. 500 Criminal Careers
39. Criminal Behavior
40. Within Prison Walls

COLUMN II

A. Sanford Bates   36._____
B. Sheldon & Eleanor Glueck 37._____
C. Lewis E. Lawes   38._____
D. Austin H. MacCormick   39._____
E. Thomas M. Osborne   40._____
F. Leo Palmer
G. Walter C. Reckless

KEY (CORRECT ANSWERS)

1.	B	11.	D	21.	B	31.	A
2.	B	12.	C	22.	E	32.	E
3.	E	13.	D	23.	E	33.	B
4.	B	14.	C	24.	C	34.	D
5.	E	15.	C	25.	E	35.	D
6.	D	16.	E	26.	D	36.	D
7.	A	17.	B	27.	E	37.	A
8.	B	18.	E	28.	A	38.	B
9.	C	19.	D	29.	C	39.	G
10.	E	20.	E	30.	B	40.	E

EXAMINATION SECTION
TEST 1

DIRECTIONS: Each question or incomplete statement is followed by several suggested answers or completions. Select the one that BEST answers the question or completes the statement. *PRINT THE LETTER OF THE CORRECT ANSWER IN THE SPACE AT THE RIGHT.*

1. Of the following, the MOST serious problem to be faced in the proper supervision of new correction officers is that, for the most part, these officers 1.____

    A. are afraid to face up to the responsibilities of their position
    B. are over-confident and have a *know-it-all* attitude
    C. have accepted this employment only as a stopgap until they find other work
    D. have had no extensive formal training in this field of work

2. An employee's performance should be evaluated quarterly during the probationary period, and at least once a year after the probationary period. Of the following, the CHIEF justification for the less frequent formal evaluation of employee performance after the probationary period is that 2.____

    A. over-supervision of experienced employees is unnecessary and undesirable and may create resentment on the part of the employee
    B. the employee has already proven himself satisfactory by passing his probationary period
    C. the older employee reacts more quickly and responsively to supervision
    D. the supervisor has already achieved a considerable degree of familiarity with the employee's capabilities, performance and need for further training

3. It has been suggested that the in-service training of employees in the correctional field be continued from the time of their employment until the time of their leaving the department. Of the following, the CHIEF justification for such a continuous program of in-service training is that 3.____

    A. a person's capacity for learning increases with age
    B. because of a natural tendency to forget what one has learned and not put into practice, training must be repeated at regular intervals
    C. employees usually are capable of further development on the job during the entire period of their employment
    D. for learning to be effective, successive stages in the learning process must be correlated and coordinated

4. Of the following, the CHIEF advantage of rotating the qualified staff of a correctional institution among the various job assignments is the 4.____

    A. development of versatility in staff members
    B. elimination of jealousy among employees
    C. establishment of bases upon which to formulate work norms
    D. lessening of the undesirable trend toward increasing specialization

5. It has been stated that the key to successful application of the majority of standards that have been set for an adult correctional institution is the proper organization, selection, training, and assignment of the staff. Of the following, the CHIEF justification for this statement is that

    A. proper selection, training, organization, and assignment of staff are often a neglected phase of institutional management
    B. proper staffing is the most complex aspect of correctional institution management
    C. staff selection, training, organization, and assignment is a continuous process
    D. the staff is the medium through which these standards must be implemented

6. Of the following, the MOST important reason why supervisors should give careful consideration to the techniques they utilize for assignment of employees to specific jobs is that

    A. an opportunity is thus offered the supervisor for periodic evaluation of the qualifications and work performance of all employees
    B. efficiency of employees is dependent in part on the techniques used by supervisory officers for selection of employees for assignments
    C. requests of employees for change in work assignments may indicate dissatisfaction with present conditions
    D. standardized techniques for the selection of employees for specific job assignments have not yet been developed

7. In the selection and appointment process for correction officers, particular care is taken to screen out the neurotic and unstable. Suppose, however, that in spite of this, as a result of your observations during the probationary period you are convinced that a new officer appointed to your command has a neurotic and unstable personality. Of the following, the BEST action for you to take as supervisor is to

    A. give restricted assignment and close supervision to this officer unless the need for more drastic action is indicated at a later date
    B. help the employee to correct this undesirable trait by giving proper and continuous training
    C. recommend that the employee be dropped at the end of the probationary period
    D. refer the employee for appropriate medical care

8. Attempts to apply police training to prison personnel will have unsatisfactory results. Of the following, the MOST probable cause of these poor results would be the

    A. difference in emphasis of the two fields of work
    B. failure to properly integrate classroom teaching with practical work
    C. poor quality of the instruction
    D. shortness of the training period generally used

9. Of the following, the LEAST desirable use of a new officer's probationary period by the supervisor is to

    A. carefully check and evaluate performance of work assigned
    B. instruct the officer in the proper performance of assigned duties
    C. observe whether the officer is capable of performing the duties of the job efficiently
    D. train the officer for promotion to the next higher rank

10. The statement has been made that correction officers have a tendency to get into a rut. If this statement is valid, the one of the following actions by an officer which BEST illustrates this tendency is

    A. continuing in the same assignment for several years without being motivated to ask for a change in assignment
    B. performing an act of alertness or heroism after the incident which might have been prevented by such act has already been precipitated
    C. releasing an inmate after partial identification, taking for granted that it must be the correct inmate
    D. using the standard, approved methods of conducting their searches for contraband instead of trying to devise more ingenious and novel methods

11. A superior, investigating why an order had not been carried out, was told by the officers concerned that they had not realized that what the superior had told them was intended as an order. This incident illustrates MOST directly an order that was not

    A. concise
    B. possible of performance
    C. recognizable as an order
    D. reviewed after issuance of the order

12. In explaining to a subordinate the importance of the tier officer's initial contact with a new admission, the superior should stress MOST the

    A. constructive influence this initial contact can have on the inmate's future adjustment to confinement
    B. desirability of getting the inmate to talk freely and without interruption
    C. harmful effect on the inmate's morale of a businesslike approach in the conduct of this initial interview
    D. value of this initial interview in impressing the inmate with the fact that violations of the rules will not be tolerated

13. In explaining to a group of new officers the reasons why their position is so important in the operations of the Department, the supervisor should emphasize MOST the fact that

    A. the inmate's attitude to the officer is basically a hostile one
    B. the largest number of uniformed personnel is in the rank of correction officer
    C. the officer represents the most frequent, direct contact of the Department with the inmate
    D. this is the rank from which the administrative positions in the Department will be filled

14. Each job assignment of personnel in the institution should be carefully described in writing, setting forth the duties, responsibilities, and special requirements of the particular job assignment. Of the following, the CHIEF advantage of this procedure is that

    A. a change in administration or supervision will not interfere with the orderly running of the institution
    B. defects in administrative organization will become apparent

C. employees will have a ready means of knowing what is expected of them in their particular assignments
D. it will be possible to transfer employees more freely from one job assignment to another

15. If, as supervisor, you find that there occur a considerable number of minor, apparently unintentional infractions of rules by inmates on one officer's post, the BEST action of the following for you to take FIRST would be to

   A. determine if the inmates on this post have a clear understanding of the rules and what constitutes violation of the rules
   B. find out the basic causes of inmate dissatisfaction on this post and correct them
   C. give this officer additional training in proper techniques for maintaining stricter discipline on the post
   D. investigate whether it would be advisable to assign a more competent officer to this post

16. Suppose you learn that an officer under your command intends to file an official complaint against an inmate for committing an infraction of the institution's rules.
Of the following, the BEST action for you to take as captain is to

   A. advise the officer that the filing of official complaints should be reserved for the most serious infractions only
   B. determine if the infraction is serious enough to warrant an official complaint
   C. make an inspection to determine whether discipline on the post is otherwise satisfactory
   D. support the officer in the interest of maintaining institution discipline and morale

17. Suppose it comes to your attention that an officer under your supervision does not give prompt consideration to all complaints and requests of inmates. Of the following, the BEST action for you to take is to

   A. discuss with the officer the harmful effect such action can have on inmate morale
   B. explain to the officer that action on complaints must be differentiated from action on requests
   C. order the officer to comply with all inmate complaints and requests promptly
   D. warn the officer and give closer supervision as something serious might result from this method of work

18. In explaining to a correction officer why an unvaried routine in the conduct of tier post inspections is not desirable, a supervisor should stress MOST the fact that

   A. a method of work that may be entirely acceptable in one situation generally proves to be unacceptable when transferred without modification to a different work situation
   B. inmates seeking to violate the institution's rules make a study of the officer's habits so that they can time their activities to forestall detection
   C. it is important to have a clear understanding of the purposes of the tier post inspection in order to be able to carry it out efficiently and intelligently
   D. the discovery of contraband is not the sole purpose of a tier post inspection

19. A superior instructed subordinates in the meaning of parole, the conditions under which it is granted, and in the rules and practices of parole supervision. The superior's action was

    A. *necessary and desirable;* the entire prison staff should have an understanding of parole if the indoctrination and orientation of the inmates with respect to parole is to be well done
    B. *unnecessary and undesirable;* only occasionally does a member of the superior's staff have any responsibilities directly connected with the parole function
    C. *necessary and desirable; while* the staff generally has no concern with parole matters and problems, they should have a well-rounded background which includes a knowledge of related agencies
    D. *unnecessary and undesirable;* the parole function is the responsibility of another agency

20. Of the following, the LEAST important rule for a supervisor to stress when instructing an officer in the fundamentals of making a count of prisoners is:

    A. Count each tier of a cell block separately and make a temporary note of the count for each tier
    B. Do not speak to prisoners or to other personnel when making a count
    C. See flesh or movement or hear prisoners speak before recording them as counted
    D. Speak the number out loud as you count each inmate so that you can actually be heard making the count

21. A supervisor instructed a group of new officers that before beginning their tier count when coming on duty, they should get the off-going officer's last count and use this as a check when making their count. The supervisor's instructions were

    A. *good,* because a new officer should receive assistance from an experienced officer
    B. *poor,* because errors in the previous count may be unconsciously duplicated
    C. *good,* because both counts must agree
    D. *poor,* because the oncoming officer is not in any way responsible for the off-going officer's count

22. A superior instructed subordinates that, at all times, the tier officer going off duty was to notify the oncoming officer of any inmate who should be particularly watched. The superior's instructions were

    A. *good,* because the on-coming officer will not be surprised if any inmate behaves strangely
    B. *poor,* because alertness and initiative on the part of the on-coming officer may be reduced
    C. *good,* because the on-coming officer will benefit from the experiences and observation of the off-going officer
    D. *poor,* because all inmates should be given careful and close custody and supervision

23. Of the following, the technique that is likely to contribute MOST to the successful control of suicides in a correction command is for the supervisor to

   A. explain to subordinates some of the most common methods by which inmates commit suicide
   B. keep subordinates informed of the latest statistics on suicides in the Department's institutions as a sobering reminder that constant attention to duty is required
   C. stress to subordinates repeatedly the serious effect on the institution of a successful suicide
   D. train subordinates in spotting the inmates who may be potential suicides

24. A supervisor stated to a group of newly appointed correction officers: *I cannot emphasize to you too much the importance of frequent patrol of your post.* The supervisor MOST probably placed such great emphasis on the importance of frequent patrol because

   A. many captains neglect to develop in their subordinates a proper understanding of and technique for the post patrol
   B. most officers do not patrol often enough
   C. patrol is the best way for an officer to keep in touch with what is happening on his post
   D. patrol is the best way of developing regular habits of work in a correction officer

25. Suppose that two experienced officers assigned to a tier post report to you that they suspect there is contraband hidden on the post but that they have been unable to locate it in spite of several searches. As supervisor, the BEST thing for you to do at this time is to

   A. advise the officers to continue to be on the alert and to make several more searches at unexpected times
   B. explain to the officers that it is pointless to persist in these suspicions when they have not been substantiated by the facts
   C. organize and supervise a special search of the tier with a selected group of officers
   D. review the techniques employed by the officers in conducting these searches and point out why they are faulty

26. A cautious and observant officer seldom becomes involved in litigation initiated by an inmate who is injured during confinement on a tier. This statement is MOST probably based on the principle that such an officer will

   A. avoid and prevent situations which might cause injury to an inmate
   B. avoid any and all disputes with inmates
   C. be able to persuade the inmate that litigation is not justified
   D. make sure that any injury to an inmate is the result of the inmate's own negligence

27. Of the following, the factor that contributes MOST to making the problem of custodial supervision in a prison so difficult is the

   A. few troublesome inmates who do not adjust
   B. lack of adequate space and facilities
   C. shortage of staff
   D. unnatural environment of a prison

28. A supervisor is summoned by a correction officer to the cell of a newly committed inmate who has been taken suddenly ill. After observing the inmate, the supervisor thinks that the inmate's condition is due to nervous excitement resulting from commitment to the institution. The supervisor should

    A. speak quietly to the inmate until a normal condition is restored
    B. give the inmate a mild sedative
    C. make the inmate comfortable and instruct the officer to keep a close watch
    D. secure medical assistance for the inmate

29. Of the following, the type of inmate in whom arrest and confinement are likely to cause the GREATEST emotional shock is the

    A. adolescent offender
    B. adult of established family in the community
    C. mental defective
    D. recidivist who was confident of not getting caught

30. The maintenance of the personal cleanliness of inmates through the medium of regular bathing assumes added importance in a prison MAINLY because

    A. it is another procedure by which the possession of contraband by inmates can often be discovered
    B. most inmates have not developed proper habits of cleanliness
    C. personal body cleanliness is important in all individuals, including prison inmates
    D. the confining nature of institutional life necessarily brings inmates into close daily contact with each other

31. From the standpoint of custody, the first concern of the correction officer in the court pen should be to lock the inmate in the pen as soon as possible. Of the following, the CHIEF justification for this statement is the fact that the officer

    A. can more easily take an accurate count of inmates confined in the pen
    B. can then give undivided attention to other important duties
    C. does not know how soon the inmate will have to be produced in court again
    D. may be the only obstacle between the inmate and escape

32. In the event that an officer discovers an attempted suicide by an inmate, the FIRST thing the officer should do is

    A. administer first aid
    B. gather all the evidence
    C. go to summon the institution physician
    D. notify the head of the institution

33. When an inmate commits a serious infraction of discipline, the supervisor is required to investigate the incident as soon as practicable, but not later than the same day. Of the following, the CHIEF justification for such prompt investigation is that

    A. an investigation delayed is usually forgotten
    B. memory of the incident will be more accurate in the minds of participants and witnesses

C. the inmate will be impressed with the seriousness of the offense
D. the various participants and witnesses concerned in the incident will have less opportunity to prepare false versions of what actually happened

34. An officer should NOT use force toward an inmate for the purpose of

    A. compelling obedience to an order
    B. curbing a riot
    C. protecting the inmate's life
    D. self-defense

35. Cell location is an important factor in the custody and security of inmates who may be potential suicides PRIMARILY because

    A. cell location has an important effect on the morale of inmates
    B. in some cells it is easier to conceal contraband
    C. the ease of committing suicide varies from cell to cell
    D. the officer can keep certain cells under close observation more easily

36. Familiarity with the statistical information about suicides and attempted suicides in the institutions of the Department is of value to supervisors MAINLY because such information

    A. can assist the supervisor in personally detecting and preventing a greater number of suicides
    B. can be used as a basis of comparison with what is happening on the correction command
    C. can be used as an aid in training subordinates in the detection and prevention of suicides
    D. gives the supervisor a broader understanding of the success of the Department in carrying out its objectives

37. In the institutions of the Department, special security procedures are observed with an inmate sentenced to death or to a long term in a state prison. Such special procedures are advisable MAINLY because the

    A. Department is only temporarily responsible for someone who is actually a prisoner of the State
    B. inmate's friends and accomplices on the outside may attempt to free the inmate by force
    C. isolation of such inmate from the rest of the prison population is not practicable
    D. severity of the sentence may impel such inmate to commit some desperate act

38. An advantage of frequent special tier searches for contraband, although often no contraband may be discovered in such searches, is that

    A. inmates are placed on notice that contraband will not be tolerated in the institution
    B. negligence on the part of the tier officer with respect to contraband control does not have serious results
    C. officers are given training in military discipline
    D. responsibility for contraband control on the post is shared equally by superior and subordinate

39. When assigned to duty in a large mess hall during inmate mess, it is important for officers to station themselves in such a way that they can see and be seen by their superior at all times. This statement is justified MAINLY because the

    A. inmates will not attempt to create any disturbance when they see that the officers and their superior are in ready communication with each other
    B. officers will be able to show their superior that they are performing their jobs properly
    C. officers will be able to tell if the superior has left the mess hall
    D. superior, who may be far away from the officers, might suddenly find it necessary to transmit an order to them quickly by means of a signal

40. The sole value of the maintenance of proper sanitation procedures on a tier post is the protection of the health of the inmates and of the prison personnel. This statement is

    A. *correct,* because the health of inmates and personnel must be protected at all times, in the interest of proper institutional administration
    B. *incorrect,* because proper post sanitation also has other values, such as morale building
    C. *correct,* because the poor physical and moral condition of many inmates creates an undue amount of sanitation problems
    D. *incorrect,* because there has been no positive evidence that cleanliness on a tier post actually affects health

41. The primary function of the prison is the safekeeping of the prisoners committed to the prison. This statement is

    A. *invalid,* because it ignores the latest concepts in correctional work, which emphasize the rehabilitative potentialities of imprisonment
    B. *valid,* because statistics on recidivism show that it is the only function capable of realization
    C. *invalid,* because the prison has several functions, each of which is greatly important
    D. *valid,* because the prison is legally responsible for the safe custody of the prisoners committed by the courts until the expiration of their sentences

42. In its inmate treatment program, a correctional institution should operate on the philosophy that well-adjusted people do more than merely sleep, eat, and work. Of the following, the MOST valid inference based on this statement is that an additional important function of the correctional institution is to

    A. give inmates an insight into the problems and conflicts of well-adjusted people
    B. prepare inmates for employment in useful work
    C. train inmates in proper use of leisure time
    D. train inmates to strike a proper balance between work and rest

43. All the processes in a correctional institution should be directed toward educating the individual for successful community living. Of the following, the factor that contributes MOST to making this task a difficult one is the

    A. absence of a clear definition as to what constitutes successful community living
    B. conflict of interest between community and institution

C. competitive nature of modern day community life
D. need to change unacceptable behavior patterns into patterns acceptable to the community

44. It has been recommended that the work week of inmates employed in a program of prison industries be the same as the work week for similar employment in private industry. From the standpoint of the major objectives of a prison industries program, the adoption of this recommendation is desirable MAINLY because

   A. it will make possible the inclusion of a wider variety of employments in the prison industries program
   B. it will tend to make the deterrent objective of imprisonment more effective
   C. the prison industries will then be more profitable to operate since production will be greater
   D. the rehabilitative process will be aided if conditions of work approach those in real life

45. The work assignment of inmates should be based on other factors in addition to their request for particular assignments. Of the following, the LEAST important reason for this is that the inmates

   A. may have questionable motives for requesting particular assignments
   B. may make a better adjustment to their assignments if they are in accord with their wishes
   C. may request assignments for which no additional institutional help is required
   D. may not be fitted for the work requested

46. Classification is a dynamic process. According to this statement, it would be MOST reasonable to assume that in the classification process

   A. an inmate's treatment program should be modified in accordance with the changing needs of the inmate
   B. an inmate's treatment program should be carefully planned to avoid the need for changes, or the inmate's cooperation will be lost
   C. interference with, or interruption of, an inmate's treatment program will have serious results
   D. there are very many contributing elements, all equally important, and all of which must operate at maximum efficiency

47. The present trend in penology is to liberalize visiting privileges for inmates as much as possible. However, the MOST important factor that keeps many prison officials from going along with this trend is the fear that liberal prison visiting will

   A. increase the danger of the introduction of contraband into the prison
   B. interfere with the operation of normal prison routines
   C. lead to a breakdown of prison discipline
   D. require major alteration in existing prison facilities for visiting

48. An important rule to be observed in the carrying out of an institutional program of inmate activities and privileges is:
Do not

   A. curtail or revoke any inmate activity or privilege after it has been instituted
   B. give privileges to one inmate which cannot be earned in the proper way by any other inmate
   C. make any activity or privilege too pleasurable for the inmate
   D. use the program as an aid to the maintenance of discipline

49. Of the following, the MOST important reason for issuing standard prison clothing to all inmates of a sentence institution, rather than permitting them to wear their own civilian clothing, is that it

   A. contributes to the maintenance of better discipline among inmates
   B. eliminates overt, visible differences among inmates which might otherwise lead to friction
   C. is virtually impossible to properly search and sterilize all civilian clothing of all inmates
   D. makes it easier for the public to recognize an escaped inmate

50. With respect to the operation of a parole system, correctional authorities GENERALLY oppose the

   A. application of strict rules forbidding the parole of persons convicted of certain serious offenses, such as first degree murder and kidnapping
   B. principle that prisoners released from long-term institutions after earning sufficient good time should be released on parole
   C. release of short-term prisoners on parole
   D. requirement of service of a minimum period of imprisonment of reasonable proportions before an inmate becomes eligible for parole

KEY (CORRECT ANSWERS)

1. D	11. C	21. B	31. D	41. D
2. D	12. A	22. C	32. A	42. C
3. C	13. C	23. D	33. B	43. D
4. A	14. C	24. C	34. A	44. D
5. D	15. A	25. C	35. D	45. B
6. B	16. B	26. A	36. C	46. A
7. C	17. A	27. D	37. D	47. A
8. A	18. B	28. D	38. A	48. B
9. D	19. A	29. B	39. D	49. B
10. C	20. D	30. D	40. B	50. A

TEST 2

DIRECTIONS: Each question or incomplete statement is followed by several suggested answers or completions. Select the one that BEST answers the question or completes the statement. *PRINT THE LETTER OF THE CORRECT ANSWER IN THE SPACE AT THE RIGHT.*

1. It is generally agreed among penologists that the system of communication in an institution should make it possible for any inmate to bring what seems to him an important problem to the attention of an appropriate staff member with the least possible delay. However, a danger to be guarded against in this connection is

    A. artificial separation of lines of authority
    B. a sudden breakdown of administrative control
    C. lack of coordination between professional and custodial staff
    D. misuse of the privilege by unstable inmate personalities

2. The one of the following which is NOT an advantage of removing certain classes of inmates from the regular type of prison to outside work on camps and farm colonies is the

    A. ending of direct contact between these inmates and the more undesirable elements in a prison
    B. gradual easing of some of the tensions of prison life for these inmates
    C. removal of the stigma of a prison sentence from these inmates
    D. reduction of inmate idleness in the regular prison

3. The suggestion has been advanced that, in correctional systems, the parole board be made a part of the Department of Correction. Of the following, the CHIEF argument in support of this suggestion is that

    A. fullest independence of the parole function and freedom of interference or influence from any source is desirable
    B. lay persons are not sufficiently familiar with correctional problems and procedures to be able to perform this function effectively
    C. since parole is really an extension of the sentence begun in the correctional institution, close integration of the two services is logically desirable
    D. the number of persons placed on parole is not sufficiently large to make administratively feasible the existence of an independent agency

4. It has been stated that the quality of the staff in a correctional institution is more important than the physical facilities of the institution. This statement is MOST probably based on the belief that

    A. a basic change in the character of the inmate can be brought about only as a result of the influence and guidance of the staff
    B. a competent staff can achieve excellent results without regard to the physical facilities available
    C. no institution can be run without a staff
    D. the physical facilities of an institution are not important when the staff is highly competent

5. In the *cottage* type of correctional institution for women, it is usually considered unnecessary and inappropriate to have disciplinary and custodial controls of the kind customarily found in an institution for men. Of the following, the factor that is LEAST significant in contributing to this difference in this type of women's institution is the

   A. comparative openness of the cottage type institution
   B. difference in preparation and training of the staff
   C. more personal and closer relationship between inmates and staff
   D. small inmate population

6. A feature that makes the *cottage* type institution particularly suitable for female offenders is the

   A. extensive facilities it has for outdoor recreation
   B. opportunities it affords for homemaking activities
   C. practicability of locating near urban centers
   D. privacy offered each individual inmate

7. All correctional institutions for women must accept offenders ranging in age from girls to senile women, and presenting a wide range of sentences and offenses, backgrounds, and training and treatment needs. This is so MAINLY because

   A. female offenders, no less than male offenders, are necessarily different in their characteristics and backgrounds
   B. of the absence and lack of understanding of modern classification procedures
   C. sentencing is a function of the courts, which are neither greatly concerned with nor very much aware of the problems of the correctional administrator
   D. the comparatively small number of women prisoners does not make economically feasible the establishment of diversified institutions for women

8. In the carrying forward of a vocational training program in a women's correctional institution, it will MOST likely be found that those women who have never engaged in systematic training of any kind will

   A. be least eager to participate
   B. be the best learners
   C. have a short interest and concentration span
   D. not make suitable material for such a program

9. Of the following, it is MOST important that the outdoor recreation provided in a correctional institution for women be, as far as possible,

   A. of a competitive, group nature
   B. of the same basic kind and variety as the outdoor recreational activities in an institution for men
   C. of the type that the women can engage in after leaving the institution
   D. limited to non-strenuous activities

10. Of the following, a course that it is particularly important to include in the education program of a correctional institution for women, more so than in a similar program of a correctional institution for men, is a course in

    A. bookkeeping   B. child guidance
    C. office practice   D. 3 R's

11. In a correctional institution, inmate discipline is directly associated with morale. Of the following, the CHIEF implication of this statement for the supervisor is that

    A. disciplinary problems are best solved by increasing the inmate's morale
    B. where morale is high, discipline will be maintained more easily
    C. where morale is low, discipline will be found to be lax
    D. where strict disciplinary measures are enforced, morale will be high

12. So small a percentage of all offenders are caught and convicted that what happens to them can have little effect on the great body of potential and actual violators of the law. This statement places GREATEST doubt on the value of _____ as an objective of imprisonment.

    A. deterrence   B. punishment
    C. reformation   D. rehabilitation

13. Suppose that case studies show that rejection by members of an inmate's family has a depressing effect on the inmate's morale. This fact can be used MOST constructively in correctional work to

    A. allow additional privileges to inmates with close family ties
    B. bring family influences to bear in assisting in the inmate's rehabilitation
    C. deny mail and visiting privileges for disciplinary reasons only as a last resort
    D. reveal other media that can be employed to boost the morale of an inmate with no family ties

14. It has been stated that, in the final analysis, the soundest security measure of all is the existence of a positive program of inmate activities. Of the following, the CHIEF justification for this statement is the fact that

    A. a good program of inmate activities will point up the need for correction of certain security weaknesses which might not otherwise be apparent
    B. inmates engaged in such a program of activities seldom resort to disturbances or escape attempts
    C. security without rehabilitation through an inmate program is not a lasting solution to the crime problem
    D. since security is the primary responsibility of the institution, it must be guaranteed by all institutional programs

15. To say that an inmate is psychotic implies MOST directly that the inmate

    A. has a split personality   B. has suicidal tendencies
    C. is mentally deranged   D. is of low mentality

16. A review in the American Journal of Correction of a book about a warden recommended that the book be on the reading list of all students of criminology and penology. The warden about whom this book was written was

    A. Bannan of State Prison of Southern Michigan, Jackson
    B. Ragen of Illinois State Penitentiary, Joliet
    C. Wallack of Wallkill Prison, Wallkill
    D. Wilkinson of U.S. Penitentiary, Atlanta

Questions 17-22.

DIRECTIONS: For each book title in Column I, select the author of the book from Column II; then write the capital letter preceding the author's name in the appropriate space at the right.

COLUMN I

17. Contemporary Correction
18. Criminology, A Cultural Interpretation
19. Five Hundred Delinquent Women
20. Jail Administration
21. Principles and Methods in Dealing with Offenders
22. Prisoners are People

COLUMN II

A. Alexander, Myrl E.
B. Barnes, Harry E.
C. Fenton, Norman
D. Glueck, Sheldon and Eleanor
E. Lindner, Robert M. and Seliger, Robert V.
F. MacCormick, Austin H.
G. Pigeon, Helen D.
H. Scudder, Kenyon J.
J. Taft, Donald R
K. Tappan, Paul W.

23. The book WHAT WILL BE YOUR LIFE? is
    A. a semi-autobiographical sketch written by a former prison inmate
    B. a textbook for prison inmates developed for use in a program of group counseling
    C. directed at potential juvenile delinquents
    D. in use in a pilot program with first offenders on probation

24. A feature of Ident-A-Band, a device for inmate identification, is that it
    A. cannot be put back if removed
    B. cannot be removed
    C. includes both the fingerprints and photo of the inmate
    D. is worn on the ankle

25. The Congress of Correction is held
    A. every six months
    B. annually
    C. biennially
    D. every four years

26. While the court is recessed for lunch, an attorney appears at a Criminal Court detention pen and wishes to pay a fine to secure the release of a defendant. The correction officer at the pen should

A. accept the fine only if the attorney presents a *Discharge on Payment of Fine* signed by the court clerk and bearing the court seal
B. check the commitment to see that the sentence includes an alternative fine before accepting it
C. refer the attorney to the court clerk
D. send the attorney to the detention prison to which the inmate would be transferred

27. It is a function of the Grand Jury to

    A. determine if a crime has been committed
    B. determine if a defendant is guilty of a crime
    C. secure the evidence necessary to bring an accused to trial
    D. take testimony from the District Attorney and his witnesses as well as from the defendant and his witnesses

28. The MOST accurate of the following statements about the use, form or content of commitments received by the Department of Correction from the Criminal Court is that the

    A. commitment on which a defendant was held for examination will be set aside by another commitment when the defendant is sentenced
    B. form of all commitments is the same
    C. phrase *sentenced that he stand committed to the City Prison, thereafter to be transferred to the workhouse for a period of* appears on a short commitment
    D. phrase *is committed to your custody pending examination or trial on* appears on a full commitment

29. The purpose of the *court recall sheet* is to

    A. list the inmates against whom there are other holds upon expiration of their present sentences
    B. list the inmates to be transferred from the court pen to the detention prison
    C. notify the court clerk of inmates who must be returned to prison even if released by the court on charge being heard
    D. notify the warden that he must produce certain named inmates in court or before the Grand Jury on a given date

30. When a judge exercises summary jurisdiction in a police case, he may

    A. commit the defendant to the Department of Correction pending further examination
    B. find the defendant guilty and impose sentence
    C. hold the defendant for a higher court
    D. hold the defendant for the Grand Jury

31. The MOST accurate of the following statements about the jurisdiction or functioning of the Criminal Court is that they

    A. cannot convict and sentence defendants arraigned but can merely hold them for other courts
    B. cannot sit as Courts of Special Sessions
    C. conduct preliminary examinations to determine whether defendants should be held for the Grand Jury or the Supreme Court
    D. rank second of the lower courts in volume of cases handled

32. The form which serves as the alphabetical register of all inmates in a Department institution is the _____ Card.

    A. Accompanying
    B. Inmate's Record
    C. Institution Locator
    D. Prisoner's Registration

33. A correction officer in a Criminal Court detention pen may permit an attorney to visit a defendant who is his client if the

    A. attorney presents a *Notice of Appearance* signed by the court clerk
    B. attorney presents a *Notice to the Warden* from the committing court
    C. defendant gives written consent
    D. visit has been cleared with and authorized by the warden of the appropriate detention prison

34. When an inmate is committed to the Department by the court on two charges, it is important that the notation *two cases* be written on records relating to the inmate MAINLY to

    A. avoid errors in daily census
    B. insure that the inmate is counted as one admission in the compilation of Department statistics
    C. insure that two commitments have been issued
    D. prevent release of the inmate before both charges have been disposed of

35. Of the following, the CHIEF reason for encouraging inmates to read, study, engage in some worthwhile hobby, or learn a trade while in prison is to help

    A. prevent major disturbances among inmates
    B. inmates forget about their punishment
    C. inmates adjust to normal life when released
    D. increase inmates' interests
    E. pass away the long hours of confinement

36. Of the following, the MOST accurate statement concerning short-term sentences is that they

    A. usually provide an opportunity to rehabilitate the minor criminal
    B. are relatively ineffective in giving the prisoner a new outlook on life
    C. are the answer to many baffling problems presented to a penal institution
    D. have been on the decrease in the United States since 1900
    E. offer adequate opportunity for moral, but not vocational, rehabilitation

37. If inmates are transferred from one institution of the Department to another, the receiving institution can quickly know the court history of these inmates during the time of their custody at any institution of the Department from their

    A. accompanying cards
    B. commitments
    C. locator cards
    D. registration cards

38. Of the following, the factor that is LEAST significant in making the problem of custody and control in a trial prison more difficult than in a sentence prison is the

    A. comparative absence of program for inmates in a trial prison
    B. different educational and social background of inmates in a trial prison

C. different legal status of trial inmates
D. heterogeneity of inmates in a trial prison

39. Of the trial inmates confined in the detention prisons, a comparison of inmates charged with misdemeanors with inmates charged with felonies shows that GENERALLY those charged with

   A. felonies are confined for shorter periods of time while awaiting trial
   B. misdemeanors are easier to control as a group
   C. felonies are in poorer physical condition
   D. misdemeanors have a lower rate of recidivism

40. With respect to communication between trial inmates and their relatives or friends on the outside, the supervisor should advise correction officers that

   A. they must closely supervise all telephone calls made by trial inmates
   B. they must make all the entries on the telephone message form carefully as it is a permanent record
   C. inmates who do not have the money to pay for a call must be given stationery to communicate by mail
   D. the right of such communication is guaranteed to trial inmates by law

41. According to the provisions of the Criminal Courts Act, persons committed to the reformatory

   A. are released at the discretion of the Parole Commission
   B. are sentenced for terms of 1 to 3 years
   C. may be felons or misdemeanants
   D. must be between the ages of 16 and 25

42. According to an analysis of attempted suicides in the institutions of the Department,

   A. most attempted suicides occur on the midnight to 8 A.M. tour of duty
   B. most attempted suicides occur on the 8 A.M. to 4 P.M. tour of duty
   C. most attempted suicides occur on the 4 P.M. to midnight tour of duty
   D. there are approximately the same number of attempted suicides on each of the three tours of duty

43. According to Department statistics, the greatest number of escapes and attempted escapes occurs on the 8 A.M. to 4 P.M. tour. This is MOST probably due to the fact that

   A. conditions are most conducive to escape when there is the greatest amount of institutional activity
   B. often escapes actually committed at night are not discovered until the next day, resulting in inaccurate statistics
   C. on a comparative basis, more personnel should be assigned to the day tour to enforce adequate security
   D. there is a relaxation of custodial supervision on the day tour, resulting in lowered security

44. Of the following, the CHIEF reason why the Department of Correction no longer considered a certain reformatory suitable for its purposes was probably that

    A. its physical plant was too big for the relatively small and select inmate population
    B. its physical plant was too old, dating back to the previous century
    C. it was proving insufficiently secure for the changing type of adolescent inmate the Department was getting
    D. it had no facilities for a satisfactory vocational program in urban occupations

45. The Department's adolescent program for youths in detention is concentrated on the age group

    A. 18 to 30   B. 16 to 30   C. 16 to 25   D. 16 to 20

46. The CHIEF value of team games, as opposed to individual sports, as a form of recreation in prisons is that they

    A. are easier to teach
    B. emphasize the social element
    C. are more enjoyable
    D. permit spectator participation
    E. cause the individual to develop skill more rapidly

47. It is generally held that, with reference to type of treatment afforded prisoners, the average American county jail is

    A. the most neglected of our penal and correctional institutions
    B. on a par with the state prison
    C. better than the state prison
    D. as good as the Federal prison
    E. remarkably in advance of general practice in penology

48. The type of control through which the behavior of an inmate is BEST directed is _____ control.

    A. group   B. imposed   C. leader
    D. self   E. dictatorial

49. John Smith has been a dope fiend for 12 years. He has served three jail sentences and paid several fines for selling dope. Today is his last day of a six-month jail sentence for having dope in his possession.
    He will MOST probably

    A. realize that his addiction to dope only brings him shame and disgrace and never use dope again
    B. begin using dope again in a short time
    C. have a high regard for law and order in the future
    D. have greater regard for the rights of other members of the community
    E. become a respectable citizen if he moves to a community where he is relatively unknown

50. Of the following, the BEST procedure to follow when an inmate has a temper tantrum while with a group of other inmates is, in general, to

   A. separate him from the group
   B. warn him that you will have to send for the warden
   C. appeal to his pride before the others
   D. reprimand him loudly
   E. advise him that he may be punished with solitary confinement

---

KEY (CORRECT ANSWERS)

1. D	11. B	21. G	31. C	41. A
2. C	12. A	22. H	32. C	42. C
3. C	13. B	23. B	33. B	43. A
4. A	14. B	24. A	34. D	44. D
5. B	15. C	25. B	35. C	45. D
6. B	16. B	26. C	36. B	46. B
7. D	17. K	27. A	37. A	47. A
8. C	18. J	28. A	38. B	48. D
9. C	19. D	29. D	39. B	49. B
10. B	20. A	30. B	40. D	50. A

TEST 3

DIRECTIONS: Each question or incomplete statement is followed by several suggested answers or completions. Select the one that BEST answers the question or completes the statement. *PRINT THE LETTER OF THE CORRECT ANSWER IN THE SPACE AT THE RIGHT.*

1. Suppose that a correction officer disagrees with the procedure which you, as supervisor, have outlined for him to follow in carrying out a certain assignment. Of the following, it is MOST desirable for you to tell this officer that

    A. in a semi-military organization orders must be carried out or discipline will be impaired
    B. the procedure you have outlined has been used successfully for many years in the past
    C. you are merely carrying out the orders of your own superior
    D. you will evaluate his objections to the procedure you have outlined

    1.____

2. An officer under your supervision refers to you for solution routine problems that arise on his post which other officers usually take care of themselves. Of the following, it would be MOST desirable for you to

    A. ask a more experienced employee to assist this officer whenever he has a problem
    B. show this officer when he refers a routine matter how to handle it himself and encourage him to do so in the future
    C. tell this officer to stand on his own two feet and assume his fair share of responsibility
    D. temporarily assign this officer to another post with less responsibility until he develops the capacity to handle his job properly

    2.____

3. A correction officer under your supervision regularly submits considerably more infraction reports against inmates than other officers with similar posts. Of the following, the MOST desirable action for you to take would be to

    A. direct this officer to be fairer toward the inmates
    B. give this officer additional training in order to strengthen his disciplinary control over the inmates
    C. reprimand this officer for his poor control over the inmates
    D. take no special action since in any such ranking there must always be one officer at the top and one at the bottom

    3.____

4. A correction superior gave his officers special training in the detection and prevention of suicides among prison inmates. Nevertheless, there still occurred two inmate suicides in his command during the year. Therefore, it would be MOST desirable for the superior to

    A. analyze the two suicides in order to develop special methods for preventing similar occurrences in the future
    B. assign a double guard to all suspected suicides
    C. change his training methods as they were obviously defective
    D. realize that there is a certain irreducible minimum of such occurrences which cannot be eliminated

    4.____

5. An efficient supervisor will make it a routine part of his job to study the inmates, whether he is assigned to a court pen, detention prison, penitentiary, reformatory or hospital ward. Of the following, the MOST direct implication of the preceding statement is that

   A. a good supervisor knows the habits of the inmates he supervises
   B. an efficient supervisor can successfully perform any assignment
   C. diversification of institutions for inmates is becoming more common
   D. the study of inmates, though not difficult, is often neglected

6. A new officer asks you for advice as to what to do if an inmate should refuse to carry out an order. As supervisor, you should advise this officer to

   A. ask himself if the order was a reasonable one
   B. avoid being drawn into a situation of this kind
   C. immediately summon his superior for assistance
   D. warn the prisoner that he will be subject to disciplinary action

7. A superior advised correction officers to prepare a schedule for the daily patrol of their posts and to adhere to this schedule every day. The superior's advice was

   A. *bad*, because the element of surprise is an important aid to successful detection of forbidden activities
   B. *bad*, because the inmates should always be kept guessing as to the officer's next move
   C. *good*, because regular habits, a desirable trait in a correction officer, will be developed
   D. *good*, because the inmate should be made to realize that he is always under observation

8. A superior assigned to a mess hall where several hundred inmates are eating their supper meal observes an inmate commit an infraction of the rules which does not immediately jeopardize the welfare of any officer or inmate.
Of the following, it would be BEST for the superior to

   A. defer disciplinary action until the inmates are returned to their cells in order to avoid the danger of precipitating a disturbance
   B. overlook the incident if nothing more serious happens as it may be part of a deliberate plan to stage a demonstration
   C. reprimand the offender at once to show the other inmates that he is in control of the situation
   D. warn the inmate that he will be subject to disciplinary action later because punishment, to be effective, must be prompt

9. A supervisor advised a new correction officer not to permit inmates to address him by his first name. The supervisor's advice was

   A. *bad*, because it creates a wider gap than necessary between officer and inmate
   B. *bad*, because no rule is applicable in every situation
   C. *good*, because familiarity between officer and inmate may lead to a breakdown of discipline
   D. *good*, because the more impersonally an inmate is treated the easier he is to control

10. An officer under your supervision reports to you that he suspects a certain inmate of suicidal tendencies. Of the following, the BEST action for you to take FIRST in this situation is to

    A. have the officer prepare a report for forwarding to your superior
    B. re-arrange the inmate's program so that he is always in the company of another inmate
    C. talk to the inmate and keep him under observation for a while in order to verify the accuracy of the officer's suspicions
    D. transfer the inmate to another cell where he may be kept under constant observation

11. A supervisor observes a correction officer deny an inmate's request to go to the medical clinic. This inmate has made similar requests in the past without cause and appears to have nothing the matter with him now. The supervisor should evaluate the officer's action as

    A. *unsound,* because if the inmate is really sick the denial of the request may have serious results
    B. *unsound,* because an officer should never be influenced by an inmate's previous record
    C. *sound,* because if the inmate is really sick he will let the officer know it soon enough
    D. *sound,* because it takes into account the inmate's previous record

12. On a tour of posts you observe that in a cell block supervised by a new officer, the line-up of inmates before reporting for work assignments is proceeding in a slow and disorderly manner. In this situation, it is MOST desirable that you, as supervisor,

    A. call the officer's attention to the fact that the line-up is not proceeding properly and then continue with your tour of posts
    B. issue a mild reprimand and take personal command of the line-up in order to prevent further confusion
    C. make a mental note of the situation and discuss the proper way of conducting a line-up at the next conference with your officers
    D. take the officer aside and instruct him in the immediate action to take in order to correct this situation

13. Of the following, it is MOST desirable that a supervisor train correction officers to

    A. carry out all assignments in a thorough-going and business-like manner
    B. impress upon inmates as soon as they are admitted that breaches of discipline will not be tolerated
    C. interpret inmates' behavior in terms of impressions formed upon admission
    D. learn all the rules and regulations thoroughly so as to be able to answer quickly any question raised by an inmate

14. Two of the officers under your supervision, who are assigned to a common post, are in frequent conflict with each other. In this situation, it is MOST desirable that you

    A. direct the officers to stop their arguments as they are interfering with efficient performance
    B. discuss with the officers the basic reasons for their conflict

C. tell both officers to refer all disputes to you for settlement
D. transfer one of the officers to another post

15. Of the following, the MOST desirable procedure for a supervisor to follow in order to keep correction officers *on their toes* is to

    A. apply disciplinary measures for the violation of department rules and regulations impartially
    B. encourage initiative by delegating responsibility to the best officers
    C. require them to prepare and submit frequent reports on their activities
    D. test their knowledge and alertness frequently

16. Suppose that on organized tier searches for contraband more contraband is usually found on the post of one officer under your command than on the post of any other officer. The one of the following which is MOST likely to be an important contributing factor in this situation is the

    A. amount of time this officer has devoted to the study of his book of rules
    B. amount of training you have given your staff in the detection and control of contraband smuggling
    C. special problems inherent in the type of post commanded by this officer
    D. thoroughness with which the different types of posts are searched

17. The one of the following which would probably contribute MOST to obtaining the maximum cooperation of subordinates in carrying out a change in a long established procedure would be to

    A. give several weeks advance notice of the proposed change in procedure
    B. hold staff conferences to explain and discuss the changed procedure prior to its adoption
    C. make provision for abandoning the new procedure if it is not accepted by the majority of the staff
    D. refrain from enforcing absolute compliance with the new procedure at the very beginning

18. Suppose that mail received by inmates of an institution of the Department is censored in a mail censoring room and then forwarded to the cell tier officer for distribution to the inmates. As supervisor, you should instruct the tier officer to

    A. distribute this mail to the inmates immediately upon receipt as it has already been censored carefully
    B. notify you whenever any mail is received by a former drug addict
    C. quickly examine the contents of each letter again as a double check before giving it to the inmate
    D. remove any enclosures which may not have been removed by the mail censor

19. A supervisor advised correction officers to approach with caution any inmate whose behavior was in any way different from normal. The supervisor's advice was

    A. *bad,* because over-caution on the part of a correction officer may be taken by the inmates as a sign of fear
    B. *bad,* because the inmate may actually be in need of immediate attention

C. *good,* because even seemingly harmless abnormal behavior may be part of a prepared plan for an attack
D. *good,* because every action of an inmate should be looked upon with mistrust

20. A supervisor detailed to assigning inmates to institutional work details should, in arriving at a decision as to the best assignment for an inmate, give LEAST consideration to the inmate's

    A. economic status
    B. educational background
    C. medical history
    D. occupational history

21. A new correction officer asks you to explain why department regulations permit officers to carry firearms only when having custody of a prisoner outside the prison, and not while on duty within the prison. Of the following, the BEST explanation of the justification for this rule is that

    A. an inmate has greater opportunities for escape when outside the prison walls
    B. an officer is not likely to be attacked by an inmate within the institution
    C. a single officer usually has custody of a prisoner outside the prison, whereas inside the prison there are always other officers present to render assistance in case of trouble
    D. firearms are dangerous weapons in the hands of inexperienced or unstable officers

22. A supervisor advised a correction officer as follows: When you take a count of inmates locked in a tier of cells, keep your eyes at such an angle as to have the occupant of the next cell in your line of vision immediately after verifying the count of the preceding cell. The advice of the supervisor was

    A. *bad,* because it is physically impossible to keep the eyes at the angle recommended
    B. *bad,* because when taking a count undivided attention to the cell being checked is essential
    C. *good,* because a surprise attack by the inmate in the next cell can better be prevented
    D. *good,* because in this way the process of taking the count will be speeded up

23. A supervisor directed correction officers to forbid inmates to accumulate back issues of magazines and newspapers in their cells. The supervisor's order was

    A. *bad,* because each inmate's case should be treated individually
    B. *bad,* because it discriminates against the inmate who likes to devote leisure time to reading
    C. *good,* because an accumulation of such material in cells is a health and fire hazard
    D. *good,* because an inmate does not have enough leisure time to read so much material anyway

24. Of the following, it is MOST desirable that a supervisor train correction officers to

    A. have no fear
    B. never depend on others for assistance
    C. obey all orders without question
    D. think before they act

25. As supervisor, you are assigned a detail of officers with whom to conduct a search of a tier of cells for contraband.
Of the following, the MOST desirable action for you to take in carrying out this assignment is to

   A. brief the officers of the detail in any special procedure to be followed in this case
   B. confer with the tier officer the day before as to which cells should receive closest attention
   C. have the entire detail of officers enter one cell at a time and search it thoroughly before proceeding to the next one
   D. notify the officer and inmates of the tier in advance of the search that they will have to be moved temporarily so that the search can be carried out with the least interference

26. A correction officer on a tour of inspection at night failed to observe any signs of life in the occupant of one cell. The officer immediately entered the cell to check further. When the officer reported this action to the supervisor, the latter was very critical. The supervisor's criticism was

   A. *justified,* because it wasn't necessary to enter the cell in order to find out if the inmate was dead
   B. *justified,* because the officer should not have entered the cell alone
   C. *unjustified,* because the officer had shown alertness and should have been praised
   D. *unjustified,* because the officer may have been unable to get help quickly at night

27. Suppose that a supervisor is required to review disciplinary reports against inmates prepared by correction officers before forwarding them to the disciplinary officer. Of the following, the report which it is MOST desirable for the supervisor to return to the correction officer for rewriting is one which

   A. fails to employ a high standard of written English
   B. fails to recommend an appropriate punishment
   C. is incomplete as to main details
   D. relates to more than one inmate

28. In a correctional institution where inmates were issued a manual of the rules, regulations, and procedures of the prison, a superior supplemented the manual by having the inmates given oral instruction in these matters upon admission. Of the following, the LEAST important reason for giving such supplemental oral instruction is that

   A. inmates can thereby be informed of new rules or changes in old rules
   B. inmates may not take the trouble to read the manual
   C. prison inmates occasionally lack the mentality to grasp even the most simply written instructions
   D. some prison inmates cannot read well enough

29. Newly appointed correction personnel should be given training of the orientation type, as well as training in their duties and in the application to their new positions of techniques or skills already acquired. Of the following topics, the one which BEST illustrates the first type of training described above is:

   A. Fundamentals of Supervisory Technique
   B. Purposes of Correctional Treatment

C. Required Dress for Correction Officers
D. The Daily Institutional Schedule

30. There are many methods of maintaining discipline among prison inmates. However, that discipline is best which disciplines least. Of the following, the MOST valid inference based on the preceding statement is that a correction supervisor should

    A. apply punitive measures only when unavoidable
    B. apply the least severe punitive measure when more than one is applicable
    C. have discipline rest mainly on good morale rather than on strict enforcement of detailed rules and regulations
    D. leave the disciplining of inmates to the correction officers and interfere only when called upon by them for assistance or advice

31. Only the highest type of officer should be assigned to the receiving room of a detention prison. Of the following, the BEST justification for this statement is that

    A. in this assignment an officer is exposed to many pressures
    B. the inmate's future conduct in prison may be decided by the first impression formed upon admission
    C. the routine of administration in the receiving room of a detention prison is more complex
    D. this may be the only contact with prison life for most prisoners

32. We should beware of assuming that a new jail necessarily means a good penal institution. This statement implies MOST directly that

    A. not all good penal institutions are new
    B. not all old jails are bad penal institutions
    C. some new jails are not good penal institutions
    D. some old jails are good penal institutions

33. A good probation department, by furnishing the judge with information regarding the guilty individual, makes possible discrimination in the use of imprisonment and, in the person of the probation officer, provides a substitute for it. Of the following, the MOST direct implication of the preceding statement is that

    A. a properly functioning probation department offers the means for effective use of probation in lieu of imprisonment for some offenders
    B. if used with discrimination by the judge, probation is sometimes in itself an indirect form of punishment
    C. probation, as a substitute for imprisonment, should be more widely used
    D. the primary function of a good probation officer is to secure background information about the offender

34. The fact that the offense is not serious does not mean that the perpetrator can be easily turned into a law-abiding citizen. Of the following, the BEST evidence in support of this statement is the

    A. high rate of recidivism among misdemeanant prisoners
    B. large number of small jails
    C. number of prisoners who violate parole
    D. reluctance of society to accept the former convict

35. The chain of prison administration is only as strong as its weakest officer. The preceding statement implies MOST directly that

    A. careful selection and proper training of personnel are not sufficiently emphasized by many prison administrators
    B. every prison employee is basically an administrator
    C. one inefficient officer can sometimes seriously impair the functioning of an entire institution
    D. the chainlike organization of prison management becomes apparent when a weak officer fails to perform his job properly

36. The industrial farm is the best type of institution yet developed for the majority of jail prisoners. Of the following, the BEST justification for this statement is that in an institution of this type

    A. strictest application of advanced classification procedures is possible
    B. the products of inmate labor in large measure pay for the cost of running the institution
    C. there is likely to be freedom from political interference because it is located away from urban centers
    D. worthwhile employment and training in desirable surroundings can be afforded every inmate

37. Several studies have shown that the majority of sentenced workhouse prisoners are recidivists. Of the following, the MOST valid inference based on the preceding statement is that

    A. commitment procedures for certain classes of prisoners should be re-studied
    B. for many prisoners custody, rather than rehabilitation, should be emphasized
    C. the rate of recidivism is greatest among workhouse prisoners
    D. while prison administrators give more attention to rehabilitative measures today, results are generally poor

38. It is desirable that the prisoners be well acquainted with the practices and procedures of the parole board. Of the following, the BEST argument in favor of this policy is that

    A. parole practices and procedures often change with a change in the make-up of the parole board
    B. prisoner participation in the formulation of parole board practices and procedures is desirable
    C. prisoners will be less prone to think they were unjustly treated by the parole board
    D. the parole board will be less subject to public criticism

39. Of the following, the MOST probable reason why public criticism of recreational programs for prisoners is much less common today than it was twenty-five years ago is that the general public nowadays

    A. accepts the rehabilitative objectives of correctional institutions more readily
    B. comprehends the real value of recreation in the correctional program
    C. is more interested in recreation and sports
    D. understands the problems involved in the maintenance of prison discipline

40. Of the following, the CHIEF value of the indeterminate sentence is that 40.____
    A. better discipline is obtained from the prisoner during the period of his incarceration
    B. the length of time to be served can be adjusted to the seriousness of the crime
    C. the sentencing power of the courts is curtailed
    D. the time spent in jail can be related to the rate of rehabilitative progress

41. Suppose that a study of prison inmates shows that a relatively small percentage of first 41.____
    offenders become second offenders, but that a very large percentage of second offenders commit subsequent offenses. Of the following, the LEAST valid inference based on the study described is that
    A. correctional procedures presently employed with second offenders are largely ineffective
    B. first offenders offer the most fertile field for rehabilitative efforts
    C. in a random sampling of prisoners, most of those sampled will have committed two or more offenses
    D. it is more difficult to attain success in the rehabilitation of second offenders than in the rehabilitation of first offenders

42. The mess hall is usually considered by prison administrators as the most sensitive spot 42.____
    in a correctional institution MAINLY because
    A. a large number of inmates is gathered together there at one time
    B. an insufficient number of officers is often assigned to the mess hall during meal periods
    C. the food in most prisons is inadequate and poorly prepared
    D. the use of eating utensils as weapons can be dangerous

43. Progressive penologists GENERALLY are of the opinion that 43.____
    A. alcoholics should be sentenced to jail for at least six months so that a cure can be effected
    B. alcoholics should receive an indeterminate rather than a definite jail term
    C. chronic alcoholism is a sickness rather than a crime
    D. treatment for chronic alcoholism should be made compulsory

44. It has been proposed that wider use be made of fines in lieu of imprisonment as a 44.____
    method of punishment for certain offenses. Of the following, the BEST argument in support of this proposal is that
    A. contact with prison atmosphere is often an effective deterrent to a repetition of the offense
    B. fines are not difficult to collect
    C. fines can be adjusted to the ability of the offender to pay
    D. imprisonment is expensive for the government

45. Penologists are generally opposed to the use of force as a method of maintaining prison 45.____
    discipline MAINLY because
    A. it is difficult to limit its use to self-defense or the enforcement of lawful commands
    B. it is of doubtful legality

C. modern escape-proof institutions have reduced the discipline problem to a minimum
D. resentment of the use of force by inmates may create, rather than correct, discipline problems

46. Of the following, the MAIN reason why it is so difficult to eradicate the smuggling of narcotics into a prison is that

   A. it is not possible to measure the personal integrity of prison personnel prior to their appointment to the service
   B. so many prison inmates are drug addicts today
   C. there are so many possible ways for the drugs to enter the prison
   D. the supply of available drugs is constantly increasing

47. Of the following, the LEAST valid argument in favor of having a commissary in a correctional institution is that the commissary

   A. contributes to the maintenance of inmate morale
   B. helps to reduce the institution's food budget
   C. is an important aid in maintaining discipline
   D. provides funds, not otherwise available, to buy recreational equipment for inmates

48. Of the following, the CHIEF argument in favor of dormitories over cells as a method of housing prison inmates is that dormitories

   A. are cheaper to construct
   B. are easier to clean
   C. make custodial supervision easier
   D. are preferred by inmates

49. In comparing the Pennsylvania with the Auburn system of penal discipline, it is MOST correct to state that in the

   A. Auburn system the prisoners were completely separated from each other except at meal time
   B. Auburn system the prisoners were not permitted to talk to each other
   C. Pennsylvania system prison visiting was prohibited
   D. Pennsylvania system the prisoners were allowed to mingle with each other only when at work

50. The proper Fahrenheit temperature which should be maintained in a cell block during the winter months is MOST NEARLY

   A. 60°   B. 65°   C. 73°   D. 75°

KEY (CORRECT ANSWERS)

1. D	11. A	21. A	31. B	41. C
2. B	12. D	22. C	32. C	42. A
3. B	13. A	23. C	33. A	43. C
4. A	14. B	24. D	34. A	44. D
5. A	15. D	25. A	35. C	45. D
6. D	16. C	26. B	36. D	46. C
7. A	17. B	27. C	37. A	47. B
8. A	18. C	28. A	38. C	48. A
9. C	19. C	29. B	39. A	49. B
10. C	20. A	30. C	40. D	50. B

EXAMINATION SECTION
TEST 1

DIRECTIONS: Each question or incomplete statement is followed by several suggested answers or completions. Select the one that BEST answers the question or completes the statement. *PRINT THE LETTER OF THE CORRECT ANSWER IN THE SPACE AT THE RIGHT.*

Questions 1-2.

DIRECTIONS: Questions 1 and 2 are to be answered on the basis of the following information and in accordance with pertinent rules and regulations.

Captain Blount is assigned to a steady 4:00 P.M. to 12:31 A.M. tour. His area of responsibility includes the Law Library.

1. Captain Blount must ensure that the Law Library is open on each of two weekday evenings for at least _____ hours.

   A. two B. three C. four D. five

2. According to rules, Captain Blount must permit detainees to use the Law Library at least _____ hour(s) on each day that the Law Library is in use.

   A. one B. two C. three D. four

3. Captain Tyrus is instructing Correction Officer Boyle in lock-in/lock-out procedures as mandated by procedures. He tells Officer Boyle that detainees shall be locked in during the day only for essential institutional business which cannot be carried out while inmates are locked out. He should also tell Officer Boyle that inmates can be locked in for this purpose for a total of no more than _____ hours in any 24-hour period.

   A. two B. three C. four D. five

4. While conducting a General Housing Area search, Officer Thomas reports to Captain Hayden that there appears to be an object in the lining of an inmate's leather jacket.
   In accordance with procedures, Captain Hayden should tell Officer Thomas to

   A. prepare a written statement to be given to the inmate before his jacket is cut
   B. cut the lining of the jacket only enough to be able to remove the object
   C. search the lining for an opening and if none is found, return the jacket to the inmate
   D. remove the lining of the jacket by cutting and ripping only the lining

5. Detainee Dalton tells Captain Mulligan that he wants to mail a letter that is required by law to be certified but he has no money in his account.
   In accordance with procedures, Captain Mulligan should tell Detainee Dalton that

   A. detainees are not allowed to mail certified letters from a Department facility
   B. he may not mail a certified letter unless he can pay for it himself
   C. he must mail the letter by regular mail at the Department's expense
   D. he can mail the certified letter at the Department's expense

6. After several incidents involving Inmate Marilyn Smith, Captain Blair decides that letting her attend communal religious services while in punitive segregation will pose a threat to the safety and security of the institution. He informs her of his determination in writing 48 hours before services will be denied to her, explaining the reason for his decision and how long the decision will be in effect. He also informs her that she will be allowed to present her case before another Captain. If the determination is upheld, she will be given another opportunity to be heard in one month.
In accordance with the law and rules, Inmate Smith was denied due process because she should have been

   A. allowed a hearing before Captain Blair reached a determination
   B. given written notice 72 hours before services were denied
   C. allowed to present her case before a duly constituted board
   D. advised that she will be allowed another opportunity to present her case in a week

7. While making a routine tour of inspection, Captain Oscar Peterson is approached by inmate Fong who informs him that he would like to mail 3 letters to friends and relatives but he has no money in his commissary account. In accordance with the Board of Correction Minimum Standards regarding correspondence, after substantiating that inmate Fong is indigent, Captain Peterson should inform him that he can receive free postage each week for _____ personal letters weighing _____ ounce(s) or less.

   A. 3; 2   B. 2; 2   C. 1; 1   D. 3; 1

8. While you are touring an adult general population housing area, the B Officer informs you that there are 6 inmates in the south-side cell corridor doing sit-ups and push-ups and 9 inmates in the north-side cell corridor playing checkers, chess, and cards. He asks you how to proceed.
According to the Board of Correction Minimum Standards regarding recreation, you should advise the officer to allow

   A. all inmates to proceed with the activities as long as they conduct themselves in an orderly fashion
   B. the inmates who are exercising to continue but send the remaining inmates to the day room to continue their games
   C. inmates playing games to continue but tell the remaining inmates they will have to wait until scheduled recreation to exercise
   D. none of the inmates to remain in the corridors but tell them they can continue their activities in the dayroom

9. You are a Captain making a routine institutional search. You observe Officer Harrison confiscate numerous sheets and pillowcases from inmate McGee's cell, leaving inmate McGee with 1 clean sheet and 2 clean pillowcases.
In accordance with the Board of Correction Minimum Standards regarding personal hygiene, you should tell Officer Harrison that the inmate is entitled to _____ sheets and _____ pillowcase(s).

   A. 2; 2   B. 3; 2   C. 2; 1   D. 2; 3

10. Detainee Perez, a member of a terrorist group, is housed in Maximum Security for armed robbery. He tells Captain Montressor that he was arrested with four other men, who are incarcerated in separate institutions. He further states that he would like to visit with his co-defendants within a week and that they have all consented to the visit.
    According to the Board of Correction Minimum Standards regarding access to co-defendants, Captain Montressor should tell Detainee Perez that

    A. his request will be granted with no stipulations
    B. detainees involved in Class A felonies are not permitted to confer with each other
    C. his request may not be granted without specific and written authorization from the district attorney
    D. his request will be granted, but the Department may require the presence of the attorney of record

11. Officer Santiago volunteers for overtime on the 3:30 P.M. to 12:01 A.M. tour after completing his regular tour of duty on the 7:00 A.M. to 3:31 P.M. tour. At the completion of the overtime tour, Santiago submits a Request to be Excused Form to the Control Room Captain requesting three hours time due beginning at 7:00 A.M. on his next tour.
    In accordance with the Board of Correction Minimum Standards regarding overtime, the Control Room Captain

    A. must grant Officer Santiago the entire 3 hours time due that was requested
    B. may grant Officer Santiago 3 hours time due at his own discretion based on the needs of the facility
    C. must grant Officer Santiago 2 hours time due and may grant the additional hour at his own discretion based on the needs of the facility
    D. must grant Officer Santiago 1 hour time due and may grant the additional 2 hours at his own discretion based on the needs of the facility

12. You are the Visit House Captain at your assigned facility. Officer Thomas, the Visit Registration Officer, informs you that a woman claiming to be the mother of three inmates housed in your facility has asked if she can visit with her three sons at the same time.
    In accordance with the Board of Correction Minimum Standards regarding visiting, you should tell Officer Thomas that the

    A. Board of Correction Minimum Standards does not permit a visit with more than two inmates at the same time
    B. facility rules and regulations only permit a visit with one inmate on each visit day
    C. Board of Correction Minimum Standards permits such a visit as long as facility regulations do not prohibit a visitor with three inmates at the same time
    D. facility regulations permit visits with several inmates on the same visit day as long as each inmate is visited separately

13. You are the Visit Captain. Officer Tomlinson informs you that inmate Ferguson, a male homosexual, is kissing his male visitor. He further states that he is personally offended by this behavior and asks you what he should do. In accordance with the Board of Correction Minimum Standards regarding visiting, you should instruct Officer Tomlinson to

    A. allow inmate Ferguson to continue his visit in the same Visit Area
    B. escort inmate Ferguson and his visitor to an isolated Visit Area
    C. tell inmate Ferguson to conduct himself properly
    D. terminate inmate Ferguson's visit with the male visitor

14. You are a Receiving Room (Intake) Captain in an adult detention facility. You are informed that inmate Smith, who just returned from court, refuses to submit to a mandatory search. You make every attempt to convince inmate Smith to comply with the rules. Inmate Smith still refuses to be searched.
In accordance with rules, the NEXT step that you should take in this situation after notifying the Tour Commander is to

    A. request that the Response Team forcibly search inmate Smith
    B. isolate inmate Smith and commence the forcible search
    C. request that the facility physician respond to the intake area
    D. return inmate Smith to his cell without subjecting him to a search

15. Control Room Captain Minali receives a telephone call from a relative of an inmate. The relative claims that she cannot visit the inmate because during regular visiting hours she must care for an ailing family member, who has a serious medical condition requiring constant attention. In accordance with the rules and regulations, Captain Minali should tell the relative that

    A. only the attorney of record may visit with the inmate at times other than the regular visiting hours
    B. she must apply for special visit privileges at the Department's Central Office
    C. only the inmate can request special visit privileges by submitting an application to the Chief of Operations
    D. she must apply to the head of the facility for a visit at a time other than during regular visiting hours

16. During an investigation of a multiple stabbing, you overhear District Attorney Jonathan Carter question Officer Julia Delgado. When Mr. Carter asks Officer Delgado what actions she took during the stabbing incident, she informs the District Attorney that she will not answer any questions without the advice of her attorney.
In accordance with the rules, you should tell Officer Delgado that she

    A. has the right to consult with her attorney before answering any questions
    B. must answer any questions relating to her official duties in the lawful investigation of the stabbings
    C. may request the advice of her union delegate before answering the District Attorney's questions
    D. may seek immunity from prosecution before answering the District Attorney's questions

17. Officer Pike notifies Captain Quincy that an inmate is refusing to get ready for his court appearance and has requested medical attention. He further informs her that the inmate is claiming to be too ill to go to court but that he has been known to fake illness in the past.
In accordance with the rules, Captain Quincy should

    A. send the inmate to the clinic for a medical evaluation
    B. instruct the inmate to go to the Receiving Room and have him fill out an Undelivered Defendant's Form
    C. enter the inmate's cell with a team of officers and have him physically removed
    D. threaten the inmate with bodily harm if he does not get ready for court

18. Captain Morrison reports for duty on the 8:00 A.M. to 4:00 P.M. tour on November 14. The Captain he is relieving reports that a routine infraction occurred on her tour at 5:45 A.M., which she was unable to process. Captain Morrison agrees to process the infraction and serves the inmate with a Notice of Infraction at 11:00 A.M. The hearing date is set for 9:00 A.M. the following day, November 15.
According to the rules, Captain Morrison's actions were

    A. *proper,* because the inmate was afforded at least 24 hours from the time of the infraction to the time of the hearing
    B. *improper,* because the inmate was not afforded at least 24 hours from the time of the fraction to the time of the hearing
    C. *proper,* because the inmate was afforded at least 24 hours from the time he was served with a Notice of Infraction to the time of the hearing
    D. *improper,* because the inmate was not afforded at least 24 hours from the time he was served with a Notice of Infraction to the time of the hearing

19. You are the Control Room Captain. Officers Murphy and Jackson have escorted inmate Smith to the hospital. The physician treating him has requested that his handcuffs be removed. Officer Murphy notifies you of the situation. In accordance with the rules, you should

    A. deny the request and inform Murphy that the handcuffs can only be removed in a serious medical emergency
    B. approve the request and instruct Murphy on necessary steps to prevent the inmate's escape
    C. deny the request and inform Murphy that the handcuffs can only be removed in a life-threatening emergency
    D. approve the request and immediately inform the Tour Commander of the situation

20. Captain Jacobson is the Receiving Room Captain at his assigned facility. At 6:00 P.M., on Thursday, the day prior to a legal holiday, Captain Jacobson is reviewing legal folders from the General Office. During this review, he notices that inmate Cohen's release date is on Saturday and that his religious beliefs do not permit him to travel or carry currency during daylight hours on that day.
In accordance with the rules, Captain Jacobson should release inmate Cohen on

    A. Saturday after dark, to permit Cohen to observe his religious beliefs
    B. Friday, because legal holidays are not a consideration when determining an inmate's day of release
    C. Thursday, because inmates are not normally released on Saturday, Sunday or legal holidays
    D. Monday, because inmates scheduled for release on Saturday or Sunday will be released on the next business day

21. You are processing bails when an inmate's father who wants to pay a $500 cash bail for his son refuses to sign the Consent of Surety Form.
In accordance with the rules, you should

    A. continue to process the bail
    B. instruct the father to pay the bail in court
    C. inform the father that his son cannot be released without a signature on the consent form
    D. inform the father that he must receive a surety examination form from the court

22. You are the Receiving Room Captain. A Correction Officer hands you an accompanying card with a red designator attached for a new inmate.
   In accordance with operations orders, Color Coded Designators, the red designator identifies the inmate as

   A. a centrally monitored case
   B. requiring protective custody
   C. a homosexual
   D. requiring mental observation

23. You are the Receiving Room Captain while inmates are being prepared for court. Officer Morris is unclear as to what items an inmate is allowed to take to court and asks for your help.
   In accordance with operations orders, Restriction of Items Taken to Court by Inmates, which of the following groups of items should Officer Morris allow an inmate to take to court in addition to legal materials?

   A. 2 handkerchieves, 2 pencils, 1 newspaper, and 1 book
   B. 2 packs of cigarettes, 2 pencils, 2 pens, and 1 book of matches
   C. 2 pencils, 2 pens, 2 packs of cigarettes, and 2 pieces of fruit
   D. 2 pens, 2 packs of cigarettes, 1 newspaper, and 1 piece of fruit

24. Captain Arnold Weissman is assigned to the Control Room on the 11:00 P.M. to 7:30 A.M. tour. At 3:00 A.M., an inmate properly processed for discharge on bail asks for carfare for a one fare zone. Captain Weissman, designated to issue carfare, notes that the inmate has $1.00 in his account.
   In accordance with operations orders regarding inmate carfare procedure, Captain Weissman should give the inmate the money in his account and

   A. no additional money
   B. an additional $1.00
   C. an additional $2.00
   D. an additional $3.00

25. Receiving Room Captain Greco is advised by Officer Joan Harvey in the General Office that Mrs. Curley is at the front gate to post bail for inmate Jim Curly using $500.00 in quarters.
   According to general orders regarding payment of bails and fines, Captain Greco should instruct Officer Harvey to

   A. accept the $500 in quarters for the bail
   B. accept $20 in quarters but tell Mrs. Curley that the rest must be in paper currency
   C. inform Mrs. Curley that the entire $500 must be converted to paper currency
   D. accept $100 in quarters but tell Mrs. Curley that the rest must be in paper currency

KEY (CORRECT ANSWERS)

1.	B	11.	A/B
2.	B	12.	C
3.	A	13.	A
4.	B	14.	C
5.	D	15.	D
6.	D	16.	B
7.	B	17.	A
8.	A	18.	D
9.	C	19.	B
10.	D	20.	C

21. A
22. A
23. D
24. D/C
25. A

TEST 2

DIRECTIONS: Each question or incomplete statement is followed by several suggested answers or completions. Select the one that BEST answers the question or completes the statement. *PRINT THE LETTER OF THE CORRECT ANSWER IN THE SPACE AT THE RIGHT.*

1. You are the Control Room Captain on the Friday, 3:00 P.M. to 11:31 P.M. tour. At 10:30 P.M., an off-duty Correction Officer, Lawrence Silver, calls you on the telephone and informs you that he was arrested at 9:50 P.M. for a domestic dispute and was issued a Desk Appearance Ticket at 10:00 P.M. by the local police precinct.
You record all pertinent information and inform Officer Silver that in accordance with General Orders regarding Arrest of Employees and Amendments to the Rules and Regulations, he must submit a written report to his command by

   A. Saturday, 9:50 P.M.
   B. Sunday, 9:50 P.M.
   C. Saturday, 10:00 P.M.
   D. Sunday, 10:00 P.M.

1.____

Questions 2-3.

DIRECTIONS: Questions 2 and 3 are to be answered on the basis of the following information and in accordance with General Orders regarding Attempted Suicide.

You are the Control Room Captain. You receive a telephone call from Officer Rentas, the *A* Officer in Housing Cell Block. She reports that the inmate in cell 14 was discovered hanging by his neck from a light fixture and that he appeared to be dead. She further reports that the *B* Officer went into the cell to cut the inmate down.

2. In the situation described above, the *B* Officer's action in entering the cell was

   A. *proper,* because an inmate who is hanging should be cut down immediately
   B. *improper,* because the *B* Officer should have requested medical assistance before entering the cell
   C. *proper,* because the inmate appeared to be dead
   D. *improper,* because he should not have entered the cell alone

2.____

3. After the inmate is cut down, Officer Rentas reports that the inmate has stopped breathing and has no pulse. Neither the *B* Officer nor Officer Rentas have been certified in Cardio-Pulmonary Resuscitation (C.P.R.), but Officer Rentas is familiar with the technique.
You should advise Officer Rentas to

   A. do nothing until the physician arrives
   B. tell the *B* Officer to administer artificial respiration
   C. tell the *B* Officer to administer C.P.R.
   D. leave the *A* post and administer C.P.R. herself

3.____

4. You are a Housing Area Captain on the midnight tour. At approximately 2:40 A.M., Correction Officer Colon reports to you that at 2:30 A.M., while alone on his post, he opened inmate Jefferson's cell. He further explains that the inmate was complaining of severe chest pains and he did not want to waste any time in getting him to the clinic. In accordance with General Orders on Inspection and Search, you should inform Officer Colon that his action of opening inmate Jefferson's cell was

4.____

A. *proper,* because he may open an inmate's cell after lock-in for medical reasons
B. *improper,* because he may not open an inmate's cell after lock-in unless the inmate is in a Mental Observation Unit
C. *proper,* because he may open an inmate's cell after lock-in if a supervisor is notified soon thereafter
D. *improper,* because he may not unlock an inmate's cell after lock-in

5. You are a Housing Area Captain. You observe the change of tour count procedure in your assigned cell block area. The on-duty Officer takes a count of inmates and remainson his post. Moments later, the relieving Officer arrives, enters the cell block, takes the inmate count, and makes a security inspection. The relieving Officer then reports to the on-duty Officer's station, where he verifies the reported inmate count and number of keys with the on-duty Officer. The relieving Officer is briefed on activities during the tour by the on-duty Officer, who then departs from the cell block with the properly signed count slip.
In accordance with General Orders, it is CORRECT to conclude that

    A. the on-duty Officer failed to adhere to proper relieving count procedure, but the relieving Officer performed properly
    B. both Officers performed their duties properly in reference to the taking of the count
    C. both Officers failed to properly adhere to the change of tour count procedure
    D. the on-duty Officer properly adhered to the change of tour count procedure, but the relieving Officer did not

6. At the completion of roll call, Officer Debra Cummings, on her first tour after being off-duty, complains to the Roll Call Captain that her Punitive Segregation *B* post was changed to a General Population post. The Captain tells Cummings that the *B* post required the routine strip frisking of male inmates in and out of the Punitive Segregation Area.
In accordance with Directives on Guidelines for Assignment of Male/Female Uniformed Personnel within Correctional Facilities, the Captain's action was

    A. *improper,* because female Officers can work Punitive Segregation even if their duties require strip frisking male inmates
    B. *proper,* because female Officers cannot be assigned posts requiring the routine strip frisking of male inmates
    C. *improper,* because female Officers can be assigned posts requiring the routine strip frisking of male inmates if those duties can be assigned to a male Officer
    D. *proper,* because female Officers can be assigned duties requiring the routine strip frisking of male inmates if a post assignment variance is issued by the Chief of Operations

7. While assigned as the General Officer Supervisor, you overhear a conversation in which Officer James is listing acceptable instruments for the payment of bails.
In accordance with General Orders on Payment for Bails and Fines, which of the following instruments should you inform James is NOT acceptable as payment for bails?

    A. Veterans Administration checks
    B. State Government checks
    C. Travelers Express Company money orders
    D. Certified personal checks

8. During your tour of inspection in the Administrative Segregation Housing Area, inmate Chadwick approaches you and states that he wants his Centrally Monitored Case Classification changed because it is based on an incident which occurred 5 1/2 years ago.
   In accordance with Directives regarding Central Monitored Cases, you instruct him to submit an appeal to the

   A. Inspector General or Commissioner
   B. Director of Classification or Warden
   C. Director of Classification or Chief of Operations
   D. Deputy Warden of Programs or Deputy Warden of Administration

9. You are the Receiving Room Captain. Three detainees have just returned from court with the following orders:
   I. Detainee A - a temporary order of observation
   II. Detainee B - a final order of observation
   III. Detainee C - an order of commitment
   Officer Stanton asks you if any of the detainees are eligible for discharge from custody.
   In accordance with Directives regarding Custody of Defendants Found to be Incapacitated Pursuant to Article 730 of the Criminal Procedure Law, which of the following should you tell Stanton?

   A. I and II, but not III, should be discharged.
   B. II and III, but not I, should be discharged.
   C. III, but not I and II, should be discharged
   D. None of the detainees should be discharged.

10. You are the Receiving Room Captain on Mondays. Officer Harvey informs you that inmate Talbot, a Central Monitored Case, has an 11:00 A.M. appointment at Bellvue Hospital on Wednesday.
    In accordance with Directives on Central Monitored Cases, the Chief of Operations should be notified of the scheduled movement on _____, between _____ A.M.

    A. Tuesday; 8:00 A.M. and 8:30
    B. Tuesday; 10:00 A.M. and 10:30
    C. Wednesday; 7:00 A.M. and 7:30
    D. Wednesday; 8:00 A.M. and 8:30

Questions 11-12.

DIRECTIONS: Questions 11 and 12 are to be answered on the basis of the following information and in accordance with Directives on the Use of Chemical Agents.

Captain Moore notifies the Tour Commander that an inmate is refusing to leave his cell for a court appearance. He further reports that the inmate is extremely big and is waving a 6" shank. The Tour Commander orders Captain Moore to use chemical agents.

11. Which of the following aerosol dispensers should Captain Moore use?

    A. #280 and #281, followed by #287
    B. #280 and #282, followed by #287
    C. #281 and #282, followed by #289
    D. #282 and #283, followed by #289

12. Captain Moore uses the chemical agents, and they have no effect on the inmate. Which of the following is the MAXIMUM amount of time, in minutes, that the inmate can remain in his cell before he must be removed by alternate means?

    A. 3   B. 5   C. 7   D. 10

13. During his tour of inspection in the Protective Custody Housing area, Captain Velez is informed by Officer Martinez that she has dismissed Inmate Observation Aide Linda Watts. Officer Martinez claims that the reason for the dismissal was that Watts was not cooperative.
    In accordance with Directives regarding Inmate Observation Aide Program, Captain Velez should NEXT

    A. review the Inmate Observation Aide logbook to ensure that the reason for Watts' dismissal has been logged, then initial the entry
    B. tell Correction Officer Martinez to write an infraction against inmate Watts for improper performance of duty as an Inmate Observation Aide
    C. review the protective custody housing area logbook to ensure that the reason for Watts' dismissal has been logged, then initial the entry
    D. tell Correction Officer Martinez to reinstate Watts because she does not have the authority to dismiss Inmate Observation Aides

14. You are the Captain of a Mental Observation Housing area. Officer Stevens informs you that inmate Brewer has smashed in the television set in the dayroom because other inmates would not allow him to put on a program he wanted to watch. An infraction and Notice of Infraction has already been prepared against inmate Brewer.
    In accordance with rules, which of the following is the NEXT action you should take regarding inmate Brewer?

    A. Void the infraction and refer inmate Brewer to the Mental Health Unit for evaluation.
    B. Process the infraction and prepare and process a Request for Evaluation of inmate Brewer's mental health status, pending disciplinary action.
    C. Process the infraction and recommend restitution since inmate Brewer destroyed City property.
    D. Transfer inmate Brewer to Administrative Segregation and place a Mental Health Observation sheet on him while he awaits a disciplinary hearing.

15. You are a Housing Area Captain. Officer Al Brown informs you that inmate Reed wants to change his religious affiliation.
    In accordance with regulations on Congregate Religious Services, you should instruct Officer Brown to

    A. inform the Deputy Warden for programs of the inmate's request
    B. tell the inmate to submit an interview slip to the Chaplain of the requested faith
    C. escort the inmate to the Receiving Room so a new identification card can be issued
    D. inform the inmate that religious affiliation cannot be changed

16. You are assigned as the Control Room Captain. At 8:00 P.M., a nurse from the clinic informs you that an inmate has a life-threatening emergency, his condition is critical, and he should be transferred to a hospital.
    In accordance with Standard Time Schedules for the Delivery of Inmate Patients to Appropriate Medical/Psychiatric Facilities, you should IMMEDIATELY

A. obtain a second medical opinion from the facility physician
B. secure the facility physician's approval for transfer to a hospital
C. contact the inmate's family for approval before transfer to a hospital
D. arrange for transportation to the nearest appropriate private or municipal hospital

17. A disciplinary hearing is held on Thursday at 10:00 A.M. and due to the fact that inmate Parker has a history of breaking telephones, he is sentenced to 7 days in punitive segregation and 7 days loss of telephone privileges. He receives written notification of his loss of telephone privileges at 6:00 P.M. the same day.
Inmate Parker may submit an appeal by no later than

A. Friday at 10:00 A.M.
B. Friday at 6:00 P.M.
C. Saturday at 10:00 A.M.
D. Saturday at 6:00 P.M.

18. You are the Control Room Captain. While inspecting the Officers at roll call, you detect alcohol on the breath of Officer Frank Jameson and notice that he is unsteady on his feet and incoherent.
In accordance with Disciplinary Procedures, how many hours can Officer Jameson be detained for his personal safety?

A. 2   B. 4   C. 6   D. 8

19. An Officer is assaulted by an inmate at a Department facility. As a result of the assault, the Officer sustains serious injuries and criminal prosecution is being considered. To document the incident and the extent of injury, photographs are taken of the injured Officer.
In accordance with Operation Orders on Unusual Incidents, the photographs should be forwarded immediately to the

A. Office of the District Attorney having jurisdiction
B. Police Precinct where the assault occurred
C. Deputy Warden for Security
D. Inspector General

20. After a contact visit, an inmate is found to be in possession of counterfeit identification.
In accordance with Operation Orders on the Search of Inmates Returning from Contact Visits, the MOST appropriate action to take next before returning the inmate to his cell is to

A. prepare an Infraction and Notice of Infraction against the inmate
B. conduct a thorough search of the inmate's cell area and his belongings
C. detain and question the inmate's contact visitor
D. provide the visitor and inmate with written notification informing them that future visits will be limited to non-contact visits

21. You are the Control Room Captain. During the 4-12 tour, two members of the Inspector General's staff arrive at your facility.
In accordance with Operation Orders on Access to Department Facilities by the Office of the Inspector General, you should

A. admit the Inspector General's staff members but notify the Tour Commander of their arrival
B. ask the Tour Commander if it is permissible to admit the Inspector General's staff members into the facility beyond the Control Room

C. tell the Inspector General's staff members that they must report to the Tour Commander before they will be granted access to the facility
D. upon presenting their shields and I.D. cards, grant the Inspector General's staff members immediate access to all areas of the facility

22. In accordance with the rules, which of the following can be considered substantial evidence in making a determination to place a detainee involuntarily into separate homosexual housing?
A

A. homosexual detainee who has physical mannerisms more often associated with women than men
B. transvestite detainee who wears female undergarments
C. homosexual detainee whose presence in the general population will pose a serious threat to his personal safety
D. transvestite detainee who is also known to be homosexual

23. Following are three statements that may or may not conform to the stipulations in the Consent Decree Ambrose vs. Malcolm:
    I. Clothing intended for a detainee who must appear in court on the following day must be delivered by 9:00 P.M. to the Department facility where the inmate is housed
    II. Visitors shall be permitted to bring clothing for a detainee to a Department facility during regular visiting hours
    III. Clothing which is personally delivered to Department facilities shall be delivered to intended recipients within 24 hours

Which of the following BEST classifies the above statements?

A. I and II conform; III does not.
B. II and III conform; I does not.
C. I and III conform; II does not.
D. I, II, and III all conform.

24. In accordance with the Board of Correction Minimum Standards regarding Legal Documents and Supplies, an inmate may be permitted to obtain legal or clerical supplies at the Department's expense if he has

A. no money in his inmate commissary account
B. grounds for a legal motion in a criminal case in progress
C. correspondence which must be prepared on legal forms
D. reasonable expectations that he may be granted an appeal for a recent conviction

25. In accordance with the Board of Correction Minimum Standards regarding Classification, when a detainee is classified in the most restrictive security status, a review of this status shall be conducted at intervals not to exceed _____ week(s).

A. 1   B. 2   C. 4   D. 8

26. Captain Velardo is contacted by a friend of his at another facility, Officer Giordello. Giordello states that he believes a Captain at his facility is accepting delivery of inferior quality foodstuffs and receiving a cash kickback. He further states that he is beginning an independent investigation to substantiate his belief and will report his findings to the Commissioner when his investigation is complete.
In accordance with Executive Order regulations, Captain Velardo should tell Officer Giordello to discontinue his investigation and report his allegations directly and without further delay to the

    A. Inspector General or Commissioner
    B. District Attorney
    C. Tour Commander at his facility
    D. Deputy Warden for Administration at his facility

27. An institution with competent superiors will be an institution well-run.
Of the following, the BEST justification for this statement is that

    A. the duties of superiors, although often supervisory, are essentially custodial
    B. competent supervision is usually reflected by competent performance of duties
    C. if subordinates are inefficient, competent supervision becomes increasingly difficult
    D. even competent supervisors need the cooperation of their superior officers

28. Prior to roll call, Housing Captain Sakota notices that two Correction Officers who are about to return from vacation are assigned to the same housing area. Sakota recalls that on several occasions when the Officers have been assigned together, they have been involved in incidents where the use of force was questionable. He reassigns one of the Officers to another housing area and advises the Tour Commander of his decision to separate the Officers. After roll call, both Officers voice their objections to being assigned to separate housing areas.
In this situation, Captain Sakota's action was

    A. *appropriate,* because it is Captain Sakota's responsibility to be sensitive to situations that may result in a threat to the good order, safety, and security of his facility
    B. *inappropriate,* because Captain Sakota does not have the authority to change personnel assignments that are made by the Office of the Deputy Warden of Administration
    C. *appropriate,* because Correction Officers should be separated after involvement in any incident where use of force occurs even if such use of force was permissible
    D. *inappropriate,* because any changes in the subject Correction Officers' assignments will be viewed by the inmates as a lack of support for the Officer's abilities to maintain order

Questions 29-30.

DIRECTIONS: Questions 29 and 30 are to be answered SOLELY on the basis of the following information.

Captain Hargrove responds to the report of a serious incident involving the possible use of weapons in his assigned housing area.

The following is a list of actions he may or may not take with regard to the incident:
  I. Question the inmate witness.
  II. Question the Correction Officers involved.
  III. Report the incident to the Tour Commander.
  IV. Conduct a search for contraband.
  V. Question the inmates involved.
  VI. Advise the inmates who are identified as the alleged perpetrators of their Miranda rights.
  VII. Notify the Office of the District Attorney in the borough of occurrence and jurisdiction.
  VIII. Make initial critical observations.
  IX. Determine if anyone is in need of immediate medical assistance.

29. Which of the following are the FIRST five actions Captain Hargrove should take in the order they are to be taken?

    A. II, IV, V, VIII, IX
    B. VIII, IX, IV, V, II
    C. II, V, VIII, IX, IV
    D. VIII, IX, II, IV, V

30. Which of the following remaining actions is NOT appropriate for Captain Hargrove to take with regards to the incident described above?

    A. Question the inmate witness.
    B. Report the incident to the Tour Commander.
    C. Advise the inmates who are identified as the alleged perpetrators of their Miranda rights.
    D. Notify the Office of the District Attorney in the borough of occurrence and jurisdiction.

KEY (CORRECT ANSWERS)

1. B		16. D	
2. A		17. B	
3. B		18. D	
4. D		19. C	
5. B		20. B	
6. B		21. D	
7. D		22. C	
8. A		23. A	
9. D		24. A	
10. C		25. C	
11. B		26. A	
12. B		27. B	
13. C		28. A	
14. B		29. D	
15. B		30. D	

TEST 3

DIRECTIONS: Each question or incomplete statement is followed by several suggested answers or completions. Select the one that BEST answers the question or completes the statement. *PRINT THE LETTER OF THE CORRECT ANSWER IN THE SPACE AT THE RIGHT.*

Questions 1-2.

DIRECTIONS: Questions 1 and 2 are to be answered on the basis of the following five paragraphs. Assume that these paragraphs are from an Incident Report in no particular order.

I. At 4:45 A.M., the City Medical Examiner arrived, officially pronounced Compton dead, and removed the body to the City Morgue. At 4:50 A.M., City Police Detectives Pintos and Cohen arrived to investigate this incident. None of the Housing Officers nor Inmate Observation Aide Geralds reported any unusual behavior by Compton prior to his suicide. At this time, this writer cannot determine the reason for Compton's suicide.

II. Blakey reports that when Geralds notified him, he responded from the rear of the corridor and observed Compton hanging. He then informed A Officer Ben Dawson, Shield #7867, who opened the cell door. Blakey then entered the cell and, with Geralds' assistance, cut the noose around Compton's neck and placed him on his bed.

III. Officer Dawson reports that immediately after opening Cell Door #5, he notified the Control Room and requested medical and supervisory assistance. The Control Room notified this writer by radio, and I contacted the doctor and responded to the scene.

IV. Submitted herein is a report of an apparent suicide by Inmate John Compton, #346-88-6718, discovered hanging in Housing Area 3 Main, Cell #5, at 2:10 A.M. on 12/5. At 2:10 A.M., Inmate Observation Aide Geralds, #349-88-1210, observed Compton hanging in his cell with a bedsheet tied to his neck and affixed to the overhead light fixture. He then notified B Officer Jim Blakey, Shield #7894, who responded immediately.

V. At approximately 2:15 A.M., I arrived on the scene with Doctor Harrison and Nurse Ashley. The examination revealed that Compton had been dead for several hours. Doctor Harrison requested that the body be removed to the Clinic, and I complied. At 2:30 A.M., I notified Tour Commander A/D/W Jim Cash, Shield #160, of what had transpired.

1. What is the MOST logical order for the above five paragraphs? 1.___

   A. IV, II, III, V, I   B. IV, II, III, I, V
   C. IV, III, II, I, V   D. IV, III, II, V, I

2. What is the name of the Officer who reported the incident to the Control Room? 2.___

   A. Blakey   B. Compton   C. Dawson   D. Geralds

Questions 3-5.

DIRECTIONS: Questions 3 through 5 are to be answered on the basis of the following information.

Captain Donald is assigned to an Adult Correctional Facility. He receives a report from a Correction Officer that Officer Blades is in the locker room in an apparent stupor and under the influence of drugs. After asking another Captain and another Correction Officer to accompany him, Captain Donald goes to the locker room to investigate. There he sees Officer Blades leaning against the wall with a dazed look in his eyes, babbling nonsense. Officer Blades' locker door is open, and Donald notices 7-8 square cellophane bags containing white powder on the locker shelf. Donald confiscates the cellophane bags and informs Blades that he will be detained for drug testing. However, Blades refuses to answer questions or be treated for drugs unless his union representative is consulted. Donald then immediately suspends him from duty.

3. Captain Donald's action in responding immediately to the scene after learning of Officer Blades' possible involvement with drugs was

    A. *improper*, chiefly because he should have notified the Inspector General's Office prior to responding
    B. *proper*, chiefly because he has reasonable cause based on a reliable informant
    C. *improper*, chiefly because he should have notified the Tour Commander prior to responding
    D. *proper*, chiefly because an immediate response was necessary due to the nature of the allegation

4. Captain Donald's action in suspending Officer Blades from duty was

    A. *proper*, chiefly because the evidence was overwhelming and beyond reasonable suspicion
    B. *improper*, chiefly because there was not reasonable suspicion based on the information he received
    C. *proper*, chiefly because the evidence suggested that Officer Blades was under the influence of drugs
    D. *improper*, chiefly because a higher ranking Officer should have been called to the scene to make the decision

5. Blades' request to consult with his union representative was

    A. *proper*, chiefly because under no circumstances may a Correction Officer be drug tested without representation
    B. *improper*, chiefly because a Correction Officer has no right to make such a request when the evidence is overwhelming
    C. *proper*, chiefly because a Correction Officer has the right to consult with a union representative before submitting to testing
    D. *improper*, chiefly because as a public official, a Correction Officer must follow orders from supervisors

Questions 6-7.

DIRECTIONS: Questions 6 and 7 are to be answered on the basis of the following information.

While inspecting your four assigned cellblock housing areas, the A Officers on each block report the following conditions, which you verify:

Housing Area #1:
The Officer reports that all the inmates appear to be buying over and beyond their normal amount of commissary food items, but the area is generally quiet.

Housing Area #2:
The Officer reports that everything appears in order and he has no problems. During his tour of inspection, he observed a high volume of commissary items in almost every cell.

Housing Area #3:
The Officer reports that he has had to constantly chastise the inmates due to the increased noise level over the past two days; purchases of commissary food items are also high.

Housing Area #4:
The Officer reports that a higher than normal volume of food items has been purchased by the inmates, and he has received many inmate requests to be transferred to another part of the institution.

6. Which of the following is the MOST appropriate conclusion you can make regarding the higher than normal purchase of commissary food items?

   A. The commissary has upgraded the quality of its food items.
   B. These inmates are more affluent than most others.
   C. A planned inmate disturbance is likely to occur soon.
   D. The inmates are all voicing their dissatisfaction for the institution's regular meal program.

7. In which housing area is it MOST likely that the inmates may be hacksawing a window bar?
   Housing Area _____.

   A. 1   B. 2   C. 3   D. 4

Questions 8-9.

DIRECTIONS: Questions 8 and 9 are to be answered on the basis of the following information.

Captain Bromley has two tasks to be delegated among the six Officers under her supervision. Officer Aaronson has shown leadership qualities in dealing with inmates. Officer Browne uses independent judgment to solve all problems. Officer Crane is able to state facts in a clear and concise manner. Officer Duncan is a hard worker, but does not submit reports on time. Officer Jennings is well-liked by the other Officers in the facility. Officer Maginn is very imaginative and has drawn illustrations for several science fiction books.

8. To which of the following Officers should Captain Bromley delegate the task of writing an injury report?

   A. Aaronson   B. Browne   C. Duncan   D. Jennings

9. To which of the following Officers should Captain Bromley delegate the task of supervising an inmate work detail?

   A. Jennings   B. Duncan   C. Browne   D. Aaronson

10. Captain Chase is supervising the noon feeding when Correction Officer Walker tells him that an inmate on the kosher meal program has asked for a regular meal instead of the kosher meal.
    Captain Chase should tell Correction Officer Walker to inform the inmate that he

    A. may substitute a regular meal for a kosher meal, but he will be removed from the kosher meal program
    B. will not be allowed to have a regular meal until he requests that his inmate identification records be changed
    C. may substitute a regular meal once without penalty, but the next time he will be removed from the kosher meal program
    D. will not be allowed to have a regular meal unless he first receives approval from the Deputy Warden of Programs

11. While you are touring your housing area, inmate Jack Kehoe approaches you and states that he was a licensed barber before his incarceration and is interested in cutting hair in the barber shop.
    You should respond by telling him the requirements for this position include

    A. clearance by the Institutional Civilian Barber and Deputy Warden for Security
    B. clearance by the Deputy Warden for Programs and the Deputy Warden for Security
    C. a recommendation by an Officer and clearance by the Facility Security Office
    D. a food handler's certificate and clearance by the Facility Security Office

12. Captain Sykes discovers that Correction Officer Frazier has not been making his half-hour cell and area inspections. When questioned, Officer Frazier reports he has not been making the inspections since there are only ten inmates housed in the area and they are locked-out and are all in the dayroom.
    Captain Sykes should inform Officer Frazier that he must patrol and inspect

    A. the dayroom every half-hour
    B. each cell and the entire post area every half-hour
    C. each cell and the entire post area at the end of the tour
    D. each cell every half-hour when at least one inmate is locked in

13. You are the Control Room Captain. Officer Stark telephones to inform you that she was not able to locate her shield when she arrived home from her tour. You notify the Tour Commander, and he orders you to notify the Communications Control Center.
    Which of the following is the MAXIMUM amount of time allowed to report the missing shield to the Communications Control Center?

    A. 5 minutes   B. 15 minutes
    C. 30 minutes   D. 1 hour

14. You are a Captain assigned to the Inmate Dining Area. You observe that inmate Wayne Mason's identification card has him pictured with a full beard and shoulder-length hair. However, inmate Mason is now clean-shaven and has a crewcut. When you question him, he tells you that he went to the barber shop earlier in the day and requested to have his hair cut and beard shaved off.
    You should instruct the Housing Officer to

    A. issue the inmate a new identification card at inmate expense
    B. write the inmate up with an Infraction for changing his appearance

C. change the inmate's facility photographs at no cost to the inmate
D. detain the inmate in the dining area until the Tour Commander has been notified

15. Officer Allen has worked steadily for the past several months in one of your housing areas. Based on her past performance, you consider Officer Allen to be responsible, conscientious, and alert. However, in the past several weeks, her performance has deteriorated. She has displayed a lethargic, lackadaisical attitude, her absences have increased, and she has had 2 AWOLs. You have attempted on several occasions to ask her if she was experiencing any problems on or off the job. Allen has responded that there are problems, but refuses to be specific.
Your BEST course of action in this situation is to

    A. refer the Officer to the Employee Assistance Program
    B. recommend that the Officer be transferred to another institution
    C. suggest that the Officer take a leave of absence
    D. suspend the Officer immediately to avoid problems in the housing area

16. Captain Castellano reports to the Mental Health Observation Area of his facility in response to a report that an inmate is in danger of becoming violent. He observes inmate Horowitz speaking of devils and goblins and threatening other inmates with a stick. Captain Castellano immediately takes the stick from the inmate and places him in handcuffs. He then calls the Mental Health Staff to request a psychiatrist to report to the scene but is informed that it may take up to 2 hours for the psychiatrist to arrive.
The MOST appropriate action for Captain Castellano to take is to

    A. transport the inmate as soon as possible to a facility where a psychiatrist is on duty
    B. immediately contact a psychiatrist at another facility to determine the appropriate psychiatric hospital for referral
    C. wait 1 hour for the facility psychiatrist, then transfer the inmate to a facility where a psychiatrist is on duty
    D. wait 1 hour for the facility psychiatrist, then contact a psychiatrist at another facility to determine the appropriate psychiatric hospital for referral

17. Captain Bello is assigned to a court pen. Correction Officer Johnson reports to Captain Bello that he just received a superceding sentence commitment from a Court Officer. Officer Johnson further reports that the super-ceding commitment is for an inmate who is currently serving a sentence in a Departmental institution, but was not produced in court. The superceding sentence commitment changes the inmate's sentence from 9 months to 6 months. Captain Bello instructs Officer Johnson to accept the superceding sentence commitment.
Captain Bello's instructions to Officer Johnson are

    A. *improper,* because he is not allowed to accept a super-ceding sentence commitment for an inmate who is currently serving a sentence
    B. *proper,* because he must accept a superceding sentence commitment that is ordered by the court system
    C. *improper,* because he is not allowed to accept a superceding sentence commitment that reduces an inmate's sentence
    D. *proper,* because he must accept a superceding sentence commitment that does not extend an inmate's sentence

18. You are assigned to the Mental Observation Housing Area on the 7:00 A.M. to 3:31 P.M. tour. At 10:00 A.M., you are informed by a steady Officer that there has been a change in inmate Roberts' behavior and that the inmate seems very depressed. The Officer tells you that he would like to deny optional lock-in to inmate Roberts for fear he will hurt himself but that there will be no psychiatrist or psychologist on duty until 8:00 that night.
You should

    A. tell the Officer that optional lock-in can only be denied by a psychiatrist or psychologist
    B. deny optional lock-in for no more than 24 hours but have the inmate examined by the first available psychiatrist or psychologist
    C. tell the Officer that optional lock-in can only be denied by the facility physician
    D. deny optional lock-in for no more than 48 hours but have the inmate examined by the first available psychiatrist or psychologist

19. You are a Housing Area Captain on the midnight tour. At approximately 3:00 A.M., the B Officer contacts you concerning a fire in an inmate's cell. When you arrive on the scene, you discover that the fire has been extinguished, but there is a slight smoke condition in the corridor and the inmates are yelling to get out of their cells.
In this situation, the FIRST action you should take is to

    A. request a support team to report to the area
    B. evacuate the inmates to the dayroom
    C. ventilate the area to clear out the smoke
    D. contact the Tour Commander

Questions 20-23.

DIRECTIONS: Questions 20 through 23 are to be answered on the basis of the following information.

You are the Housing Area Captain of Cell Block 2 at your assigned facility. At the start of a designated lock-in period, you observe an altercation develop between Officer Harris and inmate Devoe. When ordered to lock-in, Devoe ignore the order and verbally abuses Harris with racial insults. Officer Harris responds by aggressively shoving Devoe toward his cell and punches him in the back of the head. Devoe enters his cell, and all of the inmates are locked-in.

20. Which of the following BEST describes the use of force Officer Harris used against inmate Devoe?
    _____ use of force.

    A. Sequential   B. Unnecessary
    C. Excessive   D. Permissible

21. After observing the altercation, the action you should take FIRST is to

    A. have inmate Devoe examined by the facility medical staff
    B. notify Communications Control Center of the incident
    C. have a psychiatric evaluation referral prepared for inmate Devoe
    D. notify the Inspector General of the incident

22. Which of the following is the MOST appropriate action for you to take with regard to Officer Harris' and inmate Devoe's behavior?

    A. Order Officer Harris to prepare an Infraction against inmate Devoe but take no further action against Harris.
    B. Question inmate Devoe about the altercation; and if he does not complain, take no further action with regard to Devoe or Harris.
    C. Order Officer Harris to prepare an Infraction against inmate Devoe and initiate Disciplinary Charges against Officer Harris.
    D. Take no action against inmate Devoe but initiate Disciplinary Charges against Officer Harris.

23. During your investigation of the altercation, you interview Officer Crane, the A Post Officer. Crane's account of the incident agrees with your own observation, but, in addition, Crane also informs you that on several other occasions, he witnessed Harris aggressively shove, slap, or punch inmates who did not respond fast enough to his orders. You ask Crane if he reported these other incidents, and he tells you he did not because no injuries occurred and Harris' actions made the inmates more cooperative. You tell Officer Crane to submit a detailed report of this altercation and the other incidents he witnessed.
    Assume the allegations described above have been substantiated.
    Which of the following is the MOST appropriate action for you to take concerning Officer Crane's disclosure that he witnessed several similar unreported use of force incidents?

    A. After receiving the requested report, initiate disciplinary charges against Officer Crane for not reporting the other incidents where use of force was used.
    B. Explain to Officer Crane what the use of force means and inform him that he was careless in not reporting the other incidents.
    C. Tell Officer Crane that he must report all future incidents involving the use of force but take no formal action because he did not actively participate in using force.
    D. Formally request that Officer Crane be given remedial instruction on the use of force and proper reporting procedures but take no other formal action.

24. Captain Clark is the Receiving Room Captain. Transportation Division Officers arrive at her institution and report that there is a new admission inmate who refuses to leave the bus. Captain Clark first talks to the inmate but cannot convince him to leave the bus. She then contacts the institutional doctor and has him standing by. Next, she contacts the Tour Commander; and then under her direction, the Receiving Room Officers pick up the inmate by his arms and legs and carry him into the Receiving Room Clinic. There he is examined by the institutional doctor, and no injuries are found.
    Which of the following BEST describes the use of force employed to deliver the inmate into the Receiving Room?
    _____ use of force.

    A. Permissible
    B. Unnecessary
    C. Excessive
    D. Illegal

25. Correction Officer Simpson writes up a Report of Infraction on inmate Wilson Parker for breaking a departmental telephone and forwards it to Captain Howell for investigation. Captain Howell conducts an investigation, submits a report, and gives the inmate a Notice of Infraction.
If inmate Parker received the Notice of Infraction at 8:00 P.M. Monday, which of the following is the EARLIEST day and time for a hearing to be scheduled?

    A. Tuesday at 8:00 A.M.
    B. Tuesday at 8:00 P.M.
    C. Wednesday at 8:00 A.M.
    D. Wednesday at 8:00 P.M.

Questions 26-27.

DIRECTIONS: Questions 26 and 27 are to be answered on the basis of the following information.

You are the Control Room Captain when Officer Suarez calls to report a discharge of his firearm. He reports that he was running for a bus when a large dog chased him down the street. He further reports that he climbed a tree to avoid the dog and then fired two shots, killing the animal. He could not obtain witnesses since there was no one else in the area.

26. The Captain should inform Officer Suarez that his actions were

    A. *improper,* because there was no imminent danger to human life
    B. *proper,* because he had no other means of escape
    C. *improper,* because a warning shot would have scared the dog away
    D. *proper,* because a vicious dog is a danger to public safety

27. The Captain should then instruct Officer Suarez to

    A. submit a written report within 24 hours
    B. inform the local police precinct immediately
    C. report to the facility for a corrective interview
    D. wait at the scene for an investigator from the Inspector General's office

Question 28.

DIRECTIONS: Question 28 is to be answered on the basis of the following information.

Captain Chang has jotted down the following notes regarding an incident:

Officer involved:	Officer Blair
Incident:	Shield and I.D. lost
Last seen:	11-10 at 3:00 P.M. Charles' Grocery Store 37 East 60th Street Brooklyn, NY Charles Brito, Manager
Last discovered:	4:00 P.M. at Blair's residence 21 East 4th Street Brooklyn, NY

28. Which one of the following paragraphs expresses the above information MOST clearly and accurately?

    A. Officer Blair last saw his shield and ID at 3:00 P.M. on 11-10 while shopping at Charles' Grocery Store, located at 37 E. 60th Street, Brooklyn, N.Y. When he arrived at his residence at 21 E. 4th Street, Brooklyn an hour later, he noticed that his wallet containing his shield and ID was missing. Officer Blair immediately returned to Charles' Grocery Store and was informed by Manager Charles Brito that the shield and ID were not turned in.

B. Officer Charles returned to Blair's Grocery Store, located at 37 E. 60th Street, Brooklyn, N.Y. immediately after he found that his wallet containing his ID and shield in the Grocery Store at 3:00 P.M. on 11-10 and it was missing when he returned home an hour later to 21 E. 41st. Street, Brooklyn, N.Y.

C. On 11-10 at Charles' Grocery Store, Officer Blair last saw his shield. He returned to the grocery at 37 E. 50th Street later, and Manager Charles Brito told him that the shield and ID were not turned in. Blair noticed the wallet containing the shield and ID was missing at his residence at 21 E. 41st St.

D. When Blair returned to his residence at 21 E. 41st. Street, Brooklyn, N.Y., one hour later, he realized that his wallet containing his shield and ID was missing. He returned to the grocery store on 37 E. 60th Street, Brooklyn, N.Y. and was informed by Manager Charles Brito that the shield and ID had not been turned in.

Question 29.

DIRECTIONS: Question 29 is to be answered on the basis of the following information.

Captain Laforge is preparing an Incident Report using the following information:

Incident:	Inmate stabbing
Place of Occurrence:	Cell Block B
Date and Time of Incident:	November 15 at 2:00 P.M.
Inmates Involved:	Goldman and Oliver
Officers Involved:	Amsden and Urbano
Weapons Involved:	Inmates used 4-inch shanks
Disposition:	Goldman and Oliver taken to hospital for multiple lacerations

29. Which one of the following paragraphs expresses the above information MOST clearly and accurately?

A. On November 15 at 2:00 P.M., Officers Amsden and Urbano observed inmates Goldman and Oliver stabbing each other with 4-inch shanks. The Officers immediately separated and restrained the inmates. Both inmates received multiple lacerations and were escorted to the hospital.

B. Officers Amsden and Urbano separated and restrained inmates Goldman and Oliver on November 15 at 4:00 P.M. in Cell Block B. The inmates were stabbing one another with homemade shanks and had to be escorted to the hospital for lacerations.

C. Inmates Goldman and Urbano were escorted to the hospital on November 15 after stabbing each other repeatedly. At 2:00 P.M., Officers Amsden and Urbano separated and restrained the inmates, who received multiple lacerations from 4-inch homemade shanks.

D. On November 15, inmates Goldman and Oliver were fighting with each other. The Officers immediately observed and restrained them. The inmates were escorted to the hospital by Officers Amsden and Urbano at 2:00 P.M. for multiple lacerations sustained during the fight.

30. Captain Crenna responds to Housing Area C with several probe team members in response to a body alarm. *B* Officer Givens, who witnessed the incident, informs him that inmates Adams and Quesada were involved in an altercation and Adams was severely injured. Officer Givens further explains that he returned Quesada to his cell and called the facility physician. The physician reports to the scene and tells Captain Crenna that Adams must be taken to the hospital. Captain Crenna then orders Officer Givens and a probe team member to escort Adams to the hospital.
Concerning the hospital run assignments, Captain Crenna was

    A. *correct* in assigning Givens but incorrect in assigning the probe team member
    B. *correct* in assigning the probe team member but incorrect in assigning Givens
    C. *correct* in both assignments
    D. *incorrect* in both assignments

30.____

KEY (CORRECT ANSWERS)

1.	A	16.	A
2.	C	17.	A
3.	C	18.	D
4.	D	19.	D/C
5.	C	20.	B
6.	C	21.	A
7.	C	22.	C
8.	A	23.	A
9.	D	24.	A
10.	A	25.	B
11.	D	26.	A
12.	B	27.	B
13.	B	28.	A
14.	A	29.	A
15.	A	30.	B

EXAMINATION SECTION
TEST 1

DIRECTIONS: Each question or incomplete statement is followed by several suggested answers or completions. Select the one that BEST answers the question or completes the statement. *PRINT THE LETTER OF THE CORRECT ANSWER IN THE SPACE AT THE RIGHT.*

1. The way the custodial prison maintains stability of life within its walls is

    A. through the granting of privileges
    B. through the exercise of total power by guards
    C. by treating all inmates alike, in order to destroy the influence of inmate leaders
    D. by dealing with leaders chosen by the inmates

2. A prison has been described as a *total institution* in which large groups of persons live together around the clock within a circumscribed space under a tightly scheduled sequence of activities imposed by a central authority. Of the following, the MOST likely consequence of this way of life is that

    A. effective rehabilitation is easily achieved
    B. deviant behavior is unlikely to occur
    C. correctional staff and inmates will develop hostile sterotypes of each other
    D. change in the social relationships in prisons can occur if all signs of a punitive ideology are removed

3. Daily interaction between inmates and guards results in

    A. coercion of inmates by guards
    B. a tendency toward corruption of authority
    C. a desire of guards to act as policemen, and not as work foremen
    D. an increase in aloof behavior between inmates and guards

4. Studies on the Jukes and Kallikaks reflected a certain intellectual atmosphere. The one of the following statements which BEST states this atmosphere is that

    A. crime is interrelated with the social and cultural systems of total society
    B. criminal behavior is a product of the lack of religious upbringing
    C. The individual is fundamentally influenced by his family and friends
    D. criminal behavior is inherited

5. The indeterminate sentence sets

    A. a fixed maximum term and usually a fixed minimum
    B. a fixed maximum term but no minimum
    C. a fixed minimum term but no maximum
    D. neither minimum nor maximum terms

6. The *good time* system of permitting a reduction in the prisoner's sentence of an established number of days for each year of good behavior has been

A. applied in a manner which carefully discriminates between prison-wise and rehabilitation-oriented prisoners
B. accepted by most prisoners as a method of rewarding their good behavior and punishing their misbehavior
C. applied to prisoners who are assigned to routine jobs but not to those who perform such crucial jobs as cooking or maintenance
D. undermined as a rehabilitative tool by the mechanical way in which its awards are granted

7. The percent of all personnel working in local jails and institutions nationally who devote their time to treatment and training is, MOST NEARLY,

   A. 3%   B. 15%   C. 30%   D. 60%

8. To the greatest possible extent, correctional rehabilitation should be a *joint* responsibility of

   A. government and private agencies
   B. police and correction staff
   C. custodial and professional staff
   D. staff and inmates

9. Persons who are released from prison are LEAST likely to commit new crimes if they were originally convicted of which of the following?

   A. Auto theft   B. Robbery
   C. Narcotics offenses   D. Serious crimes of violence

10. Inmates who are referred to as *right guys* or *straights* are

    A. inmates reutinely thrown into very personal contact with staff
    B. at the lowest stratum of the inmate society
    C. likely to be suspected by other inmates if they have private communication with staff
    D. the inmates who most personify the *aggressive convict*

11. Many states are reporting new trends in inmate counseling. The one of the following which indicates *one* of these new trends is the

    A. use of professionals to direct and supervise sub-professionals who are performing the direct treatment task
    B. elimination of individual counseling and substitution of orientation interviews in its place
    C. movement of specialists out of dormitories and cell blocks and into special counseling rooms
    D. use of traditional psychotherapeutic efforts as the only counseling procedure

12. In recent years, corrections has seen the development of new operating methods designed to create a more *collaborative* institution which is less isolated from the community physically and in terms of values. Which of the following is LEAST likely to be part of this trend toward *collaborative* institutions?

    A. Group counseling involving institutional employees and groups of inmates
    B. Inmate involvement in institution management groups

C. Use of selected inmates to help guard and control other inmates
D. Institutional construction that emphasizes small rooms housing one inmate each

13. Changing corrections into a system with significantly increased power to reduce recidivism and prevent recruitment into criminal careers will require, above all else, many tasks to be done.
Of the following, the MOST reasonable inference which can be drawn from this statement is that

   A. most personnel in corrections are custody-oriented
   B. the main ingredient for changing people is other people
   C. training of correctional personnel has been uniformly inadequate
   D. the barriers imposed by the criminal label make rehabilitation difficult to achieve

14. The MOST promising correctional strategy today is

   A. probation   B. institutionalization
   C. parole   D. halfway programs

15. One of the MOST critical problems in developing new community-based programs has been the

   A. antagonism of staff to such programs
   B. lack of acceptance of such programs by the community
   C. conflict between staff and inmates over methods of implementing such programs
   D. negative attitude of inmates toward such programs

Questions 16 - 25.

DIRECTIONS: Each of Question 16 through 25 consists of two statements. Choose answer
   A. if both statements are correct
   B. if neither statement is correct
   C. if statement I only is correct but not statement II
   D. if statement II only is correct but not statement I

16. I. A complaint is an allegation of an improper or unlawful act of omission which relates to the business of the department.
    II. A member of the department who is not a superior officer may not make a complaint of dereliction of duty against another member of the department.

17. I. Changes or additions to the rules and regulations shall be promulgated by a special order of the department, and any change or addition shall be stated in full therein.
    II. Employees of the central office of the department shall, in the performance of their duties, be subject to the direction and control of the heads of the divisions to which they are assigned

18. I. Whenever an inmate, upon first admission to an institution, or return from outside the institution, refuses to be fingerprinted, photographed or submit to a clothing and body search for contraband, reasonable force shall be used immediately to compel him to do so.
    II. Except as required by his official duties, a member of the department shall not correspond with prisoners or former prisoners.

19. I. When an inmate is taken for treatment to any clinic which is accessible to the general public, he shall be handcuffed during the course of treatment, except when a physician or other competent person administering treatment requests that the handcuffs be removed.
    II. All matters concerning the welfare of an employee, which requires the attention of the central office, must be submitted in writing through the head of the institution.

20. I. Except when required as a part of their prescribed duties, employees assigned to the various institutions of the department will not telephone or visit central office without the express permission or direction of the respective heads of institutions.
    II. No superseding commitment will be accepted by a member of the department in the case of an inmate committed to serve a sentence in an institution of the department.

21. I. Line-ups for the purpose of identification of any inmate or inmates shall be conducted whenever requested in writing by the Police Department.
    II. Whenever a member of the department is directed by the medical director to consult his personal physician for the treatment of a condition which impairs his efficiency as a member of the department, he shall take prompt action to obtain such treatment. Failure to do so shall be deemed neglect of duty.

22. I. A member of the department shall have recorded with the head of the institution or division his correct residence, phone number, and social status, and shall promptly report any change in the foregoing.
    II. It shall be the duty of a member of the department charged with the custody of inmates at any time or place, to make an oral report of any conduct against good order and descipline by an iamate.

23. I. Members of the department shall not be granted permission to peruse their personal history folder when matters of a derogatory nature are to be filed therein.
    II. Whenever an order is received from the court for the discharge of an inmate, or his sentence expires, while said inmate is being held in a court detention pen, he shall be transferred to an institution for discharge.

24. I. No member of the department shall engage in any business or transaction or shall have a financial or other private interest, direct or indirect, which is in conflict with the proper discharge of his official duties.
    II. Under special circumstances, a correction officer may make cell, tier, floor or dormitory assignments of inmates, or change such assignments.

25. I. When it is deemed necessary at any time to search the person of any employee on duty, such search shall be made by a captain or other superior officer.
    II. Mechanical means of physical restraint other than handcuffs shall be used only when necessary in transporting prisoners, or under medical advice when necessary to prevent injury to the prisoner or to others.

KEY (CORRECT ANSWERS)

1. A
2. C
3. B
4. D
5. D

6. D
7. A
8. D
9. D
10. C

11. A
12. C
13. B
14. A
15. B

16. C
17. D
18. D
19. A
20. A

21. D
22. C
23. B
24. C
25. A

———

TEST 2

DIRECTIONS: Each question or incomplete statement is followed by several suggested answers or completions. Select the one that BEST answers the question or completes the statement. *PRINT THE LETTER OF THE CORRECT ANSWER IN THE SPACE AT THE RIGHT.*

1. The degree of security needed for the confinement of an inmate depends upon the   1.___

   A. calibre of personnel assigned to the institution
   B. personality and background of the inmate
   C. type of programs available in the institution
   D. type of security facilities within the institution

2. The one of the following which is an example of partial institutional custody is   2.___

   A. civil commitment   B. conditional release
   C. probation   D. work release

3. With regard to the custodial aspect of the criminal treatment system, which of the following is recommended?   3.___

   A. Administration of probation by the judiciary, and administration of incarceration and parole by the executive branch
   B. Greater emphasis on the difference between incarceration and the field services (probation and parole)
   C. Placing few offenders in the community as soon as possible in order to reduce the risk that they will commit new crimes
   D. Development of a single overall concept of custody which eliminates the arbitrary lines between probation, incarceration and parole

4. In the context of the criminal treatment system, the term *sanction* comprises formal community condemnation, deprivation of rights and privileges, and forfeiture of property for a purpose other than restitution or reparation, imposed and carried out by the state as a direct consequence of conduct that violates a prohibition promulgated by the state. Which of the following is NOT a sanction in the context of the criminal treatment system?   4.___

   A. Conditional discharge   B. Conviction
   C. Incarceration   D. Field supervision

5. According to *Attica: The Official Report of the New York State Special Commission on Attica,* when negotiations between inmates and officials failed in the 1971 uprising in Attica,   5.___

   A. inmates advised state officials that they expected guns to be used to retake the institution but that such a move would prove futile since inmates had full access to the Attica armory
   B. state officials assured inmates that no force would be used in retaking the institution until after the Governor had met with the inmate committee
   C. state officials did not advise inmates that they intended to retake the institution with guns nor did they make adequate arrangements for the medical care of severe casualties
   D. state officials were told by the Governor that, if any of the hostages were injured or killed, guns should be used in storming the prison

6. In the Attica report, the Commission states that one out of every _____ residents of New York City was a victim of crime in 1971.
   Which one of the following, when inserted in the blank space, makes the statement CORRECT?

   A. four
   B. fifteen
   C. thirty-seven
   D. seventy-five

7. According to a recent issue of the American Journal of Correction, medical experimentation in correctional institutions has become a major focus of attention. The article shows how the Connecticut Department of Corrections has dealt with the subject of medical research performed on inmates.
   Which of the following is a feature of Connecticut's program?

   A. A fee schedule has been established which guarantees direct payment to inmate volunteers
   B. All inmates are equally eligible to participate in the program
   C. An inmate volunteer receives reasonable assurance that if he cooperates freely in the program he will receive additional *good time*
   D. Medical research programs enjoy the highest priority higher, for example, than vocational training programs

8. Inmate disorders must be dealt with instantly and decisively. Ringleaders in a disturbance must be

   A. punished immediately as an example to the other inmates
   B. identified immediately and then isolated
   C. punished by being placed in solitary confinement
   D. turned over to a psychologist or other clinician for treatment if they have been diagnosed as psychopathic

9. The Correction Law empowers the Department of Correction to establish a furlough program for certain sentenced inmates.
   For an inmate to be eligible for consideration for this program, he must have served AT LEAST _____ months.

   A. two   B. four   C. six   D. nine

Questions 10 - 13.

DIRECTIONS: Questions 10 through 13 are to be answered SOLELY on the basis of the following passage.

Traditional correctional institutions do not change or redirect the behavior of many of their inmates. Few of these establishments are equipped with adequate resources to treat the social and psychological handicaps of their wards. Too often, far removed ideolologically from the world to which its charges must return, the institution often compounds the problems its corrective mechanisms are intended to cure. Training school academic programs, for example, range from poor to totally inadequate and usually reinforce negative feelings toward future learning experiences. Vocational programs are frequently designed to benefit the institution without regard to the inmate, and the usual low-key common denominator treatment program scarcely begins to meet the needs of many offenders.

Most correctional institutions must mobilize their limited resources in time and talent for purposes other than the ever-present concern about runaways or escapes. No one could quarrel rationally with the need to safeguard the community and control the behavior of people who may be of danger to themselves or others. It is ridiculous and tragic, however, that an overstated security approach is still the rule for the bulk of our correctional population.

10. The passage states that inmates of traditional correctional institutions are LIKELY to

    A. develop belief in radical political ideologies
    B. experience conditions that produce no betterment
    C. give major attention to devising plans of escape
    D. desire vocational training unrelated to their individual potential

11. The passage indicates that traditional training school academic programs lead inmates to

    A. adjust to the institutional setting
    B. avoid later formal learning
    C. develop respect for the values of education
    D. request more practical, vocational training

12. The passage indicates that most traditional correctional institutions, because of their ideological distance from the realities of the outside world, are MOST LIKELY to

    A. ignore the safety of the outside community
    B. favor a minority of the inmate population
    C. lack properly motivated staff
    D. increase the problems of inmates

13. The passage states that the strong custodial function in most correctional institutions is MOST LIKELY to be

    A. accorded excessive emphasis
    B. aimed at incorrigible inmates only
    C. necessary to redirect inmate behavior
    D. resented by the outside community

Questions 14 - 16.

DIRECTIONS: Questions 14 through 16 are to be answered SOLELY on the basis of the following passage.

The most widely accepted argument in favor of the death penalty is that the threat of its infliction deters people from committing capital offenses. Of course, since human behavior can be influenced through fear, and since man tends to fear death, it is possible to use capital punishment as a deterrent. But the real question is whether individuals think of the death penalty before they act, and whether they are thereby deterred from committing crimes. If for the moment we assume that the death penalty does this to some extent, we must also grant that certain human traits limit its effectiveness as a deterrent. Man tends to be a creature of habit and emotion, and when his is handicapped by poverty, ignorance, and malnutrition, as criminals often are, he becomes notoriously shortsighted. Many violators of the law give little thought to the possibility of detection and apprehension, and often they do not even consider the penalty. Moreover, it appears that most people do not regulate their lives in terms of the pleasure and pain that may result from their acts.

Human nature is very complex. A criminal may fear punishment, but he may fear the anger and contempt of his companions or his family even more, and the fear of economic insecurity or exclusion from the group whose respect he cherishes may drive him to commit the most daring crimes. Besides, fear is not the only emotion that motivates man. Love, loyalty, ambition, greed, lust, anger, and resentment may steel him to face even death in the perpetration of crime, and impel him to devise the most ingenious methods to get what he wants and to avoid detection.

If the death penalty were surely, quickly, uniformly, publicly, and painfully inflicted, it undoubtedly would prevent many capital offenses that are being committed by those who do consider the punishment that they may receive for their crimes. But this is precisely the point. Certainly, the way in which the death penalty has been administered in the United States is not fitted to produce this result.

14. Of the following, the MOST appropriate title for the above passage is 14.____

    A. Capital Offenses in the United States
    B. The Death Penalty as a Deterrent
    C. Human Nature and Fear
    D. Emotion as a Cause of Crime

15. The above passage implies that the death penalty, as it has been administered in the United States, 15.____

    A. was too prompt and uniform to be effective
    B. deterred many criminals who considered the possible consequences of their actions
    C. prevented crimes primarily among habitual criminals
    D. failed to prevent the commission of many capital offenses

16. According to the above passage, many violators of the law are 16.____

    A. intensely concerned with the pleasure or pain that may result from their acts
    B. influenced primarily by economic factors
    C. not influenced by the opinions of their family or friends
    D. not seriously concerned with the possibility of apprehension

Questions 17 - 20.

DIRECTIONS: Questions 17 through 20 are to be answered SOLELY on the basis of the following passage:

The loss of control over the use of a drug — called addiction where there is both physical and psychological dependence, and habituation where there is psychological dependence without physical dependence — is, regardless of the particular drug involved, a disease. Both chronic alcoholism and narcotics addiction are usually recognized as diseases.

It is inappropriate to invoke the criminal process against persons who have lost control over the use of dangerous drugs solely because these persons are drug users. Once a person has lost control over his use of drugs, the existence of offenses such as drug use or simple possession will not deter his use. Having lost control, he cannot choose to conform his conduct to the requirements of the law by refraining from use. He is non-deterrable.

Admittedly, there may be times before a person loses control over his use of drugs when he did have a choice of whether to use or not to use, or to stop using. Because of this, punishing him for use or simple possession would not offend the principle that to be punishable conduct must be a result of free choice.

17. Of the following, the MOST suitable title for the above passage is

    A. Drug Addiction
    B. Drug Abuse and Punishment
    C. Habituation and the Criminal Process
    D. Preventing Drug Related Crime

18. According to the above passage, addiction and habituation are

    A. *identical* in meaning because both are diseases related to drug use
    B. *identical* in meaning because both involve dependence on drugs
    C. *similar* to the extent that both involve physical dependence on a drug
    D. *similar* to the extent that both involve psychological dependence on a drug

19. According to the above passage, punishing drug abusers would be justifiable ONLY if their behavior were

    A. elective
    B. non-deterrable
    C. chronic
    D. dangerous

20. According to the above passage, punishing a person for simple possession of drugs is

    A. appropriate under certain circumstances
    B. inappropriate because the person could not have acted otherwise
    C. necessary for the protection of society
    D. unfair because it penalizes past conduct

Questions 21 - 25.

DIRECTIONS: Questions 21 through 25 are to be answered SOLELY on the basis of the following notes and charts.

NOTES

Assume that correctional facilities in the town of Libertyville have recorded the number of individual inmate escape attempts, both successful and unsuccessful, for the year. This information is presented in Chart I.

Assume also that records were kept on the amount of time which elapsed between successful escapes by inmates and their recapture. This information is presented in Chart II.

ESCAPE ATTEMPTS BY INDIVIDUAL INMATES AT LIBERTYVILLE'S CORRECTIONAL FACILITIES, BY INMATE AGE GROUP

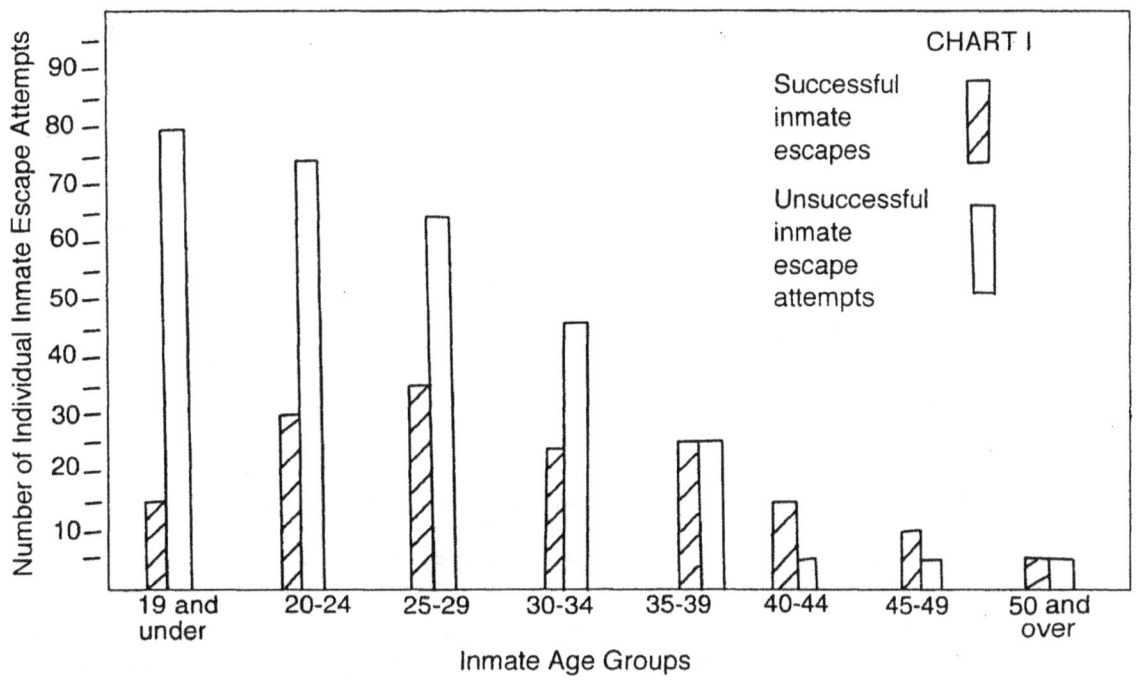

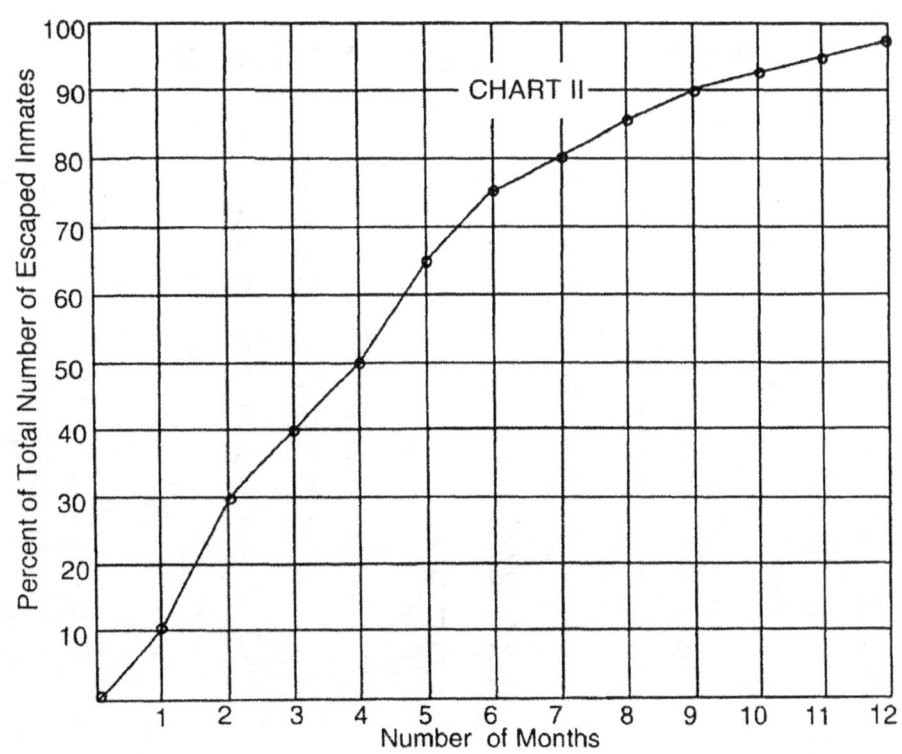

21. Which of the following age groups shows a GREATER total number of escape attempts than the next youngest age group?

    A. 20-24   B. 25-29   C. 30-34   D. 35-39

22. Which of the following MOST NEARLY indicates the number of inmates who were recaptured within nine months of their escape?

    A. 90   B. 130   C. 145   D. 160

23. Based on the total number of escape attempts for each of the following age groups, which group had the HIGHEST percentage of successful escapes?

    A. 19 and under   B. 25-29
    C. 35-39   D. 45-49

24. An inmate who attempted to escape had GREATER than a 50% chance of

    A. *succeeding* if he was in the 25-29 group
    B. *failing* if he was in the 50 and over group
    C. *succeeding* if he was in the 40-44 group
    D. *failing* if he was in the 45-49 group

25. Which of the following statements concerning escaped inmates is NOT correct?

    A. Most of the inmates who escaped were under 30 years of age.
    B. One third of the escaped inmates were recaptured withing three months.
    C. Less than 10 per cent of the inmates who escaped were over 45 years of age.
    D. Seventy per cent of the escaped inmates were recaptured within six months.

KEY (CORRECT ANSWERS)

1. B		11. B	
2. D		12. D	
3. D		13. A	
4. A		14. B	
5. C		15. D	
6. B		16. D	
7. A		17. B	
8. B		18. D	
9. C		19. A	
10. B		20. A	

21. A
22. C
23. D
24. C
25. A

READING COMPREHENSION
UNDERSTANDING AND INTERPRETING WRITTEN MATERIAL
EXAMINATION SECTION
TEST 1

DIRECTIONS: Each question or incomplete statement is followed by several suggested answers or completions. Select the one that BEST answers the question or completes the statement. *PRINT THE LETTER OF THE CORRECT ANSWER IN THE SPACE AT THE RIGHT.*

Questions 1-4.

DIRECTIONS: Questions 1 through 4 are to be answered SOLELY on the basis of the following passage.

Morally, there is no basis for the assertion that the commission of a social offense allows society to strip a human being of all his rights except those which, through some sort of *natural law* concept, he needs to survive. Rather, society is justified in punishing offenders only to the extent that it needs to protect itself; excessive retribution is *immoral.* Thus, unless society can demonstrate that a specific deprivation is necessary to its self-preservation, or to its reassertion of authority over the individual offender, it should not be entitled to enforce the deprivation. To place the burden on the prisoner to demonstrate that he should not be deprived of a particular right appears to be unfair and unjustified for two reasons: (1) the resources and skills are unequally distributed in society's favor, and (2) the concept of *proportionality* as a rudimentary value is rejected by such an approach, which even theories of retribution and vengeance do not support.

Pragmatically, too, prisoners should be viewed and treated as human beings. Ninety-five percent of all those incarcerated in prisons are returned to the free world. It violates common sense to expect a man who has been treated at best as a cipher while in prison to be enamored of a society which has not only enchained him but also has increased his torment while he is confined. When he is released, his action is likely to be antisocial rather than social. Additionally, the imposition of excessive suffering on offenders permeates society's attitudes toward others in its midst. Just as we are now realizing that violence abroad erodes the barriers against domestic violence, official hostility toward some human beings tends to add an aura of authority to hostility toward and among others. Disinclination to cherish humanity at one point in society leads to total abdication of humanity at another.

1. In the above passage, it is pointed out that

    A. it is a practical approach to treatment to take away all but the basic rights of a prisoner
    B. it is proper to remove an inmate's rights within a system of rewards and punishments
    C. incarceration should not be used for revenge against one who has offended society
    D. the inmate ought to play a primary role in determining treatment methods

1.____

2. According to the above passage,
   A. inmates who are treated badly are apt to resort to antisocial behavior when they are returned to society
   B. there is a tendency among inmates to join organizations dedicated to achieving civil rights for the victims of society
   C. society generally sees all inmates as being equal, despite inconsistent observation of prisoners' rights
   D. recidivism is a serious problem for the majority of prisoners who are released on parole

3. While criticizing the kind of treatment prisoners receive in our institutions, the above passage implies that
   A. the mistreatment of prisoners is an outcome of society's benign attitude toward the law-abiding citizen
   B. cruelty begets cruelty, and that humane treatment will make better citizens of those entrusted to our care
   C. when violence in this country spreads, it increases all over the world
   D. an aura of authority has replaced official hostility in correctional institutions

4. According to the above passage, penal authorities are justified in depriving prisoners of rights
   A. in order to satisfy society's desire for retribution against criminal offenders
   B. until prisoners can demonstrate that particular deprivations are unjustified
   C. whenever the preservation of order within the institution will be facilitated
   D. only when it is necessary to protect society or maintain control over the inmate

Questions 5-8.

DIRECTIONS: Questions 5 through 8 are to be answered SOLELY on the basis of the following excerpt from a memo circulated by a correction official for comments.

Some bargaining is virtually inevitable between those charged with enforcing institutional regulations and inmates who are supposed to be regulated for the simple reason that administrators rarely have sufficient resources to gain complete conformity to all the rules. An insufficient number of guards and cells and inadequately threatening punishments create an environment in which institutional rules are often ignored. At the same time, the attempt to impose order upon individuals deprived of normal amenities, who often lack opportunities for adequate recreation or privacy, tends to produce violent disorder. Toleration by correctional administrators and officers of constant violation of institutional rules results even if confined to a level considered by administrators to be neither very visible nor very serious. Recurring contact between guards and inmates creates ample opportunity for an ongoing informal bargaining.

Although some form of bargaining has long been recognized as a basic process of control within prisons and other total institutions, it is not clear whether a system of control which relies on private, particularized bargains between staff and inmates contributes to the goals of rehabilitation, order, or protection from arbitrary punishment. In fact, within the daily bargaining process, often the only goal sought to be achieved by the institution is short term surface order - the semblance that everything is running smoothly with no official (or public) cause for alarm.

5. According to the above passage, all of the following conditions contribute to the existence of bargaining EXCEPT

   A. difficulty in getting inmates to conform to the rules
   B. the scarcity of guards and cells
   C. the scarcity of administrators
   D. the pressures of confinement brought on by prison conditions

6. According to the above passage, which one of the following is MOST likely to create a climate for bargaining between inmates and staff?

   A. Lack of privacy
   B. Lack of opportunities for recreation
   C. Frequent interaction between guards and inmates
   D. Desires of guards to avoid enforcement of rules

7. The author IMPLIES that the practice of bargaining in institutions is a process which

   A. is not generally recognized outside institutions
   B. eliminates violent disorders among inmates
   C. should be utilized more frequently
   D. has been in existence for a long time

8. According to the above passage, which one of the following statements concerning bargaining is MOST NEARLY correct?
   It

   A. contributes to the goals of the institution because it protects inmates from arbitrary punishment
   B. impedes rehabilitation since it weakens respect for correctional personnel
   C. is a method of reducing the visibility of inmate rule violations
   D. detracts from the smooth operation of the institution because it is an ineffective system of control

Questions 9-12.

DIRECTIONS: Questions 9 through 12 are to be answered on the basis of the following portion of a report submitted by a Tour Commander to the appropriate superior about an unusual occurrence in a Detention Dormitory. The portion of the report consists of 21 numbered sentences, some of which may or may not follow the principles of good report writing.

1. Following is a report of an altercation between inmate John Doe, #441-77-9375, and inmate Henry Green, #441-77-1656.
2. At approximately 6:15 A.M. on June 15, an alarm was received in the Control Room from Officer Arthur Kinney #6214 of the 7M dormitory (General Population).
3. Captain Ronald Doaks #529 and Officer Henry James #7654 responded immediately to determine the cause of the alarm.
4. Captain Doaks reports that, upon arrival, he observed inmate John Doe, #441-77-9375, on the officer's bridge bleeding from the mouth.

5. The institutional doctor also found a stab wound in the left arm.
6. The Captain observed inmate Henry Green, #441-77-1656, locked behind the *B* gate, heard him shouting obscenities and threatening further harm to Officer Kinney.
7. He noticed a large group of inmates standing quietly in the day room.
8. Officer Kinney, who was on post alone, reports he heard a commotion in the rear of the dormitory while sitting at his desk reading the Departmental Rules and Regulations.
9. He could not see what was going on because of a large crowd of inmates.
10. He reports that inmate Doe suddenly broke through the crowd screaming toward the *B* gate.
11. Doe was being pursued by inmate Green.
12. Officer Kinney states that he sounded the alarm and allowed inmate Doe onto the bridge.
13. Since inmate Doe was bleeding from the mouth, Captain Doaks ordered Officer James to escort him to the clinic for immediate examination and treatment by Dr. James White, who subsequently suspected a broken jaw and also discovered a puncture wound in the left bicep.
14. Dr. White ordered his transfer to Harmony Hospital for x-ray of the jaw.
15. Inmate Green, who appeared free of injury, stated to the Captain that he and Doe argued over the telephone, agreed to *take it to the back* and fight.
16. Green would make no further statements.
17. No other inmate in the dormitory would admit seeing anything.
18. Inmate Green received an infraction and was transferred to the Administrative Area pending further investigation.
19. The housing area was then restored to order and normal operations were resumed.
20. Prior to his transfer to the hospital, inmate Doe stated to the Captain that he was assaulted by inmate Green for no apparent reason.
21. He was told that he has an infraction and, upon return from the hospital, would be transferred to another housing unit pending investigation.

9. Of the following, which sentence is MOST likely to be out of sequence?

    A. 2   B. 5   C. 8   D. 14

10. Of the following, which sentence indicates the GREATEST need for further clarification by the Tour Commander submitting the report?

    A. 4   B. 6   C. 9   D. 17

11. Which one of the following sentences BEST indicates the possibility of potential danger remaining in 7M because of the omission of a necessary procedure?

    A. 3   B. 14   C. 19   D. 21

12. Which one of the following sentences is LEAST significant to the report?

    A. 4   B. 7   C. 11   D. 17

Questions 13-16.

DIRECTIONS: Questions 13 through 16 are to be answered SOLELY on the basis of the following fictitious directive which may or may not conform with actual policy and procedure of the Department of Correction.

<u>DIRECTIVE NO. 15</u>   Dated March 1

Guidelines for Members of the Department when accepting packages for inmates being held in custody of the City Department of Correction.

1. <u>Receipt and Distribution of Packages</u>

All packages delivered by the postal authorities must bear the name and address of the sender. All packages regardless of whether received through the mail or delivered by an individual, during visiting hours only, must be in a cardboard box with tape sealing same so as to prevent access to contents of package. When package is received by mail, it is to be placed in the mailroom of the institution concerned by the staff member assigned to picking up the mail. In addition, the officer delivering the package to mailroom officer will get a receipt for all packages. The mailroom officer shall prepare Form P-103 in duplicate, which will document the time and description of all packages received, including the contents thereof, as well as the name and address of the sender. Packages must be weighed and weight noted on Form P-103, as no inmate is to receive an excess of 40 lbs. in packages in a six-month period. Log is to be maintained of all packages received, distributed, and returned to sender, including the weights for packages received and accepted. When a package is brought to the institution by an individual, during visiting hours only, it is to bear the name and address of person who is responsible for articles in package, who must be the individual who is delivering the package. Form P-103 is to remain with package until signed by inmate, since original of Form P-103 is the institutional record and substantiation that inmate has received his/her package.

As soon as practicable, all packages are to be searched for contraband and appropriate actions taken. If package is determined to be acceptable, inmate concerned shall be called to mailroom and shall inspect package, sign Form P-103 in duplicate, receive the duplicate copy of Form P-103, and remove package to his/her respective cell. If the inmate is not available when called for, package is to be secured in a locked closet or room and key so secured that only authorized personnel have access to area. If mailroom officer is not on duty when package is brought to institution by an individual, officer assigned to visits is to be responsible for handling and safekeeping of package according to this directive.

2. <u>Acceptability of Articles</u>

Suitable clothing may be accepted in all packages according to guidelines determined by the head of each institution. However, the institutional clothing card must be referred to so excess clothing is not accumulated and in order to maintain a strict control over same. Food and snacks are also acceptable items - no alcoholic beverages, nor glass containers are to be accepted. Sharp instruments are not to be accepted nor any item that may create a hazard or breach of security within the institution. Shaving utensils are to be distributed by the institution and are not to be accepted in packages. Under no circumstances is money or jewelry to be accepted in packages. No medications are to be accepted when included in packages or otherwise, but, when the occasion arises, inmate must be instructed that all medications are dispensed through the medical staff assigned to that institution. Prescription eyeglasses can be accepted, but must be inspected and approved by the institutional physician before distribution to inmate. Under no circumstances are cigarettes to be accepted in packages since they must be purchased through each institutional commissary.

3. <u>Appropriate Areas For Use</u>

Food received in packages cannot be removed from the housing area. Under no circumstances should an inmate bring food to the main dining room as a substitution or addition to the departmental menu. Books and magazines cannot be removed from the housing areas. Under no condition should any inmate's library privileges be cancelled or modified because he has received publications from another source. All eatable items are to be consumed either in the inmate's cell or the day room of the housing area he/she is assigned to. Any inmate who has received special permission to receive an item of clothing for sporting or athletic purposes may use said clothing only in the gymnasium of the institution, said clothing is to remain in the gymnasium, and a system for laundering determined and controlled by the Recreation Director.

4. A. <u>Safeguarding Undelivered Packages</u>

All undelivered packages will be secured in a locked closet of the mailroom or the mailroom itself. The mailroom shall be secured whenever a custodial member is not in attendance. The key to the mailroom must be secured so that only authorized personnel have access to the area. The schedule for the use of the mailroom must be arranged to create accountability for the safekeeping of all packages received for any inmate of the Department. Every effort must be made to deliver packages to inmates as soon as is practicable. However, if after ten days, the package is not delivered, it must be returned to the sender with an appropriate notation - under no condition may a package remain undelivered for more than ten days.

B. <u>Ensuring that Unacceptable Packages or Unacceptable Items Are Returned to Sender</u>

All unacceptable packages or unacceptable items must be returned to sender immediately upon being determined unacceptable. The inmate must be notified of any article or package that is being returned, but not necessarily before the items have been mailed. Upon mailing any unacceptable items to the sender, no items shall be returned which would violate postal regulations. Whenever articles are returned to sender, a return receipt must be requested of the postal authorities.

5. Procedure for the Prosecution of Persons Violating the Postal Regulations or Prison Contraband Law

Whenever serious contraband is found in a package received by mail at an institution of the Department, the supervisor investigating the incident will notify the postal authorities, cooperating with them whenever possible. The officer who actually finds contraband must be witness to any criminal proceedings that would follow. If contraband is delivered to the institution by an individual, the Police Department shall be notified, and the supervisor investigating said incident will cooperate fully with the Police Department. The officer who actually finds contraband will be a witness if any criminal proceeding is instituted. All serious contraband will be turned over to the Police Department and a voucher received for same. The supervisor will conduct a complete investigation of all discoveries of serious contraband received in packages, and submit proper reports to the head of the institution.

6. System of Appeals for Those Inmates Denied Packages or Contents Thereof

Any inmate who has been denied a package or any article included in a package and has been informed of this by the mailroom officer may request Form P-111, fill out same, and return it to the mailroom officer. This is a form of appeal and must be forwarded to the A/D/W-A/D/S in charge of security, who will investigate the complaint and render a decision on the complaint. The inmate must be interviewed by the A/D/W or A/D/S or a designated person, who will inform him/her of the reason for the denial, and the security Deputy's decision. If the inmate tells the security Deputy he/she wishes to appeal, a copy of the decision and Form P-111 will be forwarded to the D/S or D/W for a final decision. If no appeal is requested after the interview and rendering of the A/D/W-A/D/S - decision, or at the conclusion or final decision by the D/W - D/S, Form P-111 and the written copy of the decision will be filed in the inmate's folder.

7. Procedure for Receiving Special Permission for Items or Articles Not Generally Allowed the Institutional Population, Before the Package is Received

An inmate wishing to receive a specific item who has a legitimate need, may write to the head of the institution stating the need, if the item is not generally allowed in the institution. When determined necessary by the head of the institution, the inmate will be asked to submit a professional opinion substantiating the need. The request and substantiation will be submitted to a review board and their determination will be forwarded to the head of the institution for his/her approval. Only upon receipt of the approval of the head of the institution will special permission be given for possession of a specific item or article.

13. According to the above directive, which one of the following is NOT a condition for receiving a package in an institution of the Department?   13.____

    A. All packages must be weighed and logged in an effort to control the aggregate weight of packages received by each inmate at an institution.
    B. Packages may be brought to the institution by individuals during visiting hours only.
    C. If a package has been determined acceptable by a custodial officer, the inmate shall inspect the package, sign for it, and take possession of it.
    D. The log maintained by the mailroom officer is the institutional substantiation that the inmate has received the package.

14. According to the above directive, which one of the following is NOT a valid statement regarding acceptability of items in packages received for inmates in institutions of the Department?   14.____

    A. Money, jewelry, and medications are not to be accepted in packages.
    B. Prescription eyeglasses can be accepted by the institution before they are approved and inspected by the institutional physician.
    C. Shaving utensils which meet the guidelines established by the head of the institution may be acceptable when received in packages.
    D. The institutional clothing card must be consulted when determining whether to accept clothing in packages.

15. According to the above directive, which one of the following statements is NOT valid concerning actions to be taken when postal regulations or prison contraband laws are violated while sending or delivering packages to an institution?

   A. The officer who discovers serious contraband in a package, whether delivered to an institution by an individual or mailed through the postal authorities, is a witness as far as the Department is concerned.
   B. The supervisor responsible for investigating the discovery of serious contraband in a package brought to the institution by a visitor must notify the Director of Operations immediately.
   C. All serious contraband must be turned over to the Police Department and vouchered, whether or not criminal proceedings are instituted.
   D. The supervisor responsible for investigating the discovery of serious contraband in a package brought to the institution must submit his/her report to the head of the institution.

16. According to the above directive, which one of the following is a VALID statement concerning an application for special permission to receive an article not generally allowed in an institution?

   A. A professional opinion substantiating the need for the item requested must accompany the application for special permission to receive said item.
   B. A review board, upon receipt of the application and professional opinion substantiating the need for the item, will render a final decision.
   C. An inmate wishing to receive a special item, for any reason, may write to the head of the institution.
   D. The head of the institution may approve, for use by a specific inmate, a specific item or article which is not generally permitted in the institution.

Questions 17-19.

DIRECTIONS: Questions 17 through 19 are to be answered SOLELY on the basis of the following passage.

In collaboration with operating staff and research social scientists, the statistician should be responsible for installing standard measures of achievement in the information system. Reliability of measurements used by the system should be reviewed periodically. This review will be especially important if predictive devices are installed to facilitate comparison of expectations with observed outcomes.

This evaluation technique is well suited to standardized use by information systems. A standard base expectancy table is established to predict results of programs for groups, using criteria such as recidivism or completion of training. Such a device will be capable of assigning any given subject to a class of like subjects grouped by the statistical weighting of aggregated characteristics. Group expectancy for success or failure as determined by recidivism or other criteria can be expressed in percentiles.

Use of base expectancies for comparison with observed outcomes may be thought of as a *soft* method of evaluation. But its economy, in comparison with the classical control group procedure, is considerable. It eliminates the need for routine management of research controls over extended periods. Comparison of predicted with observed outcome affords a rough estimate of program effectiveness. For example, if the average expected recidivism of a group of offenders exposed to a behavior modification program is 50 percent, but the observed outcome is 25 percent, a *prima facie* indication of program effectiveness is established.

Such an indication affords the administrator some assurance that a program seriously subjected to a controlled evaluation with similar results is continuing to be effective. It may also provide a rough estimate of the value of a program that has not been evaluated under the control group method. This kind of evaluation has many limitations. A predictive device is valid only to the extent that the group observed is typical of the population used as the basis for the standard. A second objection to the use of predictive devices in evaluation rests on the tendency of the predictive bases to deteriorate. The applicability of a prediction under circumstances prevailing in year one will not necessarily be the same circumstance prevailing in year ten. Accordingly, it is good practice to audit the accuracy of the predictive device at least every five years to assure that the circumstances are the same. A final objection is that predictive devices can be used only for global indications of program effectiveness.

17. Of the following, the KEY element in the traditional approach to program evaluation that would NOT be used in the approach described in the passage is

   A. computers
   B. recidivism rates
   C. standard populations
   D. control groups

18. Of the following, the MOST appropriate title for the above passage is

   A. HOW TO PREDICT THE RESULTS OF PROGRAM EVALUATIONS
   B. A *SOFT* METHOD OF PROGRAM EVALUATION
   C. THE USE OF PREDICTIVE DEVICES IN PROGRAM EVALUATION
   D. COOPERATION BETWEEN THE STATISTICIAN AND OPERATING STAFF

19. All of the following statements describe limitations of using predictive devices to evaluate programs for the first time EXCEPT:

   A. The group under study must be typical of the group used to develop the predictive device.
   B. Predictive devices can be used only for global indications of program effectiveness.
   C. Predictive devices are more expensive to use than classical control group procedure.
   D. The circumstances prevailing in the year of the study must be the same as in the year the predictive device was developed.

Questions 20-25.

DIRECTIONS: Questions 20 through 25 are to be answered SOLELY on the basis of the following passage.

At present, in State X, whole classes of offenders are retained at unnecessarily close and expensive levels of confinement and supervision because the various decision-makers involved are required to make predictions about the future behavior of offenders which cannot, given the present state of social science, be made accurately. Items such as social and psychological history, changes in attitude, estimates of institutional progress, and anticipation of constructive responses to parole supervision are particularly useless as evaluative criteria in the disposition of offenders because such subjective evaluations are rooted in the attitudes of the appraiser and in the constructive tendencies of bureaucracies.

The result has been that while probation is used extensively (chiefly because institutions are overcrowded) parole board policy has become increasingly cautious and expensive. Although the initial choice between probation and commitment to prison is often arbitrary, the offender thus committed tends to remain incarcerated for long periods. Because the absence of a clear, positive, and legislatively authorized parole policy is a fundamental obstacle to the reallocation of funds, and because the decision problems involved are repeated at each level of the correctional system, the Committee on Criminal Penalties examined the state parole policy. It then presented model legislation which required that offenders committed to prison be automatically released to parole at expiration of the statutory minimum parole-eligible period (often only six months under present law), unless their individual histories contained substantial evidence of past serious violence. The resulting institutional savings were to be devoted chiefly to improving parole services and subsidies for improvements in local law enforcement agencies.

The basic intent of the legislation was to substitute clearly defined statutory ineligibility for release criteria based on the past actions of offenders for the present administratively defined eligibility criteria that necessarily rely on predictive data of highly questionable validity. By requiring the early release of any offender not shown to be clearly ineligible, the act would essentially remove responsibility for the disposition of doubtful cases from the parole authorities and return it to the courts.

20. Of the following, the MOST suitable title for the above passage is

    A. THE REASONS FOR GRANTING PAROLE
    B. THE COMMITTEE ON CRIMINAL PENALTIES
    C. DECISION PROBLEMS IN CORRECTIONS
    D. A NEW APPROACH IN PAROLE POLICY

21. According to the above passage, which of the following is NOT a true statement about the present correctional system in State X?

    A. Many offenders are retained at unnecessarily close and expensive levels of confinement and supervision.
    B. The offenders committed to prison tend to remain incarcerated for long periods.
    C. Probation has become more and more extensive in application chiefly because institutions are overcrowded.
    D. When reviewing cases, parole authorities often use objective criteria like the social and psychological history of inmates.

22. According to the above passage, one change from the present system of parole which would result from the enactment of the proposed system of parole is that

    A. criminals could be paroled after the minimum parole eligibility period
    B. offenders who committed serious violent acts would automatically be paroled after a specified amount of time
    C. institutions would become overcrowded
    D. responsibility for parole in doubtful cases would essentially be given to the court rather than the parole authorities

23. According to the proposed method of determining parole, an inmate would be paroled after a specified period   23._____

    A. unless ineligible by administrative criteria
    B. unless ineligible by specific legislative criteria
    C. if eligible according to administrative criteria
    D. if eligible according to specific legislative criteria

24. Under the proposed method of determining parole, parole would be granted or denied depending on the inmate's   24._____

    A. past actions
    B. present behavior
    C. present psychological adjustment
    D. probable future actions

25. According to the above passage, the one of the following that is NOT a primary reason why the Committee on Criminal Penalties presented the legislation described above was to   25._____

    A. set objective criteria for parole
    B. expedite the reallocation of funds
    C. eliminate arbitrary commitment to prison
    D. prevent overlong commitment of many inmates

KEY (CORRECT ANSWERS)

1.	C	11.	C
2.	A	12.	B
3.	B	13.	D
4.	D	14.	C
5.	C	15.	B
6.	C	16.	D
7.	D	17.	D
8.	C	18.	C
9.	B	19.	C
10.	B	20.	D

21. D
22. D
23. B
24. A
25. C

PHILOSOPHY, PRINCIPLES, PRACTICES, AND TECHNICS OF SUPERVISION, ADMINISTRATION, MANAGEMENT, AND ORGANIZATION

TABLE OF CONTENTS

	Page
MEANING OF SUPERVISION	1
THE OLD AND THE NEW SUPERVISION	1
THE EIGHT (8) BASIC PRINCIPLES OF THE NEW SUPERVISION	1
I. Principle of Responsibility	1
II. Principle of Authority	2
III. Principle of Self-Growth	2
IV. Principle of Individual Worth	2
V. Principle of Creative Leadership	2
VI. Principle of Success and Failure	2
VII. Principle of Science	3
VIII. Principle of Cooperation	3
WHAT IS ADMINISTRATION?	3
I. Practices Commonly Classed as "Supervisory"	3
II. Practices Commonly Classed as "Administrative"	3
III. Practices Commonly Classed as Both "Supervisory" and "Administrative"	4
RESPONSIBILITIES OF THE SUPERVISOR	4
COMPETENCIES OF THE SUPERVISOR	4
THE PROFESSIONAL SUPERVISOR-EMPLOYEE RELATIONSHIP	4
MINI-TEXT IN SUPERVISION, ADMINISTRATION, MANAGEMENT, AND ORGANIZATION	5
I. Brief Highlights	5
A. Levels of Management	6
B. What the Supervisor Must Learn	6
C. A Definition of Supervision	6
D. Elements of the Team Concept	6
E. Principles of Organization	6
F. The Four Important Parts of Every Job	7
G. Principles of Delegation	7
H. Principles of Effective Communications	7
I. Principles of Work Improvement	7
J. Areas of Job Improvement	7
K. Seven Key Points in Making Improvements	8

	L.	Corrective Techniques for Job Improvement	8
	M.	A Planning Checklist	8
	N.	Five Characteristics of Good Directions	9
	O.	Types of Directions	9
	P.	Controls	9
	Q.	Orienting the New Employee	9
	R.	Checklist for Orienting New Employees	9
	S.	Principles of Learning	10
	T.	Causes of Poor Performance	10
	U.	Four Major Steps in On-the-Job Instructions	10
	V.	Employees Want Five Things	10
	W.	Some Don'ts in Regard to Praise	11
	X.	How to Gain Your Workers' Confidence	11
	Y.	Sources of Employee Problems	11
	Z.	The Supervisor's Key to Discipline	11
	AA.	Five Important Processes of Management	12
	BB.	When the Supervisor Fails to Plan	12
	CC.	Fourteen General Principles of Management	12
	DD.	Change	12

II. Brief Topical Summaries — 13
- A. Who/What is the Supervisor? — 13
- B. The Sociology of Work — 13
- C. Principles and Practices of Supervision — 14
- D. Dynamic Leadership — 14
- E. Processes for Solving Problems — 15
- F. Training for Results — 15
- G. Health, Safety, and Accident Prevention — 16
- H. Equal Employment Opportunity — 16
- I. Improving Communications — 16
- J. Self-Development — 17
- K. Teaching and Training — 17
  1. The Teaching Process — 17
     - a. Preparation — 17
     - b. Presentation — 18
     - c. Summary — 18
     - d. Application — 18
     - e. Evaluation — 18
  2. Teaching Methods — 18
     - a. Lecture — 18
     - b. Discussion — 18
     - c. Demonstration — 19
     - d. Performance — 19
     - e. Which Method to Use — 19

PHILOSOPHY, PRINCIPLES, PRACTICES, AND TECHNICS
OF
SUPERVISION, ADMINISTRATION, MANAGEMENT, AND ORGANIZATION

MEANING OF SUPERVISION

The extension of the democratic philosophy has been accompanied by an extension in the scope of supervision. Modern leaders and supervisors no longer think of supervision in the narrow sense of being confined chiefly to visiting employees, supplying materials, or rating the staff. They regard supervision as being intimately related to all the concerned agencies of society, they speak of the supervisor's function in terms of "growth," rather than the "improvement" of employees.

This modern concept of supervision may be defined as follows: Supervision is leadership and the development of leadership within groups which are cooperatively engaged in inspection, research, training, guidance, and evaluation.

THE OLD AND THE NEW SUPERVISION

TRADITIONAL
1. Inspection
2. Focused on the employee
3. Visitation
4. Random and haphazard
5. Imposed and authoritarian
6. One person usually

MODERN
1. Study and analysis
2. Focused on aims, materials, methods, supervisors, employees, environment
3. Demonstrations, intervisitation, workshops, directed reading, bulletins, etc.
4. Definitely organized and planned (scientific)
5. Cooperative and democratic
6. Many persons involved (creative)

THE EIGHT (8) BASIC PRINCIPLES OF THE NEW SUPERVISION

I. Principle of Responsibility
   Authority to act and responsibility for acting must be joined.
   A. If you give responsibility, give authority.
   B. Define employee duties clearly.
   C. Protect employees from criticism by others.
   D. Recognize the rights as well as obligations of employees.
   E. Achieve the aims of a democratic society insofar as it is possible within the area of your work.
   F. Establish a situation favorable to training and learning.
   G. Accept ultimate responsibility for everything done in your section, unit, office, division, department.
   H. Good administration and good supervision are inseparable.

II. Principle of Authority
The success of the supervisor is measured by the extent to which the power of authority is not used.
   A. Exercise simplicity and informality in supervision
   B. Use the simplest machinery of supervision
   C. If it is good for the organization as a whole, it is probably justified.
   D. Seldom be arbitrary or authoritative.
   E. Do not base your work on the power of position or of personality.
   F. Permit and encourage the free expression of opinions.

III. Principle of Self-Growth
The success of the supervisor is measured by the extent to which, and the speed with which, he is no longer needed.
   A. Base criticism on principles, not on specifics.
   B. Point out higher activities to employees.
   C. Train for self-thinking by employees to meet new situations.
   D. Stimulate initiative, self-reliance, and individual responsibility
   E. Concentrate on stimulating the growth of employees rather than on removing defects.

IV. Principle of Individual Worth
Respect for the individual is a paramount consideration in supervision.
   A. Be human and sympathetic in dealing with employees.
   B. Don't nag about things to be done.
   C. Recognize the individual differences among employees and seek opportunities to permit best expression of each personality.

V. Principle of Creative Leadership
The best supervision is that which is not apparent to the employee.
   A. Stimulate, don't drive employees to creative action.
   B. Emphasize doing good things.
   C. Encourage employees to do what they do best.
   D. Do not be too greatly concerned with details of subject or method.
   E. Do not be concerned exclusively with immediate problems and activities.
   F. Reveal higher activities and make them both desired and maximally possible.
   G. Determine procedures in the light of each situation but see that these are derived from a sound basic philosophy.
   H. Aid, inspire, and lead so as to liberate the creative spirit latent in all good employees.

VI. Principle of Success and Failure
There are no unsuccessful employees, only unsuccessful supervisors who have failed to give proper leadership.
   A. Adapt suggestions to the capacities, attitudes, and prejudices of employees.
   B. Be gradual, be progressive, be persistent.
   C. Help the employee find the general principle; have the employee apply his own problem to the general principle.
   D. Give adequate appreciation for good work and honest effort.
   E. Anticipate employee difficulties and help to prevent them.
   F. Encourage employees to do the desirable things they will do anyway.
   G. Judge your supervision by the results it secures.

VII. Principle of Science
Successful supervision is scientific, objective, and experimental. It is based on facts, not on prejudices.
   A. Be cumulative in results.
   B. Never divorce your suggestions from the goals of training.
   C. Don't be impatient of results.
   D. Keep all matters on a professional, not a personal, level.
   E. Do not be concerned exclusively with immediate problems and activities.
   F. Use objective means of determining achievement and rating where possible.

VIII. Principle of Cooperation
Supervision is a cooperative enterprise between supervisor and employee.
   A. Begin with conditions as they are.
   B. Ask opinions of all involved when formulating policies.
   C. Organization is as good as its weakest link.
   D. Let employees help to determine policies and department programs.
   E. Be approachable and accessible—physically and mentally.
   F. Develop pleasant social relationships.

WHAT IS ADMINISTRATION

Administration is concerned with providing the environment, the material facilities, and the operational procedures that will promote the maximum growth and development of supervisors and employees. (Organization is an aspect and a concomitant of administration.)

There is no sharp line of demarcation between supervision and administration; these functions are intimately interrelated and, often, overlapping. They are complementary activities.

I. Practices Commonly Classed as "Supervisory"
   A. Conducting employees' conferences
   B. Visiting sections, units, offices, divisions, departments
   C. Arranging for demonstrations
   D. Examining plans
   E. Suggesting professional reading
   F. Interpreting bulletins
   G. Recommending in-service training courses
   H. Encouraging experimentation
   I. Appraising employee morale
   J. Providing for intervisitation

II. Practices Commonly Classified as "Administrative"
   A. Management of the office
   B. Arrangement of schedules for extra duties
   C. Assignment of rooms or areas
   D. Distribution of supplies
   E. Keeping records and reports
   F. Care of audio-visual materials
   G. Keeping inventory records
   H. Checking record cards and books

      I. Programming special activities
      J. Checking on the attendance and punctuality of employees

III. Practices Commonly Classified as Both "Supervisory" and "Administrative"
      A. Program construction
      B. Testing or evaluating outcomes
      C. Personnel accounting
      D. Ordering instructional materials

RESPONSIBILITIES OF THE SUPERVISOR

A person employed in a supervisory capacity must constantly be able to improve his own efficiency and ability. He represent the employer to the employees and only continuous self-examination can make him a capable supervisor.

Leadership and training are the supervisor's responsibility. An efficient working unit is one in which the employees work with the supervisor. It is his job to bring out the best in his employees. He must always be relaxed, courteous, and calm in his association with his employees. Their feelings are important, and a harsh attitude does not develop the most efficient employees.

COMPETENCES OF THE SUPERVISOR

      I. Complete knowledge of the duties and responsibilities of his position.
      II. To be able to organize a job, plan ahead, and carry through.
      III. To have self-confidence and initiative.
      IV. To be able to handle the unexpected situation and make quick decisions.
      V. To be able to properly train subordinates in the positions they are best suited for.
      VI. To be able to keep good human relations among his subordinates.
      VII. To be able to keep good human relations between his subordinates and himself and to earn their respect and trust.

THE PROFESSIONAL SUPERVISOR-EMPLOYEE RELATIONSHIP

There are two kinds of efficiency: one kind is only apparent and is produced in organizations through the exercise of mere discipline; this is but a simulation of the second, or true, efficiency which springs from spontaneous cooperation. If you are a manager, no matter how great or small your responsibility, it is your job, in the final analysis, to create and develop this involuntary cooperation among the people whom you supervise. For, no matter how powerful a combination of money, machines, and materials a company may have, this is a dead and sterile thing without a team of willing, thinking, and articulate people to guide it.

The following 21 points are presented as indicative of the exemplary basic relationship that should exist between supervisor and employee:

1. Each person wants to be liked and respected by his fellow employee and wants to be treated with consideration and respect by his superior.
2. The most competent employee will make an error. However, in a unit where good relations exist between the supervisor and his employees, tenseness and fear do not exist. Thus, errors are not hidden or covered up, and the efficiency of a unit is not impaired.

3. Subordinates resent rules, regulations, or orders that are unreasonable or unexplained.
4. Subordinates are quick to resent unfairness, harshness, injustices, and favoritism.
5. An employee will accept responsibility if he knows that he will be complimented for a job well done, and not too harshly chastised for failure; that his supervisor will check the cause of the failure, and, if it was the supervisor's fault, he will assume the blame therefore. If it was the employee's fault, his supervisor will explain the correct method or means of handling the responsibility.
6. An employee wants to receive credit for a suggestion he has made, that is used. If a suggestion cannot be used, the employee is entitled to an explanation. The supervisor should not say "no" and close the subject.
7. Fear and worry slow up a worker's ability. Poor working environment can impair his physical and mental health. A good supervisor avoids forceful methods, threats, and arguments to get a job done.
8. A forceful supervisor is able to train his employees individually and as a team, and is able to motivate them in the proper channels.
9. A mature supervisor is able to properly evaluate his subordinates and to keep them happy and satisfied.
10. A sensitive supervisor will never patronize his subordinates.
11. A worthy supervisor will respect his employees' confidences.
12. Definite and clear-cut responsibilities should be assigned to each executive.
13. Responsibility should always be coupled with corresponding authority.
14. No change should be made in the scope or responsibilities of a position without a definite understanding to that effect on the part of all persons concerned.
15. No executive or employee, occupying a single position in the organization, should be subject to definite orders from more than one source.
16. Orders should never be given to subordinates over the head of a responsible executive. Rather than do this, the officer in question should be supplanted.
17. Criticisms of subordinates should, whoever possible, be made privately, and in no case should a subordinate be criticized in the presence of executives or employees of equal or lower rank.
18. No dispute or difference between executives or employees as to authority or responsibilities should be considered too trivial for prompt and careful adjudication.
19. Promotions, wage changes, and disciplinary action should always be approved by the executive immediately superior to the one directly responsible.
20. No executive or employee should ever be required, or expected, to be at the same time an assistant to, and critic of, another.
21. Any executive whose work is subject to regular inspection should, wherever practicable, be given the assistance and facilities necessary to enable him to maintain an independent check of the quality of his work.

MINI-TEXT IN SUPERVISION, ADMINISTRATION, MANAGEMENT, AND ORGANIZATION

I. Brief Highlights

Listed concisely and sequentially are major headings and important data in the field for quick recall and review.

A. Levels of Management
Any organization of some size has several levels of management. In terms of a ladder, the levels are:

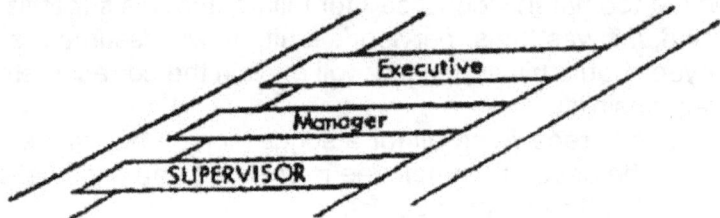

The first level is very important because it is the beginning point of management leadership.

B. What the Supervisor Must Learn
A supervisor must learn to:
1. Deal with people and their differences
2. Get the job done through people
3. Recognize the problems when they exist
4. Overcome obstacles to good performance
5. Evaluate the performance of people
6. Check his own performance in terms of accomplishment

C. A Definition of Supervisor
The term supervisor means any individual having authority, in the interests of the employer, to hire, transfer, suspend, lay-off, recall, promote, discharge, assign, reward, or discipline other employees or responsibility to direct them, or to adjust their grievances, or effectively to recommend such action, if, in connection with the foregoing, exercise of such authority is not of a merely routine or clerical nature but requires the use of independent judgment.

D. Elements of the Team Concept
What is involved in teamwork? The component parts are:
1. Members
2. A leader
3. Goals
4. Plans
5. Cooperation
6. Spirit

E. Principles of Organization
1. A team member must know what his job is.
2. Be sure that the nature and scope of a job are understood.
3. Authority and responsibility should be carefully spelled out.
4. A supervisor should be permitted to make the maximum number of decisions affecting his employees.
5. Employees should report to only one supervisor.
6. A supervisor should direct only as many employees as he can handle effectively.
7. An organization plan should be flexible.

8. Inspection and performance of work should be separate.
9. Organizational problems should receive immediate attention.
10. Assign work in line with ability and experience.

F. The Four Important Parts of Every Job
1. Inherent in every job is the *accountability* for results.
2. A second set of factors in every job is *responsibilities*.
3. Along with duties and responsibilities one must have the *authority* to act within certain limits without obtaining permission to proceed.
4. No job exists in a vacuum. The supervisor is surrounded by key *relationships*.

G. Principles of Delegation
Where work is delegated for the first time, the supervisor should think in terms of these questions:
1. Who is best qualified to do this?
2. Can an employee improve his abilities by doing this?
3. How long should an employee spend on this?
4. Are there any special problems for which he will need guidance?
5. How broad a delegation can I make?

H. Principles of Effective Communications
1. Determine the media.
2. To whom directed?
3. Identification and source authority.
4. Is communication understood?

I. Principles of Work Improvement
1. Most people usually do only the work which is assigned to them.
2. Workers are likely to fit assigned work into the time available to perform it.
3. A good workload usually stimulates output.
4. People usually do their best work when they know that results will be reviewed or inspected.
5. Employees usually feel that someone else is responsible for conditions of work, workplace layout, job methods, type of tools/equipment, and other such factors.
6. Employees are usually defensive about their job security.
7. Employees have natural resistance to change.
8. Employees can support or destroy a supervisor.
9. A supervisor usually earns the respect of his people through his personal example of diligence and efficiency.

J. Areas of Job Improvement
The areas of job improvement are quite numerous, but the most common ones which a supervisor can identify and utilize are:
1. Departmental layout
2. Flow of work
3. Workplace layout
4. Utilization of manpower
5. Work methods
6. Materials handling

7. Utilization
8. Motion economy

K. Seven Key Points in Making Improvements
1. Select the job to be improved
2. Study how it is being done now
3. Question the present method
4. Determine actions to be taken
5. Chart proposed method
6. Get approval and apply
7. Solicit worker participation

l. Corrective Techniques of Job Improvement
Specific Problems
1. Size of workload
2. Inability to meet schedules
3. Strain and fatigue
4. Improper use of men and skills
5. Waste, poor quality, unsafe conditions
6. Bottleneck conditions that hinder output
7. Poor utilization of equipment and machine
8. Efficiency and productivity of labor

General Improvement
1. Departmental layout
2. Flow of work
3. Work plan layout
4. Utilization of manpower
5. Work methods
6. Materials handling
7. Utilization of equipment
8. Motion economy

Corrective Techniques
1. Study with scale model
2. Flow chart study
3. Motion analysis
4. Comparison of units produced to standard allowance
5. Methods analysis
6. Flow chart and equipment study
7. Down time vs. running time
8. Motion analysis

M. A Planning Checklist
1. Objectives
2. Controls
3. Delegations
4. Communications
5. Resources
6. Manpower

7. Equipment
8. Supplies and materials
9. Utilization of time
10. Safety
11. Money
12. Work
13. Timing of improvements

N. Five Characteristics of Good Directions
In order to get results, directions must be:
1. Possible of accomplishment
2. Agreeable with worker interests
3. Related to mission
4. Planned and complete
5. Unmistakably clear

O. Types of Directions
1. Demands or direct orders
2. Requests
3. Suggestion or implication
4. volunteering

P. Controls
A typical listing of the overall areas in which the supervisor should establish controls might be:
1. Manpower
2. Materials
3. Quality of work
4. Quantity of work
5. Time
6. Space
7. Money
8. Methods

Q. Orienting the New Employee
1. Prepare for him
2. Welcome the new employee
3. Orientation for the job
4. Follow-up

R. Checklist for Orienting New Employees   Yes   No
1. Do you appreciate the feelings of new employees when they first report for work? ___ ___
2. Are you aware of the fact that the new employee must make a big adjustment to his job? ___ ___
3. Have you given him good reasons for liking the job and the organization? ___ ___
4. Have you prepared for his first day on the job? ___ ___
5. Did you welcome him cordially and make him feel needed? ___ ___

		Yes	No

6. Did you establish rapport with him so that he feels free to talk and discuss matters with you? ___ ___
7. Did you explain his job to him and his relationship to you? ___ ___
8. Does he know that his work will be evaluated periodically on a basis that is fair and objective? ___ ___
9. Did you introduce him to his fellow workers in such a way that they are likely to accept him? ___ ___
10. Does he know what employee benefits he will receive? ___ ___
11. Does he understand the importance of being on the job and what to do if he must leave his duty station? ___ ___
12. Has he been impressed with the importance of accident prevention and safe practice? ___ ___
13. Does he generally know his way around the department? ___ ___
14. Is he under the guidance of a sponsor who will teach the right way of doing things? ___ ___
15. Do you plan to follow-up so that he will continue to adjust successfully to his job? ___ ___

S. Principles of Learning
1. Motivation
2. Demonstration or explanation
3. Practice

T. Causes of Poor Performance
1. Improper training for job
2. Wrong tools
3. Inadequate directions
4. Lack of supervisory follow-up
5. Poor communications
6. Lack of standards of performance
7. Wrong work habits
8. Low morale
9. Other

U. Four Major Steps in On-The-Job Instruction
1. Prepare the worker
2. Present the operation
3. Tryout performance
4. Follow-up

V. Employees Want Five Things
1. Security
2. Opportunity
3. Recognition
4. Inclusion
5. Expression

W. Some Don'ts in Regard to Praise
1. Don't praise a person for something he hasn't done.
2. Don't praise a person unless you can be sincere.
3. Don't be sparing in praise just because your superior withholds it from you.
4. Don't let too much time elapse between good performance and recognition of it

X. How to Gain Your Workers' Confidence
Methods of developing confidence include such things as:
1. Knowing the interests, habits, hobbies of employees
2. Admitting your own inadequacies
3. Sharing and telling of confidence in others
4. Supporting people when they are in trouble
5. Delegating matters that can be well handled
6. Being frank and straightforward about problems and working conditions
7. Encouraging others to bring their problems to you
8. Taking action on problems which impede worker progress

Y. Sources of Employee Problems
On-the-job causes might be such things as:
1. A feeling that favoritism is exercised in assignments
2. Assignment of overtime
3. An undue amount of supervision
4. Changing methods or systems
5. Stealing of ideas or trade secrets
6. Lack of interest in job
7. Threat of reduction in force
8. Ignorance or lack of communications
9. Poor equipment
10. Lack of knowing how supervisor feels toward employee
11. Shift assignments

Off-the-job problems might have to do with:
1. Health
2. Finances
3. Housing
4. Family

Z. The Supervisor's Key to Discipline
There are several key points about discipline which the supervisor should keep in mind:
1. Job discipline is one of the disciplines of life and is directed by the supervisor.
2. It is more important to correct an employee fault than to fix blame for it.
3. Employee performance is affected by problems both on the job and off.
4. Sudden or abrupt changes in behavior can be indications of important employee problems.
5. Problems should be dealt with as soon as possible after they are identified.
6. The attitude of the supervisor may have more to do with solving problems than the techniques of problem solving.
7. Correction of employee behavior should be resorted to only after the supervisor is sure that training or counseling will not be helpful.

8. Be sure to document your disciplinary actions.
9. Make sure that you are disciplining on the basis of facts rather than personal feelings.
10. Take each disciplinary step in order, being careful not to make snap judgments, or decisions based on impatience.

AA. Five Important Processes of Management
1. Planning
2. Organizing
3. Scheduling
4. Controlling
5. Motivating

BB. When the Supervisor Fails to Plan
1. Supervisor creates impression of not knowing his job
2. May lead to excessive overtime
3. Job runs itself—supervisor lacks control
4. Deadlines and appointments missed
5. Parts of the work go undone
6. Work interrupted by emergencies
7. Sets a bad example
8. Uneven workload creates peaks and valleys
9. Too much time on minor details at expense of more important tasks

CC. Fourteen General Principles of Management
1. Division of work
2. Authority and responsibility
3. Discipline
4. Unity of command
5. Unity of direction
6. Subordination of individual interest to general interest
7. Remuneration of personnel
8. Centralization
9. Scalar chain
10. Order
11. Equity
12. Stability of tenure of personnel
13. Initiative
14. Esprit de corps

DD. Change

Bringing about change is perhaps attempted more often, and yet less well understood, than anything else the supervisor does. How do people generally react to change? (People tend to resist change that is imposed upon them by other individuals or circumstances.

Change is characteristic of every situation. It is a part of every real endeavor where the efforts of people are concerned.

1. Why do people resist change?
   People may resist change because of:
   a. Fear of the unknown
   b. Implied criticism
   c. Unpleasant experiences in the past
   d. Fear of loss of status
   e. Threat to the ego
   f. Fear of loss of economic stability

2. How can we best overcome the resistance to change?
   In initiating change, take these steps:
   a. Get ready to sell
   b. Identify sources of help
   c. Anticipate objections
   d. Sell benefits
   e. Listen in depth
   f. Follow up

II. Brief Topical Summaries

   A. Who/What is the Supervisor?
      1. The supervisor is often called the "highest level employee and the lowest level manager."
      2. A supervisor is a member of both management and the work group. He acts as a bridge between the two.
      3. Most problems in supervision are in the area of human relations, or people problems.
      4. Employees expect: Respect, opportunity to learn and to advance, and a sense of belonging, and so forth.
      5. Supervisors are responsible for directing people and organizing work. Planning is of paramount importance.
      6. A position description is a set of duties and responsibilities inherent to a given position.
      7. It is important to keep the position description up-to-date and to provide each employee with his own copy.

   B. The Sociology of Work
      1. People are alike in many ways; however, each individual is unique.
      2. The supervisor is challenged in getting to know employee differences. Acquiring skills in evaluating individuals is an asset.
      3. Maintaining meaningful working relationships in the organization is of great importance.
      4. The supervisor has an obligation to help individuals to develop to their fullest potential.
      5. Job rotation on a planned basis helps to build versatility and to maintain interest and enthusiasm in work groups.
      6. Cross training (job rotation) provides backup skills.

7. The supervisor can help reduce tension by maintaining a sense of humor, providing guidance to employees, and by making reasonable and timely decisions. Employees respond favorably to working under reasonably predictable circumstances.
8. Change is characteristic of all managerial behavior. The supervisor must adjust to changes in procedures, new methods, technological changes, and to a number of new and sometimes challenging situations.
9. To overcome the natural tendency for people to resist change, the supervisor should become more skillful in initiating change.

C. Principles and Practices of Supervision
1. Employees should be required to answer to only one superior.
2. A supervisor can effectively direct only a limited number of employees, depending upon the complexity, variety, and proximity of the jobs involved.
3. The organizational chart presents the organization in graphic form. It reflects lines of authority and responsibility as well as interrelationships of units within the organization.
4. Distribution of work can be improved through an analysis using the "Work Distribution Chart."
5. The "Work Distribution Chart" reflects the division of work within a unit in understandable form.
6. When related tasks are given to an employee, he has a better chance of increasing his skills through training.
7. The individual who is given the responsibility for tasks must also be given the appropriate authority to insure adequate results.
8. The supervisor should delegate repetitive, routine work. Preparation of recurring reports, maintaining leave and attendance records are some examples.
9. Good discipline is essential to good task performance. Discipline is reflected in the actions of employees on the job in the absence of supervision.
10. Disciplinary action may have to be taken when the positive aspects of discipline have failed. Reprimand, warning, and suspension are examples of disciplinary action.
11. If a situation calls for a reprimand, be sure it is deserved and remember it is to be done in private.

D. Dynamic Leadership
1. A style is a personal method or manner of exerting influence.
2. Authoritarian leaders often see themselves as the source of power and authority.
3. The democratic leader often perceives the group as the source of authority and power.
4. Supervisors tend to do better when using the pattern of leadership that is most natural for them.
5. Social scientists suggest that the effective supervisor use the leadership style that best fits the problem or circumstances involved.
6. All four styles—telling, selling, consulting, joining—have their place. Using one does not preclude using the other at another time.

7. The theory X point of view assumes that the average person dislikes work, will avoid it whenever possible, and must be coerced to achieve organizational objectives.
8. The theory Y point of view assumes that the average person considers work to be a natural as play, and, when the individual is committed, he requires little supervision or direction to accomplish desired objectives.
9. The leader's basic assumptions concerning human behavior and human nature affect his actions, decisions, and other managerial practices.
10. Dissatisfaction among employees is often present, but difficult to isolate. The supervisor should seek to weaken dissatisfaction by keeping promises, being sincere and considerate, keeping employees informed, and so forth.
11. Constructive suggestions should be encouraged during the natural progress of the work.

E. Processes for Solving Problems
1. People find their daily tasks more meaningful and satisfying when they can improve them.
2. The causes of problems, or the key factors, are often hidden in the background. Ability to solve problems often involves the ability to isolate them from their backgrounds. There is some substance to the cliché that some persons "can't see the forest for the trees."
3. New procedures are often developed from old ones. Problems should be broken down into manageable parts. New ideas can be adapted from old one.
4. People think differently in problem-solving situations. Using a logical, patterned approach is often useful. One approach found to be useful includes these steps:
   a. Define the problem
   b. Establish objectives
   c. Get the facts
   d. Weigh and decide
   e. Take action
   f. Evaluate action

F. Training for Results
1. Participants respond best when they feel training is important to them.
2. The supervisor has responsibility for the training and development of those who report to him.
3. When training is delegated to others, great care must be exercised to insure the trainer has knowledge, aptitude, and interest for his work as a trainer.
4. Training (learning) of some type goes on continually. The most successful supervisor makes certain the learning contributes in a productive manner to operational goals.
5. New employees are particularly susceptible to training. Older employees facing new job situations require specific training, as well as having need for development and growth opportunities.
6. Training needs require continuous monitoring.
7. The training officer of an agency is a professional with a responsibility to assist supervisors in solving training problems.

8. Many of the self-development steps important to the supervisor's own growth are equally important to the development of peers and subordinates. Knowledge of these is important when the supervisor consults with others on development and growth opportunities.

G. Health, Safety, and Accident Prevention
1. Management-minded supervisors take appropriate measures to assist employees in maintaining health and in assuring safe practices in the work environment.
2. Effective safety training and practices help to avoid injury and accidents.
3. Safety should be a management goal. All infractions of safety which are observed should be corrected without exception.
4. Employees' safety attitude, training and instruction, provision of safe tools and equipment, supervision, and leadership are considered highly important factors which contribute to safety and which can be influenced directly by supervisors.
5. When accidents do occur, they should be investigated promptly for very important reasons, including the fact that information which is gained can be used to prevent accidents in the future.

H. Equal Employment Opportunity
1. The supervisor should endeavor to treat all employees fairly, without regard to religion, race, sex, or national origin.
2. Groups tend to reflect the attitude of the leader. Prejudice can be detected even in very subtle form. Supervisors must strive to create a feeling of mutual respect and confidence in every employee.
3. Complete utilization of all human resources is a national goal. Equitable consideration should be accorded women in the work force, minority-group members, the physically and mentally handicapped, and the older employee. The important question is: "Who can do the job?"
4. Training opportunities, recognition for performance, overtime assignments, promotional opportunities, and all other personnel actions are to be handled on an equitable basis.

I. Improving Communications
1. Communications is achieving understanding between the sender and the receiver of a message. It also means sharing information—the creation of understanding.
2. Communication is basic to all human activity. Words are means of conveying meanings; however, real meanings are in people.
3. There are very practical differences in the effectiveness of one-way, impersonal, and two-way communications. Words spoken face-to-face are better understood. Telephone conversations are effective, but lack the rapport of person-to-person exchanges. The whole person communicates.
4. Cooperation and communication in an organization go hand in hand. When there is a mutual respect between people, spelling out rules and procedures for communicating is unnecessary.
5. There are several barriers to effective communications. These include failure to listen with respect and understanding, lack of skill in feedback, and misinterpreting the meanings of words used by the speaker. It is also common

practice to listen to what we want to hear, and tune out things we do not want to hear.
6. Communication is management's chief problem. The supervisor should accept the challenge to communicate more effectively and to improve interagency and intra-agency communications.
7. The supervisor may often plan for and conduct meetings. The planning phase is critical and may determine the success or the failure of a meeting.
8. Speaking before groups usually requires extra effort. Stage fright may never disappear completely, but it can be controlled.

J. Self-Development
1. Every employee is responsible for his own self-development.
2. Toastmaster and toastmistress clubs offer opportunities to improve skills in oral communications.
3. Planning for one's own self-development is of vital importance. Supervisors know their own strengths and limitations better than anyone else.
4. Many opportunities are open to aid the supervisor in his developmental efforts, including job assignments; training opportunities, both governmental and non-governmental—to include universities and professional conferences and seminars.
5. Programmed instruction offers a means of studying at one's own rate.
6. Where difficulties may arise from a supervisor's being away from his work for training, he may participate in televised home study or correspondence courses to meet his self-development needs.

K. Teaching and Training
1. The Teaching Process
Teaching is encouraging and guiding the learning activities of students toward established goals. In most cases this process consists of five steps: preparation, presentation, summarization, evaluation, and application.

   a. Preparation
   Preparation is two-fold in nature; that of the supervisor and the employee. Preparation by the supervisor is absolutely essential to success. He must know what, when, where, how, and whom he will teach. Some of the factors that should be considered are:
   1) The objectives
   2) The materials needed
   3) The methods to be used
   4) Employee participation
   5) Employee interest
   6) Training aids
   7) Evaluation
   8) Summarization

   Employee preparation consists in preparing the employee to receive the material. Probably the most important single factor in the preparation of the employee is arousing and maintaining his interest. He must know the objectives of the training, why he is there, how the material can be used, and its importance to him.

b. Presentation
In presentation, have a carefully designed plan and follow it. The plan should be accurate and complete, yet flexible enough to meet situations as they arise. The method of presentation will be determined by the particular situation and objectives.

c. Summary
A summary should be made at the end of every training unit and program. In addition, there may be internal summaries depending on the nature of the material being taught. The important thing is that the trainee must always be able to understand how each part of the new material relates to the whole.

d. Application
The supervisor must arrange work so the employee will be given a chance to apply new knowledge or skills while the material is still clear in his mind and interest is high. The trainee does not really know whether he has learned the material until he has been given a chance to apply it. If the material is not applied, it loses most of its value.

e. Evaluation
The purpose of all training is to promote learning. To determine whether the training has been a success or failure, the supervisor must evaluate this learning.

In the broadest sense, evaluation includes all the devices, methods, skills, and techniques used by the supervisor to keep himself and the employees informed as to their progress toward the objectives they are pursuing. The extent to which the employee has mastered the knowledge, skills, and abilities, or changed his attitudes, as determined by the program objectives, is the extent to which instruction has succeeded or failed.

Evaluation should not be confined to the end of the lesson, day, or program but should be used continuously. We shall note later the way this relates to the rest of the teaching process.

2. Teaching Methods
A teaching method is a pattern of identifiable student and instructor activity used in presenting training material.
All supervisors are faced with the problem of deciding which method should be used at a given time.

a. Lecture
The lecture is direct oral presentation of material by the supervisor. The present trend is to place less emphasis on the trainer's activity and more on that of the trainee.

b. Discussion
Teaching by discussion or conference involves using questions and other techniques to arouse interest and focus attention upon certain areas, and by doing so creating a learning situation. This can be one of the most

valuable methods because it gives the employees an opportunity to express their ideas and pool their knowledge.

    c. Demonstration
The demonstration is used to teach how something works or how to do something. It can be used to show a principle or what the results of a series of actions will be. A well-staged demonstration is particularly effective because it shows proper methods of performance in a realistic manner.

    d. Performance
Performance is one of the most fundamental of all learning techniques or teaching methods. The trainee may be able to tell how a specific operation should be performed but he cannot be sure he knows how to perform the operation until he has done so.
As with all methods, there are certain advantages and disadvantages to each method.

    e. Which Method to Use
Moreover, there are other methods and techniques of teaching. It is difficult to use any method without other methods entering into it. In any learning situation, a combination of methods is usually more effective than any one method alone.

Finally, evaluation must be integrated into the other aspects of the teaching-learning process.

It must be used in the motivation of the trainees; it must be used to assist in developing understanding during the training; and it must be related to employee application of the results of training.

This is distinctly the role of the supervisor.

CONTROL AND MANAGEMENT OF PRISON INMATES
TABLE OF CONTENTS

FACTORS IN PRISONER UNREST 1
    External Factors 1
        Indifference.. 1
        Politics... 1
        Unwise commitment and release procedures.. 2
        Overcrowding...2
        Emotional tone of the community... 2
    Internal Factors 2
        The society of prisoners 2
        The society of personnel 3
        Social caste in institutions 4

PREVENTIVE MEASURES 4
    Personnel Administration.. 5
        Development of correctional careers.. 6
        Support of staff development programs.. 6
        Removal of job dissatisfactions... 6
    Policies and Operating Procedures 7
        Prisoner rights and attention to complaints.. 7
        Communication.. 8
        Correspondence regulations 9
        Visiting regulations 10
        Prisoner discipline 11
    Improvement of Correctional Programs..13

HANDLING EMERGENCIES 14
    Escape Plans 14
        Prevention   15
        Sounding the alarm   15
        Mobilization of resources   15
        Establishing control   16
        Returning to normal 16
    Plans for Riots and Disturbances 17
        Containment 18
        Use of force and defensive equipment 18
        Post-riot procedures 19
    Plans for Civil Disorder 19
    Plans for Civil Disaster 20
    Fire Plans 20

CONCLUSION 20

CONTROL AND MANAGEMENT OF PRISON INMATES

FACTORS IN PRISONER UNREST

". . . and him safely keep," whether directly expressed or not, is the universal mandate that accompanies every order of commitment to a lock-up, jail, prison or other correctional facility. Ultimate responsibility for this rests upon the administrator of the facility, together with responsibilities for the training, use and performance of personnel. He also bears stewardship responsibilities for the proper care and use of government property and the wise expenditure of public funds. For these reasons, if no other, the institution administrator is very much concerned over the ever-present potentials of prisoner disorder.

The possible consequences of prisoner unrest, whether expressed in misconduct, escape or riot, can be serious. At the least, disorder of any significant magnitude can interfere with the efficient operation of the institution. For example, staff time and energies that are devoted to handling an excessive number of misconduct reports detracts from more productive pursuits of the personnel involved. Escapes not only can be disruptive of normal operations but require the deployment of personnel who have other primary duties to perform. In extreme degree, a major riot which results in extensive property damage can cripple an institution for months. Beyond this, disorder can produce negative reactions in officials and the general public by undermining confidence in the management of the institution and by reinforcing existing rejective attitudes toward offenders and employees as classes of people.

It is generally true that the potentials for disorder within an institution are in inverse ratio to the effectiveness of institutional management and control. But this explains nothing and any attempt either to apply preventive measures or to cope successfully with incidents as they occur can fall short unless there is, first, some understanding of the many factors which figure prominently in prisoner unrest. In the discussion that follows, an arbitrary distinction is made between "external" and "internal" factors. This distinction may not appear in real life. Likewise, the discussion deals with a number of separate items when, in reality, all may be interrelated.

EXTERNAL FACTORS

Indifference. It is entirely possible that what appears as indifference is actually a perfectly "natural" reaction of people who look upon irrational, irresponsible and, at times, unpredictable and threatening behavior with a mixture of fear, frustration and frank bewilderment. Rather than indifference, the reaction may be outright rejection. The term "offender," alone, expresses an attitude of rejection. Certainly imprisonment is a form of rejection or banishment, however brief.

Whatever the reasons for it, the most visible evidence of indifference is withholding support. The expenditure of public funds for the operation of prisons and jails is politically unpopular under ordinary circumstances. Hospitals, schools, highways, aid to needy children and other competing demands on the public treasury have far more appeal than the correctional needs of offenders. Hand-to-mouth budget practices and deficit financing can account heavily for the inadequacies of personnel, facilities and programs.

Politics. Typically, jail management is the responsibility of elected local officials. Unlike schools, hospitals and mental health programs, where the need for competent, trained and full-time leadership has long been recognized, the administration of local correctional facilities is more often than not one of the many responsibilities of the sheriff. He, in turn, must rely on subordinates who ordinarily have had no preparation for their jobs.

In any institution there can be less visible but more insidious kinds of politically-motivated activity which sap the vitality and undermine the integrity of operations. Some of these involve pressures to extend improper favors to certain prisoners, efforts to obtain early releases, favoritism in the assignment of personnel and misuse of institutional property and supplies.

Unwise commitment and release procedures. Prisoners, like other people, tend to excuse and rationalize their own behavior. Unfortunately, many of the excuses are easily found in the machinery of criminal justice where there are all-too-obvious inequities and injustices. Problems in this area are numerous.

The system which permits accused persons with money to be free awaiting trial while those without resources have to stay in jail is both a blot on our notions of equal justice and the cause of many people being in jail needlessly. The mystique of a "taste of jail" is still popular in the minds of police, prosecutors and judges with the resultant confinement of many people who otherwise might have been released on bond or their own recognizance, placed on probation or assessed a fine.

Disparity in sentencing practices is a prime source of prisoner discontent. All judges do not think alike about how the law should be administered. Legislatures may impose unwise limits on judicial discretion, as when laws are enacted that require long minimum sentences or which establish ineligibility for probation or parole. In addition, decisions to release from jail are often viewed by prisoners as having been based on prejudice, caprice, or the "right connections."

Overcrowding. Emotional tensions are developed by the irritations of people upon each other. The more congested the conditions under which they must live, the greater the risks of frustration, anger and open conflict. All too frequently institutions have to operate over capacity. Two beds being placed in cells built for one, mattresses spread on corridor floors, overtaxed facilities, overworked personnel and failure generally to meet the most elementary requirements of differentiating among prisoners and maintaining acceptable standards of decency.

Emotional tone of the community. Prisoners are not nearly so isolated from the free community as may be supposed. They are aware of the attitudes of employees and visitors who live in the outside world. They have access to newspapers, radio, television and other means of communication with the outside. It is widely believed by institution people that the emotional tone of the free community is reflected inside the walls as truly as upon other groups. In fact, there are many who believe that the tone is magnified because prisoners are held in confinement under duress and they tend to seek support for their own reactions to real or fancied wrongs.

INTERNAL FACTORS

Seeds of discontent abound in the very nature of life in a prison, jail or other correctional facility. An institution is a community of people set apart. It has its society of inmates, its society of personnel, and its own peculiar culture of many conflicts.

The society of prisoners. Of the hundreds of thousands of offenders who pass through correctional institutions in the course of a year, some are committed irrevocably to criminal careers while others subscribe to quite conventional values or are aimless and uncommitted to goals of any kind. Some are alcoholics, some narcotic addicts, some sexual deviates and so on through the catalog of human frailties and personal problems. Behind the visible few who are conspicuous by their offenses are nameless numbers of nondescript human beings, more characterized by imprudence and inability to cope with the demands of a complex society than by any pattern of malicious willfulness.

Many offenders are members of minority groups whose values and objectives may be quite different from the middle class standards to which members of the staff subscribe and upon which correctional goals are based. Poverty may be a common denominator among them. They may have a language barrier. A sense of low status may lie at the root of the frustration and hostility that often mark minority attitudes toward the dominant society. Almost all minority groups will have had some bad experiences with authority.

Confinement is a stressful experience under the best of circumstances. Under the worst, it can become intolerable. There are many sources of stress for the prisoner. The closing of the front gate behind him is a denial of his freedom, a frustration of his accustomed ways of life, a humiliation and a label of being an undesirable member of society. Isolation, inflexible routine and monotony are characteristic of most correctional institutions. Its most visible feature is enforced idleness which imposes a heavy burden on all concerned and may produce deterioration in once-able people who leave with neither the ability nor the will to earn an honest living.

The society of personnel. Not all institutional problems of management and control are generated by the society of prisoners. A second set of problems can be created by the staff.

Without question, the greatest single resource for correctional management and control is personnel. Prisons and jails are run by people. The quality of the operation depends directly upon the skills, experience, performance standards and morale of the staff. Well qualified and promising recruits can be attracted to correctional work only as they are offered appropriate salaries and conditions of service which encourage life-time rather than casual, periods of employment. Lack of a sufficient number of employees to provide adequate supervision for safety, to say nothing of correctional programs, is too often the rule rather than the exception. In many jurisdictions, the number of positions allowed is usually far below an acceptable level of efficient service and safe coverage.

Employees who are expected to promote the aims of the institution in keeping with philosophies and procedures laid down for them, and who are the first to bear the brunt of inmate pressures, are human beings too. To a great extent, their effectiveness is determined by what they and the administration perceive their roles to be.

There are many factors which may result in a curious combination of laxity, harshness and even brutality. One is insensitivity to the legitimate needs and rights of prisoners. Another is inattention to bona fide complaints and grievances. Laxity may result from the necessity of using prisoners to perform work which should be done by personnel. Compensation for these services may be in the form of unwarranted trust or special and unusual privileges. Laxity can be found where personnel are unqualified for the jobs they perform.

Staff failure to recognize the existence of cultural differences among offenders or to understand why people who are shaped by them fail to respond "like everybody else" can interfere seriously with working relationships between inmates and staff. When intolerance and lack of understanding foster beliefs among members of the staff that prisoners are possessed of traits that are unacceptable, inferior or repugnant, effective working relationships are impossible. Personnel are subject to emotional stress too and when this happens they are inclined to be less tolerant of beliefs which they consider to be different from their own. This may result in their unwillingness to accept policies and programs established by the administration, as well as the philosophies upon which they are based. They may become intolerant of anything that disturbs their own perceptions, their sense of knowing where they stand. They tend to resent challenges to the familiar signposts of values upon which they have counted.

Social caste in institutions. Life in a correctional institution is actually a caste system in which prisoners and personnel are divided into two distinctly separate groups. The prisoner caste is at the bottom of the ladder and even though some inmates may share some of the same values and ways of behaving as staff members, they cannot enjoy the same status and rewards. As a result, communication and collaboration between inmates and staff are hindered. The pressures upon inmates to adapt themselves to social relationships within their own caste may be greater than pressures for them to identify with the upper caste.

Traditional prisons and other correctional institutions are highly authoritarian communities. Mass handling, countless ways of making inmates subservient to rules and orders and special forms of "etiquette" have the effect of creating and maintaining social distance between keepers and prisoners. Frisking of inmates and regimented movement about the institution tend to depersonalize prisoners and make their stance toward authority increasingly obdurate. The admonition "do your own time" is a slogan which endorses alienation and indifference to the interests of both staff and other inmates.

PREVENTIVE MEASURES

Many of the factors in prisoner unrest—forces that influence the environment in which prisoner management and control takes place—cannot be changed immediately or directly. The institution manager by himself can do little about public indifference, overcrowding, political meddling or unwise commitments and releases. These are matters for which responsibility must be shared with others outside the institution. There are, however, many things that can be done to improve the climate within the institution.

Borrowing from military experience, it is too easy to think of the problems of prisoner management and control as being represented by good morale or poor morale among inmates and personnel. Not only is this a dangerous over-simplification of the problems involved but, like the military formula of command—organize, deputize, supervise, it is not particularly instructive. A short-sighted resolve to improve morale, alone, can result in misspent effort and a further complication of the underlying problems that contributed to poor morale in the first place. For example, an unwise institution manager may be tempted to accede to demands (real or anticipated) for more privileges. Unless the privileges sought will contribute directly to operational and program objectives, to grant them would risk strengthening the manager's own position at the expense of the total responsibilities he holds. Moreover, by pursuing such a course of action long enough he might discover one day that he had no more privileges to offer. The basic error in such an approach, however, is that the symptoms, rather than the causes, become the object of attention. It is not unlike taking aspirin for the temporary relief of a headache which may have serious unrelieved causes.

Obviously, the immediate purposes of prisoner management and control are security and the protection of persons and property. But there are additional concerns that are consistent with the broad objectives of imprisonment and that contain the clues to the manner in which management and control is achieved. These involve (a) reducing the damaging effects of confinement, (b) minimizing the offender's alienation from the rest of society, (c) maintaining human dignity and self-respect and (d) developing a sense of constructive purpose.

These concerns do not stem from maudlin sympathy toward offenders at all. They are based on facts. One fact is that there is nothing in the language or intent of existing statutes that says prisoners should be subjected to degradation, humiliation, privation or that confinement should be a debilitating, handicapping experience. On the contrary, there is a growing body of court decisions which state that, while prison and jail administrators must be accorded wide latitude in their actions, this shall not be disproportionate to the latitude accorded officials at every other point along the process of criminal justice. The thrust of these decisions is that prisoners do have rights, including rights to humane and equitable treatment, and that it is incumbent upon institution administrators to achieve essential security without imposing adverse restrictions. *

The other basic fact is that with few exceptions every person committed to a jail or prison is released sooner or later. A large percentage of awaiting trial prisoners are released on bail within days and many others do not return from court because they were acquitted or have been fined or their sentences were suspended. Most of the sentenced prisoners committed to jail are released in a matter of days, weeks or months. If released prisoners are bitter, hostile or further incapacitated by the experience of confinement, the institution has done nothing to contribute to the control of crime—to say the least.

The manner in which prisoner management and control is achieved is largely in the hands of the administrator and his staff. For the administrator this becomes a matter of applying philosophies and techniques to personnel management, the formulation of policies and operating procedures and the improvement of correctional programs.

PERSONNEL ADMINISTRATION

The preceding chapter identified a number of personnel problems. There is another that should be mentioned here. According to a recent survey conducted for the Joint Commission on Correctional Manpower and Training, correctional workers feel that their programs must be improved. Their concern over existing program results causes frustration and can lead to apathy or cynicism. Competent personnel faced with system shortcomings they cannot overcome will resign rather than continue their association with an organization which appears to them to be prone to failure. While dissatisfaction with the ineffectiveness of programs is general among correctional personnel, the higher the educational achievement of employees, the greater is their dissatisfaction. The field of corrections, which has always found it difficult to recruit highly trained personnel, can ill afford to suffer steady loss of those it succeeds in hiring. Moreover, when a sizable group of workers in an institution or agency holds views opposed to those of the administration, disruptions in correctional operations can be expected.

Development of correctional careers. It is an established fact that careers in correctional work are not well defined. The manner and conditions of entry into this work differ widely from one jurisdiction to another and between correctional agencies. The circumstances also differ considerably from entry into education, social welfare and other government programs or private industry. Job dissatisfaction soon arises from awareness that promotions are slow in coming and may bear little apparent relationship to experience and ability.

The need to provide real career opportunities in correctional work is obvious. Correctional managers must begin the development of such careers by taking the initiative in aggressive recruitment of qualified people, as industry, education and other public services have done for a long time. Correctional agencies must begin to compete seriously for qualified or trainable people if they are not to continue to be second and third career choices for applicants years after graduation from school and probably on the heels of dissatisfactions in other jobs.

But even the most aggressive recruitment will fail unless program managers are given more freedom in offering jobs. Age and residence requirements, which are now imposed formally or informally, should be eliminated. Some requirements of previous experience should be reconsidered if young people are to be attracted to available jobs.

Education and training must be recognized in the corrections career ladder. Management trainee posts should be established. Young people today are attracted to jobs which offer challenge and some potential for personal success. Once a person starts in correctional work, he should be able to look upon his choice as a career matching others in prestige, salary and opportunity for advancement.

Support of staff development programs. In today's world, knowledge increases so rapidly that the need for continuing education and training for most occupations is generally acknowledged. There is no reason to dispute this need in corrections. While few correctional systems now offer well-developed training programs, many have the capability for this, either by utilizing their own resources or in collaboration with nearby industries and institutions of higher learning. These programs should include training in principles of management and supervision, as well as in the dynamics of human behavior, community relations, law and correctional methods.

If staff development is to be improved in both quality and quantity, correctional leaders will need to provide the necessary funds and other forms of support required. Legislators and government officials must be impressed with the urgency of the need for staff development. This is a broader need than training alone. It includes exchange of personnel, tuition support for employees who wish to take academic courses, opportunities to conduct research, visits to other agencies and involvement in professional organizations.

Removal of job dissatisfactions. Since administrators are responsible for the establishment of policy, they must be continually alert to employees' dissatisfactions with this work. Aggressive efforts should be made to obtain higher salaries and to provide opportunities for upward mobility. Other sources of dissatisfaction are no less important. Understaffing is more than a matter of overwork for the employees on duty. The necessity of dealing with excessive numbers of offenders may result in less than adequate supervision and control, gross inefficiency and inability to help any of them. There is need to reexamine traditional utilization of personnel in the light of techniques which will improve program effectiveness. Even the nature of the services themselves should be studied carefully.

Much more than this needs to be said about personnel. But personnel administration is not the only area which can contribute to reduction of management and control problems.

POLICIES AND OPERATING PROCEDURES

There is an old prison saying to the effect that an institution is but the lengthened shadow of the warden. In a literal sense, this is only a part truth since the shadow is actually a composite of many. However, it is meant to imply that institutional programs and policies and the operating procedures which dictate the ways in which things are done reflect an underlying administrative philosophy of correctional treatment and control. There is also the accurate inference that this philosophy pervades all activities throughout the entire institution, as well as the relationships which exist between the institution and other agencies, organizations and the public. Broadly, the physical appearance of the institution and every regulation, activity and personal contact has a bearing on prisoner management and control. Four representative situations have been singled out for attention here.

Prisoner rights and attention to complaints. It has long been established that lawful imprisonment necessarily causes the withdrawal or limitation of many rights to which the average citizen is fully entitled. This does not mean that the institution manager can do as he wishes without fear of criticism, censure or judicial intervention. Neither does it mean that a prisoner is without rights. One of the great problems for the administrator is determination of what restrictions and conditions may appropriately be imposed upon prisoners when the guidelines seem to be ever-changing. Yesterday's preposterous expectations can well be today's privileges and tomorrow's rights. It is nearly impossible to predict which administrative decisions will become the subject of judicial disapproval or new legislation, but there are many indications to be found. The earlier reference to a particular issue of The Prison Journal is only one of many sources of information. The trick is to utilize these indications to insure that reasonable rules are established which will insure fair treatment of prisoners and, at the same time, allow the administrator to do his job without undue hindrance. Prisoner rights comprise only one point of view from which the new administrator should carefully study the rules and policy decisions which he inherits. This is only one reason why all regulations and procedures should be reexamined frequently.

Food service is an example of the importance of other reasons. It is assumed that every prisoner has the legal right to be adequately nourished throughout his confinement. Presumably, this means that his food intake for an average day will be in ample quantity and nutritive value to sustain him. From a nutritional point of view this amounts simply to meeting needs based on such factors as age, weight, size, sex, physical activity and conditions of health. But in jails and prisons, as elsewhere, adequate food service depends upon budgetary allowance, procurement, storage, preparation, the manner in which meals are served, sanitation, appearance and many other considerations. Not the least of them is menu planning. Menus can be effective substitutes for calendars in determining the day of the week, or they can provide variety and reflect the particular tastes of the people being fed.

Numerous similar examples can be found in the day-to-day operation of any institution. Take clothing. A prisoner's right to human dignity demands that his nakedness be covered. His right to humane treatment requires that this covering be appropriate to the climate and circumstances in which he finds himself. Health standards dictate that clothing shall be free from vermin and reasonably clean. But these are not the only considerations. If an institution is to furnish clothing, it should also be reasonably well-fitting and in an acceptable state of repair.

Beyond the issue of rights, the problems underlying the examples given are less a matter of what policies and rules may require than of how they are carried out. Thus, the administrator should be concerned both with the substance or content of programs, policies and rules and with the ways of implementing them. In part, this becomes a matter of sensitizing personnel to the fact that they deal with fellow human beings, even though they be prisoners. To illustrate further: every correctional institution conducts a "count" several times a day. This can be done promptly, accurately and with a minimum of confusion, or it can be a recurring aggravation and unnecessarily harassing inconvenience to the inmates. A strip search for contraband can be conducted efficiently, privately and with as much dignity as circumstances permit, or it can be a disgusting, humiliating spectacle. A cell "shake-down" can accomplish its purpose and leave authorized personal belongings in good order, or it can make a shambles of the cell with ruthless destruction of "junk" items which the prisoner happens to value highly.

The kinds of sensitivity and good judgment that apply to operating procedures and daily activities are equally applicable to the attention given prisoner complaints. Inattention to prisoner complaints can lead from uncertainty and dismay to distrust and rebellion that may produce an incident to attract attention. This is particularly likely to happen if the prisoner believes that his problem would be solved if it reached the proper officials. Areas in which complaints and grievances are most often expressed are: food, handling of mail and visits, disciplinary procedures and punishments, and work or quarters assignments which are thought to be inappropriate for some reason.

It goes without saying that legitimate complaints should be heard and the condition corrected as soon as possible. Not all situations can be corrected. In this event, the matter should be discussed with the complaining prisoner and dealt with openly. A number of jurisdictions have adopted a technique having at least psychological value. A special mailbox is installed in a prominent place within the institution. Any prisoner, at any time, may deposit a letter for prompt mailing without inspection or censorship to listed government officials whose office has some responsibility for the handling of prisoners' cases or for the operation of the institution.

Communications. It is probable that maintaining effective communications in a prison or jail is more of a problem than in other organizations. In addition to communications between management and staff, there must be communication between prisoners, staff and management.

There are many ways in which communication occurs. The choice of method may well depend upon circumstances, but it should also be considered in terms of why communication is necessary. Obviously one purpose is to instruct personnel. This can be accomplished by staff training, whether formal or informal, the issuance of policies and rules, written post orders which contain a detailed listing of duties, staff meetings, roll-call announcements and conversations with supervisors. Another purpose is to keep management informed of what is going on. There is no good substitute for day-to-day personal observations of management personnel, but these can be augmented by personal interviews, whether scheduled or casual, staff meetings, reports and reviews of records. Communication is an inevitable part of effective planning. Various techniques of utilizing subordinate personnel in planning assignments claim the advantages of employing staff knowledge and skills and, at the same time, insuring a sense of involvement on the part of staff in the solution of problems, program development or other planning purpose.

Adaptations of these methods are equally applicable to communications between prisoners and staff. It is just as important that prisoners know from official sources, rather than from rumors, what is expected of them and what management is doing or planning that affects their welfare. Similarly, management needs to know what the prisoners are thinking and how they feel about things in general. Beyond this, is only by increasing communications between staff and inmates that correctional programs, such as counseling, can be introduced or improved. Additional benefits are that loosening of inmate-to-staff and inmate-to-inmate communication tends to reduce the inmate politicians' power and to minimize the traditional stigma and physical danger of cooperating with the staff.

Correspondence regulations. Correspondence with members of the family and with close friends and associates is essential to the morale of all confined persons and may form the basis for both present and future good adjustment.

Traditionally, inmate correspondence has been surrounded by restrictions designed to limit the number of letters which could be posted or received, including elaborate record-keeping systems to assure that quotas were not violated. Close scrutiny of both outgoing and incoming mail was considered essential to the security of the institution and for the maintenance of prisoner discipline and control. Censorship was thought to be necessary to prevent the introduction of contraband, to minimize involvement in criminal activities and to prevent correspondence becoming a tool for planning escapes or plots of violence. Experience in a number of jurisdictions has demonstrated that some of these restrictions can be eliminated with safety in certain institutions and substantially revised in others, without loss of essential control and with important savings in time, expense and inconvenience.

The size and complexity of each institution, the status and degree of sophistication of the inmates confined, along with other variables, will determine the extent of regulations required. Generally, they should include the following:

Ordinarily there should be no question about the propriety of correspondence with members of the immediate family. Friends, former business associates and others may be considered whenever it appears that the proposed correspondence will not be detrimental to the inmate or the correspondent. Inmates should be permitted correspondence with attorneys of record or attorneys under contract without limitation. Such correspondence should be regarded as privileged in that it should be subjected to inspection only to prevent the introduction of contraband or other threat to the good order and security of the institution.

A number of institutions have demonstrated that it may not be necessary to limit the number of persons on the approved correspondence list.

Similarly, to the extent that administrative considerations permit, no limit need be placed on the number of outgoing letters authorized for mailing. (Experience has shown that the volume of correspondence remains fairly constant whether or not limitations are imposed). Recognizing the importance of maintaining family and community contacts, the institution should expect to pay postage on a "reasonable" number of letters if the inmate is substantially lacking funds.

At time of commitment, each prisoner should be expected to sign an authorization for the head of the institution or his representative to open, read and inspect all mail. Failure to sign this authorization may result in withholding of all correspondence privileges.

While all mail of a particular inmate may need to be subjected to close scrutiny, more flexible procedures for reading, scanning or otherwise spot-checking incoming and outgoing mail will suffice for most prisoners. This should be done frequently enough to maintain security, to learn about any particular problem confronting the inmate or to alert other members of the staff to any matter that may help in evaluating the inmate. "Censorship" of mail for any purpose is indefensible. That which violates postal regulations can be referred for possible prosecution. The institution cannot assume responsibility for the content of incoming or outgoing letters.

Prisoners should be informed of the reasons for which incoming and outgoing mail will be rejected and they should understand that they and their correspondents are responsible for the contents of their letters.

Petitions, motions, appeals and other legal papers related to a prisoner's commitment or sentence, or touching upon some legal question affecting his status in the institution, should be forwarded promptly to the appropriate court.

Visiting regulations. The formulation and administration of visiting regulations should encourage as much visiting as personnel and facilities will permit. The setting in which visits take place should also be as informal and attractive as facilities will permit with due regard for necessary controls. Visits should be conducted and supervised in such manner that an atmosphere of friendliness and lack of tension is achieved.

> The following general principles underly the reasons for granting visit:
>
> Like correspondence, visits are a means of maintaining family ties and wholesome personal relationships with relatives and friends.
>
> These ties and relationships are important factors in prisoner morale and future adjustment.
>
> Visits by family and friends provide an opportunity for closer relationships with staff members for the purpose of more effective program planning.
>
> Properly handled, visits can contribute to good public relations and a better understanding of the institution's objectives.

The practical considerations which impose limits on visits include the size of visiting facilities, the time and expense of supervision and the need for maintaining other important institutional activities without unnecessary or extended interference.

Generally, persons who can be approved as correspondents are suitable as visitors. While it is reasonable to expect that most of the essential legal work which a recognized attorney performs for an inmate will be handled on the basis of correspondence between the attorney and his client, personal visits will be necessary when pending legal problems require, especially with persons awaiting trial and sentence. Such visits should be supervised by observation only for the purpose of contraband control and good order. The attorney and his client should be permitted to converse privately.

As with correspondence, both the prisoners and their visitors should clearly understand what the visiting regulations are.

Prisoner discipline. There probably is no aspect of correctional institution management more filled with emotion and less open to calm appraisal than that of discipline. Yet, there is no activity more in need of objective study and complete overhauling than the traditional ways of handling prisoners who misbehave and violate institution rules. Not only does tradition exact a double standard of behavior but frequently it may ignore guarantees of civil rights and due process.

The objectives of prisoner discipline and control should be fully consistent with the correctional objectives of the institution, the focus being on (a) individual adjustment to the programs, behavior standards and limitations imposed by the administration and (b) the general welfare of the institution community. Disciplinary policy and methods should reflect this statement of purpose and recognize that disciplinary sanction is but one factor in correctional treatment and control. As applied to a prisoner who has misbehaved, this means that the sole objective is his future voluntary acceptance of certain limitations which are being imposed upon him.

Following are essential principles in acceptable and effective disciplinary policy and procedures.

1. Disciplinary action shall be taken only at such times and in such measures and degree as is necessary to regulate a prisoner's behavior within acceptable limits.
2. Prisoner behavior must be controlled in a completely impersonal, impartial and consistent manner.
3. Disciplinary action shall not be capricious nor in the nature of retaliation or revenge.
4. Program assignments and changes are made to achieve treatment goals, not as punishment or reward.
5. Corporal punishment of any kind is strictly prohibited.
6. The initiation of disciplinary measures against any prisoner is the responsibility only of staff members (preferably a committee) to whom this authority has been defined and delegated.
7. Disciplinary action should be taken as soon after the occurrence of misconduct as circumstances permit.
8. Case records should include misconduct reports, their dispositions and should also include evaluative staff statements regarding them.

Delegation of disciplinary authority: Basic authority for the administration of prisoner discipline should be delegated by the chief executive officer of the institution. Where circumstances permit, this delegation should be to a committee of at least three staff members who are competent and who broadly represent the primary areas of correctional treatment. Such delegation should be accompanied by a specific charge which outlines duties and responsibilities.

In addition to receiving reports of misconduct, conducting hearings, making findings and imposing disciplinary actions, the adjustment committee should make referrals for diagnosis and special handling, make program changes indicated and otherwise have authoritative concern policies and operating procedures which affect discipline. The committee should also be concerned with evaluating the effectiveness of its decisions and other factors which have a bearing upon prisoner discipline and morale.

The adjustment committee should be given a broad range of dispositional alternatives. Its choice of alternatives in the disposition of each case should be consistent with the objectives of disciplinary policy. Committee action should be a composite group judgment which takes cognizance of the reasons for the adverse behavior, the setting and circumstances in which it occurred, the involved prisoner's accountability and the correctional program goals set for him. The choice of disposition goes far beyond mere compliance with regulations. To be fully effective, the prisoner must understand and accept the reasonableness of the limitations being imposed upon him. A system should be devised to provide follow-up of at least the more serious and persistent behavior problems dealt with.

Use of segregation: In most institutions there is a separate housing unit for prisoners who, at times, need to be segregated from the regular population. In keeping with the statement of disciplinary policy, above, this unit should be operated in accordance with the following basic requirements of control and supervision.

1. Segregation conditions. The quarters used for segregation should be well ventilated, adequately lighted, appropriately heated and maintained in a sanitary condition at all times.
2. Cell occupancy. Except in emergencies, the number of prisoners confined to each cell or room should not exceed the number for which the space was designed. Whenever an emergency arises which indicates that excess occupancy may be needed temporarily, an immediate report should be made to the head of the institution and his approval obtained.
3. Clothing and bedding. All prisoners should be admitted to segregation (after thorough search for contraband) dressed in normal institution clothing and should be furnished a mattress and bedding. In no circumstance should a prisoner be segregated without clothing except when prescribed by the institution physician for medical or psychiatric reasons. If a prisoner is so seriously disturbed that he is likely to destroy his clothing or bedding, the institution physician should be notified immediately and a regimen of treatment and control instituted with his concurrence.
4. Food. Segregated prisoners should be fed three times a day on the standard ration and menu of the day for the institution.
5. Personal hygiene. Segregated prisoners should have the same opportunities to maintain the level of personal hygiene available to all other prisoners. This should include the availability of toilet tissue, wash basin, drinking water, comb, eye glasses, dentures and opportunities for shaving and brushing teeth.
6. Duration of segregation. Consistent with the need for segregation, no prisoner should be held in this status longer than necessary. Special care should be taken that segregation does not become a haven for those who persistently fail to face their problems. The adjustment committee should be responsible for the program needs of prisoners who require or demand long-term segregation. The committee should conduct a formal review of such cases at least once each month and make recommendations to the head of the institution.

7. Supervision. In addition to the direct supervision afforded by the unit officer, each segregated prisoner should be seen daily by the institution physician or medical technician and one or more other responsible officers designated by the head of the institution.
8. Correspondence and visits. In the absence of direct and compelling reasons to the contrary, prisoners in segregation should not be required to forfeit correspondence and visiting privileges.
9. Records. A permanent log should be maintained in the segregation unit. All admissions should be recorded indicating date, reason for admission and the authorizing official. All releases from the unit should be similarly recorded. Officials required to visit the unit should sign the log, indicating time, date and purpose of visit. Unusual activity or behavior of individual prisoners should be recorded in the log with a follow-up memorandum to the head of the institution.

IMPROVEMENT OF CORRECTIONAL PROGRAMS

The third general area in which the administrator can effect improvements in prisoner management and control is program. While this is not the place to attempt a blueprint of program design, it is appropriate to examine the philosophy of correctional treatment and certain program premises.

To a great extent, many of the problems of correctional institution management are based on philosophical conflicts and controversies. Foremost among them, of course, is the argument of punishment versus treatment. Most administrators today tend to believe that correctional institutions serve to protect the public by keeping offenders locked up, as ordered by the courts, and by making an effort to at least reduce the future threat of offenders through correctional treatment. This is not a universal point of view. Thus some of the problems of management relate to false ideas that punishment and treatment are *inconsistent objectives. This may help account for the fact that, despite the belief of* administrators, the vast majority of correctional institutions still operate in traditional ways, in which the motive force is punishment, vengeful in character and expression.

Thoughtful observation has produced another point of view. While the philosophy of individualism has done much to advance correctional treatment, it has also produced a number of distortions. For example, both the law and operation of the criminal justice system tend to focus responsibility for crime and guilt on the individual offender. Thus the courts and correctional agencies become preoccupied with reforming the individual offender as an isolated problem. By channeling resources exclusively on the reformation of the offender, attention is diverted from correcting conditions in the community which encourage development of criminal behavior. Moreover, the treatment preoccupation with individual offenders has tended to obscure the fact that they do not function as unrelated individuals. As prisoners they are members of a social system, as they were in the community, and they are subject to the heavy impact of the total confinement experience.

The framework within which program planning and development are beginning to occur consists of a number of assumptions, because the state of the art of correctional treatment is still not very far advanced. Other than the theories that have been advanced, very little is known about the direct causes of criminal behavior. More discriminating selection factors with which to classify offenders are needed. Much more must be learned about the character types which can make the most and least effective use of correctional programs and services. There is a basic need for knowledge with which to train staff and prisoners in the specific behaviors which are required to master the specific tasks for successful adjustment in the community. In the meantime, primary program assumptions are:

1. The focus of corrections is intervention in delinquent and criminal careers, through management and control of crises and programs and services designed to overcome handicapping deficiencies.
2. The deeper an offender has to be plunged into correctional processes and the longer he has to be locked up, however humanely, the greater the cost and the more difficult the road back to the point of socialization that will permit successful reentry in the community
3. A person's needs for control or for help are not necessarily related to his legal status.

These assumptions have lead to a number of alternatives to confinement that are being tried in a number of jurisdictions and they suggest new functions and new program directions which open the possibility of more efficient and constructive uses of correctional institutions. As realistic programs are developed, the majority of prisoners will be eager to participate in them, both because of the opportunities they afford and because their mere existence is evidence that somebody cares.

HANDLING EMERGENCIES

In the first chapter a number of factors in prisoner unrest were discussed. Whether any of these, singly or in combination, can be identified as causing a particular problem or incident is another matter. Similarly, inattention to the control of locks and keys, arms and ammunition, tools, items of contraband and security inspections may well contribute to problems of management and control or, in a particular situation, become the cause of a particular emergency. The preceding chapter dealt with a number of preventive measures. Not all problems and incidents can be prevented and not all of them occur as emergencies. Being prepared is both a form of prevention, among others, and a means of minimizing the magnitude of disorder when it occurs.

The kinds of emergencies with which correctional institutions are most likely to deal are escapes and riots or disturbances. This chapter will be devoted mainly to the handling of these problems. But in these days of mass social protest and challenge of authority, local jails and correctional institutions, especially, are likely to be involved in the control of civil disorder in the community. For this reason, attention will be given the problem of emergency detention occasioned by mass arrests. Fire and civil disaster are emergency situations which will be mentioned.

ESCAPE PLANS

Although escapes or attempted escapes are comparatively rare in well-managed institutions, the entire staff must be constantly alert to prevent them. It is possible to reduce successful escapes to a minimum only through cooperative and coordinated planning. While the methods and circumstances of an escape will vary, certain basic policies and procedures are applicable to all of them. Every correctional institution should maintain a carefully developed and detailed plan for the prevention and apprehension of escapes. It is important that the plan be reviewed frequently and kept up to date. A copy should be furnished each employee with the requirement that all become thoroughly familiar with its contents.

In developing a comprehensive plan, an escape should be viewed as an incident which must be assessed in phases or series of action steps.
1. The alert—a period of time in which it may be possible to prevent the incident or to prepare for it.
2. Sounding the alarm—a brief interval for decision that an incident has occurred and for notifying others.
3. Mobilizing resources—final preparation for command and action.
4. Establishing control—thwarting the attempt or apprehending the escapee and assuring security of the institution.
5. Returning to normal operations—including investigations, reports and necessary repairs.

The elements of a comprehensive escape plan will establish policy, define responsibility and outline procedures to be followed in each of these phases. The plan itself should be developed around the following action steps.

Prevention. The plan statement should indicate the most common and immediate ways of preventing escapes. This should include reference to such items as: alertness to detect and report signs of unrest or tension; observation of anything unusual about participation in programs and activities; expression of complaints and requests for change; prompt and decisive action when the occasion demands; thorough security inspections and counts; and effective methods of selecting prisoners for work and quarters assignments.

Sounding the alarm. The plan should provide that any unauthorized absence from a work detail, living quarters or other location will be reported immediately to the supervisor in charge. When it is determined from the information at hand that an escape has occurred, prearranged signals should be sounded to notify all employees. The plan should distinguish the kinds of signals and the circumstances of their use as the sounding of a general alarm can create unnecessary tension and excitement.

Mobilization of resources of resources. A list of all employees with addresses and telephone numbers should be maintained and arranged so that a maximum number of employees may be contacted with a minimum number of calls. As soon as an escape occurs, an employee should be designated to contact the off-duty employees required and have them report for duty immediately.

The security posts and maintenance operations essential to continued functioning of the institution during an escape emergency should be identified. All other posts should be vacated and non-essential activities shut down so that all available personnel can report promptly to a central place for special duty assignments. Personnel in charge of non-essential activities should place all tools in a convenient, safe place, secure the area and check their prisoners in. The officer assigned to the armory, with whatever additional help may be needed, should prepare immediately to issue arms, ammunition and other equipment that may be requisitioned. The record clerk should be to issue escape notices, including identification pictures, for prompt distribution and mailing.

Concurrent with the initial assignment of personnel to escape posts and duties, one employee should be designated to notify all law enforcement agencies in the surrounding area by telephone or radio. Addresses and telephone numbers of the agencies to be notified should be part of the escape and apprehension plan. (In the development of the plan it will be helpful to determine with local law enforcement officials exactly what involvement each agency will have. A confidential copy of the plan might well be furnished each law enforcement agency for reference.) The possibility of asking nearby radio and television stations to assist by spot announcements of escape essentials should not be overlooked.

Establishing control. A complete list of all posts to be covered during a search should be maintained. These may be divided into various categories. The posts to be manned will depend on the information available as to the time the escape occurred, means of departure, direction of travel and other factors that will help insure that the search effort can be pinpointed as closely as possible. An instruction kit should be prepared for each post and handed to the officer at the time he is assigned. For posts located beyond the immediate vicinity of the institution, the instruction kit should include a map of the area, directions for transportation, the duties to be performed and other information, such as location of the nearest telephone, and anticipated relief schedule, that will be helpful to the officer assigned to the post.

The establishment of a special communications center, apart from the command post, can be most useful in conducting an orderly, efficient search. The person in charge of this center is usually authorized to issue press releases, answer numerous inquiries, receive and place telephone or radio calls and otherwise process and record messages and information incidental to the search.

While task forces are being deployed, the plan should establish procedures for starting the investigation. This may include the assignment of an employee to search the personal locker and effects of the escapee for evidence that may provide clues for the hunt. At this time, too, the preliminary investigation should be organized, starting with interviews with both staff members and prisoners who were in a position to know the escapee well and who might be able to shed some light on the escape.

It should be clearly established in policy that if a hostage is taken in an attempt to escape, all personnel should have clear instructions that orders given by any person under duress, including executive officers, are not valid and under no circumstances should the prisoner be permitted to escape from the institution.

The plan should make clear what authority is granted for the use of firearms and in what circumstances these should be used. Generally, firearms should be used as a last resort to prevent escape, prevent injury or loss of life to personnel or prisoners not involved and to protect property. Orders to halt or desist should be given first and, if ignored, a warning shot should be fired. Should this be ignored, subsequent shots should be aimed to disable rather than kill.

Also, the plan should include instructions to all personnel on all posts regarding the importance of tact and good judgment in contacts with other people, the authority granted for stop and search and the tasks that are to be performed in collaboration with representatives of other law enforcement agencies.

Returning to normal. As soon as the decision is made to discontinue the initial search effort, all law enforcement agencies, news media and other persons who were notified of the escape should be informed.

When an escape involves cutting of bars, window sash or other property damage, a careful record, both photographic and written, should be made and arrangements made for repairs. Attention should be given the gathering and safekeeping of other evidence that may be important to prosecution. Particular care must be taken in interviewing the apprehended escapee and other suspects. It is best that this be done only with the advice of the prosecuting attorney.

One of the important concluding steps in handling an escape incident is assessment and report of the experience. The adoption of a general reporting format will facilitate the process involved and provide clues to the lessons that can be learned from the incident.

PLANS FOR RIOTS AND DISTURBANCES

Prisoner disturbances are of two basic types: (a) a disturbance of a riotous nature between two or more prisoner factions which is related to animosities between prisoner groups and may not be well organized; and (b) a more general disturbance directed against the institution because of some real or fancied grievance or other objective, such as mass escape. Whenever prisoners or personnel are under great stress "spontaneous" disturbances can erupt for any reason. Once a disturbance starts, the measures taken to regain control may be the same, regardless of its type or precipitating causes. Yet, it is important that distinctions be made among them because of the few moments of decision as to how to proceed and because of the critical importance of keeping the disorder as isolated and as small as possible.

While it is impossible to detail the procedures that should be followed for the effective handling of all kinds of disturbances in all institutions, experience has shown that the following guidelines are generally applicable.

That each correctional institution should maintain a carefully developed plan for handling group disturbances of all kinds, that the plan be kept up to date and that all employees be familiar with its contents is evident enough. The steps involved in handling a riot or disturbance, as with an escape, must be thought through. These are: the interval of alert, sounding the alarm, mobilizing resources, establishing control and returning to normal. The same basic policies and principles expressed in the preceding discussion of an escape plan are applicable to plans for riots and disturbances.

As with escapes, there usually are signs of tensions among prisoners which portend a group disturbance. It is known that precipitating factors may be unresolved racial problems, complaints over food, dissatisfaction with the performance or attitudes of personnel, complaints over recreation, visiting or formation. With this knowledge, promptness in detecting and reporting unusual mail privileges, complaints over medical treatment, gang problems and misinformation. With this knowledge, promptness in detecting and reporting unusual activity or bad "climate" may enable getting at the root of the trouble and possibly forestalling incidents that could result in a riot.

An action plan should be developed from the primary responsibilities of institution management and in this order: public safety; safety and welfare of hostages; prevention of loss of life or injury to other personnel; prisoner welfare; protection of property.

When, despite all efforts to prevent them, riots or disturbances do occur, they begin with startling suddenness, spread rapidly and can cause major damage. Prompt activation of the riot plan, in which the following elements are incorporated, is absolutely necessary.

Containment. Immediate steps to close any possible avenues of escape are mandatory. The trouble should be localized and access to other areas cut off to prevent the disorder from spreading. Careful appraisal of the situation should be made before rushing in or committing personnel to a situation that might result in their being taken hostage. The immediate objective should be determined, the necessary reinforcements called and equipment required assembled. The safety of employees and prisoners must be considered if it becomes apparent that force and the use of defensive equipment will be necessary. Force and the use of defensive equipment should be used only when ordered by the head of the institution or his representative. Any person held hostage has no authority while under duress, regardless of rank.

It is noteworthy that even in the worst prison riots only a relatively small percentage of the total prisoner population has been actively involved. It is important that prisoners not wishing to participate be given an opportunity to withdraw from the area of disturbance. They should be provided safe conduct to secure quarters.

Employees should be instructed to observe the activity closely to identify ringleaders and subsequently report their participation. Recurring efforts should be made to determine the cause of the disturbance and participants should be urged to select one or more spokesmen to confer with the head of the institution or his representative. No promises should be made to demands other than assurance of fair hearing.

Use of force and defensive equipment. When the decision has been made to use force or defensive equipment, the kind and amount will be dictated by the situation but only for the purposes of control and protection.

Riot squads. As part of a basic riot control plan, it is assumed that a number of personnel will have been selected, organized and trained both in the proper use of special equipment and in the tactics to be used in various situations. When it is necessary to use riot squads, their members should be properly equipped. Injury should not be risked unnecessarily. Each squad should be instructed in the specific tasks it is to perform. Squads should enter the area of disturbance simultaneously from as many entrances as are available.

Water. A riot can often be brought under control by the effective use of water. The riot control plan should identify the location of hydrants and other water outlets, the availability of hose and other fire fighting equipment. Further, the plan should afford protection of hydrants, valves and exposed water pipes during a disturbance. Water may be used to disperse participants, to bring sporadic fires under control and to create dampness necessary to the most effective concentrations of gas should its use be required.

Gas. Gas of various types may be useful in situations where it would otherwise be hazardous to break up a rioting group. Sufficient gas should be used in the first attempt. (Minimum and maximum amounts that can be used safely under various circumstances should be computed in advance and this information should be incorporated in the riot plan). Provisions must be made for follow-up. Gas will break resistance, but participating prisoners may have to be removed forcibly. A squad equipped with gas masks should be assigned this task. The gas should be permitted to develop fully, but not to dissipate, before the squad enters the area. Sometimes a single gas shell or grenade will break up a large group so that smaller groups can be split off. When this tactic is used, the group will quickly re-form unless the follow-up is properly timed. Whenever gas is to be used in an enclosed area, it should be determined in advance that dispersed participants can exit easily.

Firearms. As with escapes, firearms should be used only as a last resort to prevent escapes, injury or loss of life of personnel or prisoners held hostage and to protect property. Orders to halt or desist should be given first and, if these are ignored, a warning shot should be fired. Subsequent shots should be aimed to disable rather than kill.

Post-riot procedures. Steps should be taken as soon as the disturbance is under control to insure that nobody has escaped and that the institution is physically secure. Initially, all participants in the disturbance should be confined and supervision augmented to insure that the disturbance will not break out anew. Extra help should also be assigned to all living quarters and other areas where it is necessary for groups of prisoners to congregate until it is certain that the disorder has completely subsided. If necessary, all non-essential activities can be suspended and feeding schedules rearranged to provide supervision over smaller groups and to meet supervision needs elsewhere.

The remaining steps are similar to those identified for escapes in the preceding section: photographic and written reports of damage, repair of damage, collection and preservation of evidence, notification of persons and agencies that had been informed of the disturbance and, finally, assessment and report of the experience.

PLANS FOR CIVIL DISORDER

The local jail or correctional institution is very likely to be involved in community efforts to control group protests and demonstrations. When mass arrests are made temporary detention facilities will be needed for large numbers of people, including women and juveniles. Obviously, correctional officials should participate in advance law enforcement planning for such emergency and the plans should include definitions of what specific services temporary detention facilities will be expected to provide for what numbers and kinds of arrested persons. It is possible that these services can be provided by existing jail and detention facilities under emergency conditions. In this event, operating problems will center around vast overcrowding, the processing of large numbers of people in and out of the institution and such accommodations as housing, feeding, telephone calls, visits and interviews with investigating officials and attorneys.

When it is known that existing facilities lack the capabilities required to meet anticipated needs, a much greater planning problem will involve the staffing and operation of an emergency detention center in some other setting, such as an armory, stadium or warehouse. Based on two such experiences of its own, the Bureau of Prisons has published an Emergency Detention Manual, copies of which are available upon request.

It is possible that situations may arise in which trained personnel of the local jail or correctional institution will be called upon to assist law enforcement agencies in controlling civil disturbances in the community. The riot squads referred to in the preceding section would be appropriate for this purpose under emergency conditions. Service of this kind should be based on important high-level policy decisions and careful planning.

PLANS FOR CIVIL DISASTER

The local institution may be a valuable resource for emergency services to the community in the face of disaster brought about by flood, fire, earthquake or other major happening involving extensive property damage, personal injury or large-scale displacement of people. The precise needs in such dire circumstances and the capabilities of local institutions to provide services vary so greatly that generalizations about them would be of little value. The institution manager should confer with local police, fire and civil defense officials about such matters. While it may not be possible to formulate definite plans in advance, at least general agreement can be reached as to the kinds of services the local institution might offer under given conditions.

FIRE PLANS

That the institution manager bears responsibility for the protection of lives and property goes without saying. It is equally evident that this responsibility cannot be borne without planning for fire prevention and fire fighting. Fire marshals and other officials can assist greatly in the development of such plans, in training personnel and prisoners in firefighting techniques and in making periodic inspections and investigations.

CONCLUSION

Disorder, including violent and destructive behavior of prisoners, is not unknown to jails, prisons and other correctional institutions. Mass demonstrations, organized social protest and natural disasters not only can cause institutions to operate under emergency conditions but they can contribute directly to emotional stress in prisoner populations.

The potential dangers inherent in these situations are sobering, indeed, especially when it is realized that so many of the basic causes, and even the triggering incidents, are beyond the immediate control of institution managers and personnel. Yet, there need be no feeling of alarm. On the contrary, institution managers and personnel can draw much self-assurance from the knowledge that they can acquire the capability of handling disorder and are prepared for it.

The preceding discussions have emphasized the importance of planning for emergency conditions. This is a difficult, time-consuming and continuing task. Yet, only in this way can the unnecessary handicaps of surprise, confusion and costly indecision be avoided.

www.ingramcontent.com/pod-product-compliance
Lightning Source LLC
Chambersburg PA
CBHW081808300426
44116CB00014B/2277